The Jossey-Bass Nonprofit Sector Series also includes:

Achieving Excellence in Fund Raising, *Henry A. Rosso and Associates*

The Board Member's Guide to Fund Raising, *Fisher Howe*

Board Overboard, *Brian O'Connell*

Boards That Make a Difference, *John Carver*

Care and Community in Modern Society, *Paul G. Schervish, Virginia A. Hodgkinson, Margaret Gates, and Associates*

The Catholic Ethic in American Society, *John E. Tropman*

The Charitable Nonprofits, *William G. Bowen, Thomas I. Nygren, Sarah E. Turner, Elizabeth A. Duffy*

The Commons, *Roger A. Lohmann*

Creating and Implementing Your Strategic Plan, *John M. Bryson, Farnum K. Alston*

The Drucker Foundation Self-Assessment Tool for Nonprofit Organizations, *The Peter F. Drucker Foundation for Nonprofit Management*

Executive Leadership in Nonprofit Organizations, *Robert D. Herman, Richard D. Heimovics*

The Jossey-Bass Handbook of Nonprofit Leadership and Management, *Robert D. Herman and Associates*

Managing Change in the Nonprofit Sector, *Jed I. Bergman in collaboration with William G. Bowen and Thomas I. Nygren*

Marketing Social Change, *Alan R. Andreasen*

Nonprofit Boards and Leadership, *Miriam M. Wood, Editor*

Nonprofit Management and Leadership (quarterly)

Nonprofit Organizations in a Market Economy, *David C. Hammack, Dennis R. Young*

Principles of Professional Fundraising, *Joseph R. Mixer*

Reinventing Fundraising, *Sondra C. Shaw, Martha A. Taylor*

Remaking America, *James A. Joseph*

The Seven Faces of Philanthropy, *Russ A. Prince, Karen A. File*

Strategic Planning for Public and Nonprofit Organizations, Revised Edition, *John M. Bryson*

Understanding Nonprofit Funding, *Kirsten A. Grønbjerg*

Welcome to the Board, *Fisher Howe*

Winning Grants Step by Step, *Support Centers of America*

Women and Power in the Nonprofit Sector, *Teresa Odendahl, Michael O'Neill*

Leading and Managing the Expressive Dimension

Leading and Managing the Expressive Dimension

Harnessing the Hidden Power Source of the Nonprofit Sector

David E. Mason

Jossey-Bass Publishers • San Francisco

Substantial discounts on bulk quantities of Jossey-Bass books are available to corporations, professional associations, and other organizations. For details and discount information, contact the special sales department at Jossey-Bass Inc., Publishers (415) 433–1740; Fax (800) 605–2665.

For sales outside the United States, please contact your local Simon & Schuster International Office.

 Manufactured in the United States of America on Lyons Falls Pathfinder Tradebook. This paper is acid-free and 100 percent totally chlorine-free.

Library of Congress Cataloging-in-Publication Data

Mason, David E., date.
    Leading and managing the expressive dimension : harnessing the hidden power source of the nonprofit sector / David E. Mason—1st ed.
      p. cm.—(The Jossey-Bass nonprofit sector series)
    Includes bibliographical references and index.
    ISBN 0-7879-0143-1
    1. Nonprofit organizations—Management. I. Title. II. Series.
HD62.6.M369 1996
658'.048—dc20   95-34021

HB Printing   10 9 8 7 6 5 4 3 2 1   FIRST EDITION

The Jossey-Bass Nonprofit Sector Series

Contents

Preface

We often start and sustain organizations because we *want to do* something as much as because we *want something done*. Voluntary nonprofit organizations lend themselves to *doing for the sake of the doing*. They are a positive, expressive arena of choice, not a last resort.

We are not compelled to be involved in the voluntary sector. We get involved because nonprofit organizations can fulfill both our desire to act and our desire to accomplish. Nonprofit organizations are concurrently instruments for people who want something done and arenas for people who seek expressive involvement. Those who want to understand these organizations profoundly and operate them at full capacity must comprehend and use both their instrumental and their expressive dimensions.

Expressive behavior is action for direct rather than for indirect gratification. It is play for the sake of the play; work for the sake of the work; energy spent for the sake of the spending. This book is about expressive behavior and how expressive outputs can be optimized within organizations, particularly voluntary nonprofit organizations.

Voluntary nonprofit organizations predate written history. Our need for expressive behavior may be our most basic reason for banding together in groups, older than organizing to make a profit or to govern. Early peoples formed families, hunting bands, sports groups, secret societies, and religious communities. Today, we form trade unions, museums, professional associations, universities, social service agencies, and hospitals to accomplish more together than by struggling alone. When there is a need that requires others for its accomplishment, people readily join in formal and informal organizations to satisfy it. This tradition goes back to our human beginnings and is as vital to our society today as it has ever been. While home, family, and friends fulfill some needs best, our governments other needs, and our profitable businesses yet others, our participation in voluntary nonprofit organizations accomplishes still other things, things that the other sectors cannot do as well.

We have only recently recognized the commonalities among the diverse entities that make up the voluntary nonprofit sector. Indeed, *voluntary nonprofit sector* is itself a new term, and the study of the sector is still maturing. Gifted scholars and other talented observers and commentators are shining their bright lights into many dark crevices and making significant discoveries. Yet an endemic problem affects their studies: many of them know more about their foundation discipline than they do about the inner reality of voluntary nonprofit organizations. Moreover, they start with constructs and theories initially developed for other species of organizations. And when they look at nonprofit organizations through theories developed in other types of organization, they search for a reality that is not the nonprofit reality, and they often ignore the expressive dimension.

As a result, there are critics of the independent sector who see it as consisting of organizations that need healing because they are not like businesses. The cure, they think, is to make profits and eliminate volunteers. Believing that economic production is the only reasonable motive for human effort, they think that any entity that fails to generate a surplus of wealth is dysfunctional.

Indeed, there are ineffective nonprofits, and we can improve them. We can transform them into superb associations that enhance people's capacity, but let us not downgrade them to marginal businesses or second-rate government agencies.

If organizations in the voluntary nonprofit sector are an aberration, if professionalism must replace voluntarism, if all non-government entities should make a profit, then were the people who founded the Methodist Church, the Boy Scouts, Harvard University, and Rotary International all dunces? They must somehow have made a good choice, because some of these organizations and many like them have endured for centuries and, today, nonprofits are among the fastest growing of human endeavors.

If such vitality defies logic, perhaps we have missed a premise. If profit were the only sensible motive, sensible people would abandon the voluntary nonprofit format altogether. Only fools would be starting new voluntary sector organizations every day. Since this is patently not the case, perhaps there is something the critics do not understand.

Nonprofit organizations have been society's experimental cutting edge. Their lack of a mandate to show a profit has allowed them to pioneer new institutions and professions. This sector educates and trains most of the technical, professional, and managerial talent of our nation; houses much of its health care; and feeds its artistic, spiritual, and other nonmaterial hungers. As a democracy, our social system depends on the involvement of citizens. Voluntary organizations have deep taproots because their noble values and profound purposes do involve citizens. As organizations that emphasize human values apart from contribution to profit or loss, they often elicit great commitment and loyalty. They are communities where individuals can function without economic pressures and restraints and reach goals consistent with their personal agendas. They are incubators for innovation without utilitarian pressures. They are where individuals are loved and appreciated for who they are. In short, they are our primary expressive arenas.

Leading and Managing the Expressive Dimension offers a multidisciplinary approach that will help both leaders and scholars expand their influence over the nonprofit organizations and situations in which they participate. The book identifies the expressive outputs that organizations produce in addition to their instrumental outputs and shows how these expressive outputs are natural, legitimate, ubiquitous, and of surpassing value in nonprofit organizations. It shows leaders and other professionals how they can enhance their competency in managing their organizations and reaching their goals while expanding both the expressive and instrumental outputs of their organizations.

Leading and Managing the Expressive Dimension is intended to provide all those with positions of responsibility in nonprofit organizations with a new and larger frame of reference, a more accurate way of thinking about and discussing their sector than they have ever had before. The book is meant to equip paid and unpaid staff ranging from CEOs and board members to leaders of volunteers and small task groups with conceptual and practical tools for reaching many goals that they may have thought beyond their control or out of their reach.

There has long been a gap between management theory and what people experience every day in organizations. I have suggested how nonprofit personnel, consultants, and researchers can start to bridge that gap by understanding the satisfactions that people find in their work beyond meeting organizational goals, and I have suggested specific tools that can be used to increase those satisfactions and thereby improve the overall work of the organization.

Many voluntary sector leaders have long reckoned with the motivational power of expressive behavior; however, they have either covered it from view because it did not coincide with instrumental theory or they tolerated it as a phenomenon incidental to their organization's true purpose. I propose to air out what we know of the importance of directly gratifying behavior so that leaders and managers will put it on today's agenda and uncover its potency as a positive attribute, one worthy of enhancement and exploitation. I intentionally integrate rather than segregate theory and practice, tempering theory with existential reality and applying sound theoretical concepts to effective management and leadership practice.

Practical tools include a catalogue of organizational functions that enhance the expressive output, discussion of applying current management and leadership theory to expressive motivation, the expressive uses of specialized concurrent management functions and of the stages of a typical management cycle (such as a year-long program), and a method that has been proven effective for building ongoing organic growth into an organization's systems.

Audience

Among those who could benefit from reading this book are nonprofit leaders, managers at all levels, volunteer coordinators, administrators in nonprofit institutions, professional staff (whether paid or unpaid), board members, researchers in the various nonprofit areas as well as students of the sector, teachers of nonprofit management, and consultants.

Overview of the Contents

This book moves from concepts to competencies. My approach is first that of an explorer seeking to reveal what is already there. Then, I move into an inventive mode, offering a number of how-to chapters.

The first four chapters address the needs of both scholars and practitioners by assembling relevant theory and leadership concepts. Chapter One defines the subject, distinguishes expressive outputs from instrumental outputs, and argues for an acknowledgment of expressive behavior as a legitimate dimension of organizational life. Chapter Two peels away the veils that have hidden the importance of expressive activity. It discusses the magnitude of expressive outputs among various organizations, the expressive motivations of classes of participants, and the degree to which one can lead an organization toward expressive outputs. Chapter Three reviews the scholarly literature on involuntary and voluntary expressive behavior, emphasizing those findings that are significant for nonprofit and voluntary organizations. Chapter Four describes the contrasting management attitudes that bear on expressive outputs in organizations, because how we think about the expressive dimension affects how well we can manage it.

In the remaining chapters, I describe the leadership and managerial competencies that affect the expressive dimension and that can be applied toward constructing and operating more effective organizations. Chapter Five discusses organizational culture, illustrates how culture inheres in small task and affinity groups, and describes the dominant role of culture in normative organizations (that is, organizations that must rely on cultural norms to moderate and guide people's behavior). Chapter Six looks at the importance of cohesion in nonprofit organizations and describes how the factors that bind participants together can be encouraged. Chapter Seven takes the reader through a typical management sequence in considerable detail, from the initial assessment of position and clarifying of purpose through the feedback and evaluation processes and the revision for the next cycle. It shows how the steps in this sequential management process can be modified to enhance an organization's expressive aspect. Chapter Eight examines concurrent management activities, such as building redundant capacity into functions to ensure that goals are met and improving delegation practices, again showing how each activity can enhance organizational outputs.

Chapter Nine examines leadership functions in expressive contexts and describes how organizations can optimize their relations with strong leaders. Charismatic leaders can be of dramatic benefit to nonprofits, and this chapter analyzes charismatics' typical strengths and weaknesses.

Chapter Ten reveals how nonprofits grow most successfully. It spells out the steps of a growth campaign that uses the motive power of the small expressive workgroups that taken together are the organization.

Each chapter closes with suggestions for further research and a summary of the key actions that organizational leaders and managers can take to build their organizations and make them more effective. The final chapter, the Conclusion, summarizes explanations and prescriptions.

Scholars as early as Darwin and as eminent as Freud have addressed expressive behavior. With the few exceptions noted in Chapter Three, current commentators neglect the subject or sublimate its importance. *Leading and Managing the Expressive Dimension* attempts to reverse that trend.

This book should enable researchers, academics, and leaders and managers at all levels to understand the expressive dimension in organizations and begin to answer the many theoretical puzzles that nonprofits have posed. It will give leaders and other professional and volunteer participants in the voluntary sector a conceptual orientation for what they have intuitively known all along, that people do not join a nonprofit simply to accomplish that organization's instrumental goals.

In addition, leaders can use the ideas and practical suggestions in this book to organize and facilitate discussions at board retreats, planning sessions, and staff meetings. Portions of the book could also serve as the basis for a presentation at a convention, conference, or annual meeting; for a seminar; or for a required reading program for organizational leadership.

The individuals who examine, diagnose, and manage complex organisms need a workbench filled with precise tools and flooded with ample light. My purpose in this book is to provide better tools and turn up the light on the rich, multidimensional, and multiply rewarding voluntary nonprofit organizations that contribute so much to our values, our purposes, and our reasons for living.

Acknowledgments

I cannot attempt to acknowledge individually all of the people who have given me important insights over many years, but I thank all those mentors and comrades, in many organizations, with whom I worked and discovered many of the practical ideas that follow; the writers whose ideas I have absorbed; the staff at the Corpus Christi Public Library, and especially those who helped shape the final form of the manuscript for this book: Elspeth MacHattie, David Adams, Thomasina Borkman, Nancy MacDuff, Vic Murray, Ed Seeger, Alan Shrader, David Horton Smith, and Jon Van Til.

Corpus Christi, Texas   DAVID E. MASON
September 1995

The Author

David E. Mason is a consultant, scholar, and entrepreneur, with thirty-six years' experience as a CEO of local, regional, and international nonprofit organizations. He has also served on the boards of organizations representing the fields of health, education, social welfare, culture, religion, recreation, and trade associations. He is vice president for administration of the Association for Research on Nonprofit Organizations and Voluntary Action. Mason received his B.A. degree (1949) from Louisiana State University, his B.D. (1953) and Th.M. (1954) from Southern Baptist Theological Seminary, his M.A. degree (1964) from Syracuse University, and his D.D. degree (1960) from what is now Texas Agricultural and Mechanical University at Corpus Christi. This is his eleventh book and his second in the field of nonprofit management, the first being *Voluntary Nonprofit Enterprise Management* (1984).

Mason has consulted with seven Fortune 500 companies at their corporate headquarters, with six foreign governments, with scores of businesses, and with hundreds of voluntary nonprofit organizations. For ten years, he produced and hosted a weekly television program, interviewing nonprofit leaders about their activities and community issues on the ABC affiliate in New Orleans. His speaking, writing, business interests, and consulting have taken him to more than ninety nations.

In addition to being listed in *Who's Who in America* since 1965, he is in both *Who's Who in Finance and Industry* and *Who's Who in Religion*. He and his wife, Bette, operate Mason Enterprises, with real estate, oil and gas, and ranching operations.

Leading and Managing the Expressive Dimension

Chapter One

The Importance of Expressive Outputs in Nonprofit Organizations

"It was very strange," said Dr. Zilberman, head of cardiology at the St. Petersburg Children's Hospital, after a team of pediatric surgeons from Oakland, California, had visited his hospital. "We tried to understand for what purpose did they come. What did they want? And then I realized they wanted to help us, and that's all. It was very unusual for Soviet people, to think that somebody wants to help you without expecting something from you. We've never seen it before" (*60 Minutes*, May 29, 1994).

The Oakland surgeons had mystified Dr. Zilberman at first. They wanted to set up a Russian center to heal children with damaged hearts and to teach local doctors their technology. But before Zilberman could understand the magnitude of this cornucopia of free benefits, he first had to accept the voluntary service perspective. He had to leap beyond his skepticism that a rational self-interested individual would voluntarily participate in providing a collective good without tangible incentives. Only after the Russian physician accepted the Americans' motives and understood their perspective could the healing begin. Nothing changes things as much as point of view.

Some organizations not only get things done but also help people do something—the organizational activities are ends as well as means. *Leading and Managing the Expressive Dimension* examines people's intrinsic expressive motivations for starting or joining many voluntary nonprofit organizations, and it suggests a new point of view about nonprofit organizations' reasons for existence. It uncovers why many nonprofits have prospered and explains how these organizations can dramatically increase their effectiveness and why they perform a legitimate indispensable function. It demonstrates that voluntary nonprofit enterprises are not second-choice alternatives to business or government entities but the first choice of their participants.

This introductory chapter contrasts voluntary expressive behavior in organizations with the instrumental behavior that typically produces organizational products or services. It argues that opportunities for human fulfillment through expressive behavior are a legitimate output of voluntary nonprofit organizations and that these outputs not only meet many human needs but also produce energy and motivation for organizations to draw on.

This point of view understands voluntary nonprofit organizations from the traditional mind-set of the organizations themselves. Nonprofits see individuals as whole persons, not merely as units used in production. The nonprofit sector does not view the larger society exclusively as a market that drives people only through competition for gain. It sees that people have other, expressive needs, and it serves as an incubator and an arena for their expressive behavior. It fosters *activity for its own sake, looking only to itself for justification: participation for the sake of the participation; work for the sake of the work; energy spent for direct rather than for indirect gratification.*

Organizations can feed virtually every human need. Even a hunger for isolation can be satisfied—by the organization we know as a monastery. There would be no organizations if we could satisfy all our needs without them.

Researchers' compilations of human needs range from Freud's simple "*lieben and arbeiten*" (to love and to work) to H. A. Murray's catalogue of thirty needs (see Chapter Three). And most needs on most scholars' lists are expressive; they provide intrinsic rewards. Those who lead and manage organizational processes need to understand all they can about human needs if they are to motivate their followers and workers.

All of us have physical, psychological, emotional, social, and spiritual needs. We have extrinsic needs to survive, to drink and eat, to protect ourselves, to grow and be healthy, to procreate, and to have material possessions. We have intrinsic needs for love, accomplishment, variety, identity, mastery, autonomy, and opportunities for distinction. We need prestige, personal power, attainment of dominating positions, and pride of workmanship. We seek a sense of adequacy, altruistic service, loyalty to organizations, and aesthetic and religious feeling. We like to feel we are playing a role in important events. Understanding these kinds of needs helps us, then, to understand both the expressive activity that satisfies needs directly and the instrumental activity that satisfies needs indirectly.

We spend lifetimes asking questions of meaning such as, Who am I? Why am I here? What do I want? There are probably as many answers to these questions as there are human personalities, but of one thing we can be certain: those answers will reveal that we have many needs—some extrinsic, many intrinsic—and we do not satisfy them all by having, doing, or being any one thing.

The Voluntary Nonprofit Arena

We can see the diverse nonprofit arena as a complex primordial stew of formal and informal entities that meets a wider range of needs than the more specialized sectors of government and business and that meets expressive needs in particular. Any examination of voluntary association that omits its expressive dimension is as incomplete as an explanation of the universe that omits the dimension of gravity.

How many bridge clubs, garden clubs, and churches exist solely as venues for playing cards, discussing flowers, and worshipping God? How many hospital board members, university alumni, and United Way workers function solely because of their concern for people's health, education, or welfare? In addition to the ends just named, these organizations also provide direct personal gratification, satisfying activities, and opportunities for cultivating friendships, having one's ego stroked, and socializing. People participate in and support both member-benefit and public-benefit entities some of the time because there is something they want to do (an expressive need) and some of the time because they want something done (an instrumental need). Voluntary sector organizations can accommodate either purpose. They can "transport" an individual as music, drama, and being in love do, so that he or she is playing an octave higher than the mundane. This expressive action need not seek anything beyond itself for gratification; it needs no extrinsic reward, promotion, or direct or indirect approbation. Actions such as the caring for the sick, the teaching of the student, the molding of the clay, the saving of the lost, the meeting of the group, the running of the course, the writing of the concept, the raising of the funds, the striving toward the goal, or the marshaling of the forces become ends in themselves. The work produces results, but the results are lagniappe, something extra. No extrinsic reward can substitute for the intrinsic rewards of the work itself.

The traditional role of the voluntary organization in the larger society is as a place where people do what they want to do, usually when they want to do it, adapting to the needs of others because that is the organization's cultural norm, not because they are coerced or think that such adapting will be utilitarian. In both households and nonprofit entities, expressive (direct gratification) activity is okay. Instrumental (indirect gratification) activity is also okay. Blend the two, and that is still okay. Here, work equals expressive and/or instrumental activity.

Many organizational specialists understand how economies and systems use organizations as means to worthy ends. However, when they then examine nonprofit organizations, they find aspects that defy their standard explanations. They may ask questions such as, Who are the owners? Who are the customers? If not for profit, for what? When governments and businesses conform to the specialists' theories about how organizations should perform and nonprofits do not, the specialists see the former as rational and predictable and the latter as enigmatic or dysfunctional. Rather than expand their paradigms to include the legitimate realities of voluntary nonprofit enterprises, the specialists prescribe remedies to cure nonprofits and distort them into businesses. But if the specialists altered their perspective, they would find that nonprofits do function well as what they are, voluntary organizations that simply do not need to make a profit.

The nonprofit world is full of communities in which personal desires, fun, common concerns, values, hurts, love, a desire to be fair and right, and work for the sake of work mingle. Roger Lohmann recently resurrected the concept of "the commons" to describe nonprofit collectivities in which uncoerced participation, sharing, mutuality, and fairness are important (1992, p. 254). He discusses such expressive values as enlightenment, virtue, beauty, rapture, truth, salvation, perfection, community, and art for its own sake, values that "stand on their own merits as human endeavors. They do not need to be thought of in terms of utility maximization or goal attainment to be seen as reasonable pursuits" (p. 15). The behavior of individuals across the various kinds of organizations including nonprofits shows clearly that individuals do not always behave as rational economic actors. They are complex beings with multiple motives and values, driven as much by feelings and social pressures as by facts and interests. Individuals as members of groups have commitments stronger than their personal self-interest (Scott, 1987, p. 57). Viewing nonprofit entities as mere economic units is like trying to understand the family as a mere economic unit.

We have voluntary nonprofits because people support organizations that provide services—like expressive activity—whose market value is not measurable. Economists call it market failure (Hansmann, 1980). Organizations like Case Western Reserve University, the Metropolitan Museum of Art, the Kidney Foundation, Goodwill Industries, and the Mother's Day Out program at the Presbyterian church around the corner continue to thrive.

Expressive and Instrumental Activities

Up to now, we have looked at expressive activity as the implicit opposite of instrumental activity, yet the two kinds of activity are by no means mutually exclusive.

An entity is *instrumental* (like a tool) when it is producing an output to its external environment. It is expressive when it meets its own needs through an activity. All activities are means to ends. They are tools for getting what we want. We work from nine to five to earn money, throw out the garbage to have a sanitary house, plant a garden to have vegetables to eat, or engage in certain unspeakable activities to produce heirs. All these processes can produce both an instrumental output to an organization or a society that is external to the individual and an expressive input to the individual.

Individuals can do the same things for a variety of reasons;

therefore, one person's instrumentality may be another's expression. The yacht owner out for a Wednesday afternoon sail has a mind-set that makes expressive fun out of activities that would be just another day's instrumental work for a professional sailor. Kinship can turn a nanny's chore into a granny's joy. An organization may be expressive for its members, instrumental for its managers, expressive for its professional and volunteer service providers, and instrumental for its support staff. The local chapter of a nonprofit may be 90 percent expressive, and the national office 100 percent instrumental. Ambiguity and unpredictability may make the expressive activity more difficult to study than the instrumental product, but most human interests are more engaging than most human artifacts, just as two-year-old toddlers are a lot more interesting than two-year-old footstools.

Individuals hunger for a variety of experiences. These expressive and instrumental hungers are not necessarily mutually exclusive. One may express one's values by serving the dying, and the activity may become instrumental in one's earning the Nobel prize for peace. Moreover, expressive needs do not have to be congruent with the instrumental needs of the organizations that satisfy them. A foundation might bring the arts to a ghetto (instrumental), but an avid fundraiser might volunteer for the project for the sake of camaraderie with friends (expressive). The fact that expressive experience is often concomitant with although not parallel to instrumental experience is one of the principles leaders need to understand about intrinsic expressive motivation.

In addition, individuals work in both nonprofit and profit-seeking organizations for instrumental reasons other than money. The work may be a step to a broader career or may provide prestige or a social or protective benefit (Clary, Snyder, and Ridge, 1992, pp. 336–337). Professionals may not be motivated by all the same things as unpaid workers. For example, staff members of Safari Club International may have instrumental goals and enjoy extrinsic rewards even though the organization is expressive for its members. Yale faculty may fulfill themselves expressively while the extrinsic rewards of the institution's instrumental ends motivate the administrative and clerical personnel. Expressively motivated paid personnel are prevalent in the voluntary sector, and these people have multiple motivations.

Different organizations meet different degrees of both instrumental and expressive needs. (Organizations have no emotions, so no organization can really be expressive; however, I use the term *expressive organization* to refer to those entities that *facilitate expressive activity*.) When we classify organizations to better understand them—for example, lumping groups of friends and family into one sector, business organizations into another, governments into another, and organizations in which people voluntarily cooperate to help themselves and society into another (Adams, 1986, p. 161; Smith, 1991)—we are recognizing that different kinds of organizations perform different functions. Observing whether organizations are instrumental means to reach some end and/or expressive ends in themselves is one largely unacknowledged way in which we distinguish organizations. Yet we also need to recognize that satisfying expressive needs is a major motivating source of energy not only for primarily expressive organizations but also for organizations with significant commitments and obligations for measurable instrumental outputs. Thus, an enhanced understanding of expressive activity can serve both for-profit and nonprofit organizations.

Deep Taproots

Organized voluntary expressive activity is no fad. Its deep roots penetrate human development to its beginnings. When we first found tasks that required more than one person to accomplish, we gathered in informal organizations. We have formed groups for religious purposes and to meet the demands of tribal living for at least twenty-five thousand years. Whenever we have needed to solve a problem or to seize an opportunity that required cooperation, we have organized ourselves into voluntary groups.

The earliest hunter-gatherers, making the transition to agriculture, painted on cave walls, carved images, and made prayer sticks, totems, and other religious objects. Males probably enjoyed gathering around the campfire to tell stories about hunting and fighting (activities also involving cooperation), the good old days, or some unexplained event. The females probably found it satisfying to gather around common chores and to jointly advise a new mother about the antics of an infant or the misbehavior of her mate. Initiation rituals into stages of life such as puberty are a universal expressive activity among tribal peoples. For example, the Samo people of New Guinea spend two years preparing for an elaborate three-day initiation ceremony. Prehistoric life was seldom an unrelieved struggle for survival. Early people also poured energy into expressive activities, and as Lohmann points out, "must have spent substantial amounts of leisure time developing, learning, and performing myths, rituals, and ceremonies to produce the artifacts that have already been discovered and to sustain the legends and traditions that have come down to us" (1992, p. 87).

Long before the development of commerce, our remote ancestors found that they could accomplish more by cooperating than by laboring alone. Hunting in bands enabled them to kill the larger animals with relative safety, and they could defend themselves better when several families lived together. So the family, clan, hunting group, and other prehistoric arrangements for task specialization, common safety, and the exchange of goods (subsistence barter) existed as nonprofit entities before the establishment of either profit-making or government entities. Not until it was necessary to enforce matters that were for the common good but that required some form of coercion were official governments formed. Not until a surplus developed was it possible to have profit.

Thus, there is nothing new about organizations fulfilling both expressive and instrumental needs. Stone Age foraging groups were both instrumental in feeding their communities and expressive in bonding. Early religion was instrumental in eliciting God's help with bounty in the harvest and victory in combat and expressive for people's primary feelings. Anthropologists and other scholars see the same pattern in tribal societies today (Ardrey, 1966; Morris, 1969; Mason, 1988; Tiger, 1989; Young, 1986). And these earliest informal groupings are the roots of many current formal entities.

People often call nonprofit organizations in the aggregate the third sector, after business and government. I believe that historically, nonprofits came first. With the appearance of profit seeking, however, some previously cooperative not-for-profit activities began to move into the realm of business. These activities included the distribution of virtually all tangible items. Goods, unlike services, are easy to weigh and measure, and they quickly establish a market value based on their utility to the user and independent of their value to those who provide them. When a service evolved to the point where it could be assigned a measurable market value, an entrepreneur would often find a way of making a profit from offering it, too. However, needs remained that while important to the society, were difficult to assign a value. The family filled some of these needs, such as child care and early education. The society as a whole handled others, such as keeping up mores and customs through acceptance or ostracism, punishment or reward. Governments provided peacekeeping and defense from enemies. Religious institutions attended both to spiritual affairs and a wide range of services that later spun off into a variety of educational, cultural, governmental, health, and welfare organizations. Religious experience, and hence activities within a religious organization, tends to be diffuse, ambiguous, and undifferentiated. Therefore, the more understood, specialized, and differentiated a religiously sponsored activity becomes, the more likely it is to spin out of the religious sphere and into its own secular orbit.

A new and rich seedbed in which volunteer enterprise was to reach a full flourishing was the opening of the New World to Europeans. The establishment of a new nation on the edge of a vast frontier precipitated a rapid flourishing of cooperative voluntary activity and helped shape the vigorous U.S. nonprofit as we know it today. Pioneers awoke each morning to the sounds of the unexplored frontier outside their western windows. On the frontier, one's past—be it rich or poor—counted for little. There were no long traditions and no established institutions to sustain the unfortunate, the poor, and the weak. The challenges were always there, and the specter of ever-present survival needs always loomed. People on the frontier could look to no one except their comrades to meet these needs and seize the opportunities raised by the challenges. Indeed, "the frontier was not simply a place; it was a state of mind—a state of mind in which neighbor had to depend on neighbor and in which a complex of voluntary associations flourished" (Turner, 1937, p. 287). It was through such voluntary groups that the frontier promoted democracy. The ideal of liberty and justice for all, the idea of a voluntary church independent of the state, the dream of a vital middle class, and similar concepts were not born in the New World, but the frontier provided the conditions in which they could be often articulated and acted on.

The frontier gave Americans an opportunity to do more than affirm the emerging ideas of equality. It forced the implementation of these ideas in a specific social context. Voluntary associations gave individuals a piece of the action in decisions that affected the total society. In voluntarism, we engage in the social phenomena of institutional articulation, strong commitment, the expenditure of energy, the redistribution of power, and the separation of powers (Adams, 1986, p. 173). And this is precisely what the early settlers did, initiating a broad and intense voluntary sector in the United States. "No other country," says Drucker, "has the tradition of the frontier with its isolated communities forced to work together and to be self-sufficient, combined with the pluralism of self-governing churches, independent of state and government, and therefore, dependent on their congregations. No European culture, not even the closely knit Latin family, could nurture this kind of community" (1989a, pp. 205–206).

The deep roots of voluntary nonprofit enterprises in human experience give us some idea why nonprofits will persist in providing experiences that are expressive and difficult to measure, even in an age of Big Brother government and businesses that squeeze every unprofitable aspect from their services.

These roots also suggest why some businesses are taking a new look at the role of expressive behavior and the stimulation of intrinsic motivation. Organizational theorist Vic Murray notes: "Business has been working very hard to build the expressive dimension into its organizations. All the emphasis on Japanese management and transformational management strikes me as being about how to build commitment to the organization and provide employees with intrinsic involvement in their tasks and a concern for the fate of the organization as a whole (through empowerment, quality circles, team management, culture shifts, Total Quality Management and the like)" (Vic Murray, personal correspondence with author, Dec. 15, 1992).

Businesses where people enjoy what they do as much as they enjoy the resulting material benefits are on the expressive edge of the marketplace. People in such businesses include a man whose woodworking shop provides a comfortable living while he does what he loves best, shaping fine-grained wood with the smell of fresh sawdust in the air. A Wyoming rancher routinely collects his big check at the cattle auction twice a year but revels in riding the range as master of all he sees the rest of the year. A feature writer for the *New York Times* makes a healthy salary creating stories she knows millions appreciate. Public officials in the government sector enjoy campaigning as well as serving in elected office. They thrive on public attention. NASA scientists live in a nerd heaven as they work for the joy of the work itself.

Still, for the most part, there is a profound cultural chasm separating the business and government sectors on the one hand and the household and voluntary sectors on the other. Typically, business owners and supervisors think that expressive activity may undermine profits; to them, it is dysfunctional. So they work to reduce and minimize expressive activities or to harness them as means to the instrumental end. Their norms say, "Do that sort of thing on your own time. You are here to work!" Whereas, in nonprofit organizations, we optimize expressive activities; we often see them as ends rather than means. In short, we see them as legitimate work in themselves.

Government's coercive power controls. Businesses' exchange mechanisms produce profit. Nonprofits, according to Drucker, produce changed human beings (1990, p. xiv). Similarly, Jeavons writes, "The work of business revolves around wealth. The work of government revolves around power. Around what, then, does the work of . . . nonprofit organizations revolve? I would contend that the answer to this question is values" (1992, p. 406). Nonprofits are engaged in both "providing a service and making a statement about the values that undergird their motivation for and commitment to service" (p. 415).

Pendulum Swings

Expressive behavior—directly gratifying activity for its own sake—is characteristic of our species. We have been forming organizations to expand and enhance such natural activity for as long as we can remember. We need expressive activity. We hunger for it. We are going to have it. If the government outlawed it, we would go underground to get it. On the other hand, we also like to improve things that are external to us. We spend much energy cleaning these things, putting them in order, and improving on them. We like to fix broken things. Occasionally, our ardor pushes us to fix unbroken things.

I saw this urge to improve begin to swing like a heavy pendulum in the direction of voluntary nonprofit organizations in the early 1960s. American business was doing so many good things for U.S. citizens following World War II that some of us wondered how to apply this efficient know-how to our nonprofit organizations. When we tried it, it worked. Our nonprofits became more efficient, more effective, and more accountable. They grew and prospered and spawned more organizations. Outsiders began to notice the voluntary sector as if it had just been born.

I think the pendulum may now have swung too far. Nonprofit organizations' burgeoning prosperity is attracting those who should be in business. They want nonprofit tax benefits, so they devise joint ventures to link those benefits to the profit motive. They try to transform nonprofits into for-profits. Some even start their new businesses under a nonprofit cloak. Some financially challenged nonprofit leaders have piggybacked on the trend. The changes they have made in the functioning of their organizations verges on throwing the baby out with the bath water. They are losing the motive power that nonprofits gain from expressive behavior. The swing of the pendulum has helped the sector by bringing in some positive business practices, but it is now time for the pendulum to swing toward the center again, before it ceases to be a pendulum and becomes a wrecking ball.

Specifically, the nonprofit sector has swung far away from its voluntary base of broad voluntary participation and too far toward the practice of hiring paid professionals to do what volunteers once did. It has swung too far away from support by contributors and too far toward fees for service. It has swung too far away from principle and toward expediency, away from affiliation toward efficiency, away from serving participants toward serving managers, and away from independence toward dependence on government, corporate, and foundation grants. Most of all, it is swinging away from the expressive dimension.

We need to acquire a new point of view. We need to recognize and understand nonprofit organizations' relationship to people's expressive needs. That new perspective may move the pendulum's swing in a better direction, conserving the best from our recent gains but also capturing our new enlightenment.

The Other Output

Are expressive behaviors a valid organizational output? If they are, that understanding will call for a revolutionary orientation that will take expressive behavior out of the dark shadows to which we have relegated it. That new perspective will open an unexplored vista of opportunities, while scholars and commentators who have had a problem fitting nonprofit voluntary organizations into their paradigms will solve that puzzle with the model of the double-benefit nonprofit with both instrumental outputs and expressive utility.

Expressive outputs, unlike instrumental outputs, are often unstated. Yet satisfied expressive participants are both major users, or consumers, of nonprofit organizations and a principle product of those organizations. Should we not have organizations that feed the hungers of people whose other activities restrict their expressive behavior? Is that not a legitimate goal? For example, an adult literacy program involving volunteer tutors has the instrumental output of X number of adults increasing their reading ability by Y number of grade levels. It also has the expressive output of A number of tutors learning B number of skills and experiencing C amount of satisfaction. One might add the serendipitous benefit of Z amount of cross-cultural rapport. Who can say that the output to the quality of life of the learners is more important than the output to the quality of life of the tutors? Surely, no one can say that both benefits do not contribute to society.

Any organization will appear inefficient if an observer compares its costs to only part of its outputs. Effective evaluation of nonprofit organizations must include both their instrumental and expressive outputs. There is no reason to see expressive behavior as dysfunctional and to attempt to purge it. Our society has a robust business sector for organizations that exclude "unnecessary" expressive action. But where the expressive dimension of organizational participation is a significant component of certain organizations, then it follows that it is normative for that organizational culture. If it contributes positively to that culture, the culture should consciously acknowledge, enhance, encourage, and enshrine it among the cultural norms.

Overriding Benefits

I am an unapologetic convert to organizational enhancement of expressive outputs. I say "convert" because I spent my first sixteen years as a nonprofit manager trying to squeeze expressive behavior out of the way of instrumental goals. Then, I envisioned expressive outputs not only as legitimate but also as potent motivators for accomplishing instrumental visions. I found that enhancing expressive outputs substantially helps both the organizations and their participants.

Expressive activity in organizations is important not only because people *need it as an end in itself,* but also because *the opportunity for expressive activity attracts and motivates participants to work for instrumental purposes.* While some voluntary nonprofit organizations exist specifically for facilitating expressive behavior, others have traditionally used the intrinsic motivation of direct expressive satisfaction to achieve indirect instrumental goals. All leaders and managers but especially those with significant commitments to measurable instrumental outputs should appreciate expressive outputs as a major source of energy and other resources. As just one example, volunteers who work for charitable causes are more likely than other people to contribute money to charity (Hodgkinson and Weitzman, 1992).

Consider the potency of an organizational community that generates multiple desirable individual experiences while meshing them with significant societal benefits. Participants are anchored within such a community by solid moral and emotive personal underpinnings. They see the organization's being and purposes as their own. They are deeply committed and see the group as an empowered "we" rather than as a restraining "they" (Etzioni, 1988, pp. ix–x). Such organizations give participants a sense of security. In working toward common goals and helping each other, the participants develop a sense of control over their environment. In the small forums even the largest of these organizations provide, members solve their communication problems by interacting with groups of a manageable size and learning the expectations of this otherwise overwhelming new society.

Participation in expressive organizations influences decisions that affect people's lives. Listen in at an informal reunion of people who once worked together on a long-past campaign or project. The conversation will revolve around humorous, difficult, or even unsuccessful problem solving and decision making. Participation "plugs in" a person, giving her or him a functional identity. It binds the individual into the society's patterns of interrelationships. Consider how often we base our images of individuals on the information we have concerning their group affiliations. Participation establishes part of our reality. It provides consensual validation for individuals as well as an accepting body for people to bounce their views off in order to test perceptions or reality. We see this particularly clearly when a person we know changes one of his or her affiliations and then begins to see the world from a different point of view.

Since nonprofits do not have to produce a profit, they are the ideal vehicles in which individuals can band together to accomplish a wide variety of purposes. They are the means by which people's diverse motivations find expression and then reach significant ends that enrich life. Voluntary enterprises have access to vast amounts of human energy through the time, effort, funds, and talents contributed by volunteers. In return, these enterprises amplify the voices of their constituents for myriad causes and provide avenues of expression available nowhere else. Though they often bemoan their lack of funds, it is their very freedom from the tyrannies of cost effectiveness that gives them more freedom than for-profit organizations to explore uncharted territory.

Within the voluntary nonprofit environment, pure democracy can flourish. What a marvelous training ground exists in a voluntary group's committees, intrigues, human interplay, personal influences, and meetings, meetings, meetings. Nowhere else do we find our human values so emphasized. *We* are what such organizations are all about; *we* are something more than organizational machinery and the amassing of material goods. Those who work full-time in the voluntary sector have boundless resources for personal satisfaction and the practice of their chosen professions. The voluntary enterprise is responsive to creativity, new approaches, and specialized interests. It sanctions glory in the doing.

Nonprofit organizations are one of the primary creators of civilization and one of civilization's greatest creations. Their ability to satisfy many expressive needs has given them an invigorating vitality and the motive power to achieve the instrumental objectives of their causes. However, the leadership of organizations with major expressive components is complex. Leading them well is as much an art as a science. If this art were to atrophy, the essence could be squeezed out of the sector and nonprofits could be transformed into unimaginative government agencies or third-rate businesses.

Leaders in the nonprofit sector must be able to deal with nonconforming free spirits and welcome flexibility, innovation, and creativity. The commons is a culture of many speeches and publications, which as often identify individuals by their beliefs as by their deeds. If business is an environment of numbers, then the voluntary sector is an environment of words, words concerning beliefs, ideals, and appeals. It is also an environment that feeds the ego better than the bank account and in which honor and recognition replace bonuses and stock options. Leaders must be able to recognize the words and the rewards that will be meaningful.

Because nonprofits have multiple purposes, leaders with a need for clear-cut goals, measurable objectives, and unity of purpose may not be comfortable in them, particularly if an organization's goals change often and its priorities mix expressive and instrumental outputs. Conversely, the general complexity found in the nonprofit sector often attracts people who enjoy juggling many things at once or who have a holistic way of thinking that allows them to embrace complexity. These people have to find their satisfaction in the doing of work, for they usually cannot know precisely where they stand in terms of tangible accomplishment.

Voluntarism Is Not a Last Resort

The public cannot consciously recognize the legitimacy of expressive organizations and the expressive aspects of instrumental organizations until those of us in the sector recognize them, until we show that voluntarism is a positive good, not a last resort that makes up for lapses in the business and government sectors as some commentators maintain. Voluntary action may be an autonomous experience of human life (Adams, 1976, p. 8); its power is shown in the way people have established entire organizations to satisfy expressive needs or to provide opportunities for the exercise of voluntarism. The public should acknowledge expressive meaning as the motive force in the voluntary sector and see expressive output as a potent asset to the society, organizations, and individuals. Organizations should visualize the vast benefit of harnessing the power of expressive meaning for maximum effectiveness.

One individual involuntarily expresses fear when hearing the sudden buzz and movement of a rattlesnake in the path. Another involuntarily expresses joy with a clap of the hands and a burst of laughter at the first step of a baby girl. Another voluntarily expresses deep sorrow or lofty love with the lilting melody of song or the graceful line and brilliant colors of a painting. Still another, with a cup of cold water and a loaf of bread, voluntarily expresses compassion for a hungry beggar or, with a warm bed and needed medication, for a sick child. With as many levels of action as there are layers of meaning, human beings squeeze out what is within them—their feelings, their values, and their commitments. When a solo or small ensemble is insufficient, a full orchestra and chorus may be required in which individuals join not only to express what they feel and to do what they must do but also to express who they are.

African Americans symbolically marching across the bridge at Selma, knowing they could disperse and flee and play the part many expected of them but also knowing they must overcome the skewed norms of their white neighbors, marched on, marched on, because they were changed, changed men and women pouring out in courage the new beings they now were, marching toward Montgomery and what they were determined to become.

General Booth, with one hand out to suffering mankind and another to a loving God, by force of will pushed out from within himself the genius and energy to conceive and establish the Salvation Army. Florence Nightingale went where women had not gone before, into the battlefield to nurse, to heal, to soothe, to bind, and to console the wounded and dying of the Crimean war. Albert Schweitzer left not only his beloved Alsace but also the acclaim of intellectuals for his scholarship and the acclaim of musicians for his interpretations of Bach because the compassion that was within his heart drove him to steaming equatorial Gabon to minister to people of a materially poorer culture than his who were dying from such common treatable ailments as appendicitis. Mother Teresa comforts the diseased and dying found in the streets of Calcutta because her need to do so is as great as their need to have her do it. All these individuals and millions of others exemplify the flowing over of the human need to express something within oneself that compels one to act.

The voluntary sector's centerpiece is its capacity for expressive as well as instrumental ends. Unpaid personnel maintain an environment in which organizational members can legitimately foster their own interests and satisfy needs that made membership in a nonprofit organization first desirable. The organization does not have to be predictable or profitable or even practical. It is free to explore on the cutting edge. It has the endurance to persevere down the tunnel, even when no light is evident at the other end. Within its rich mixture of forces, personalities, ideas, and needs, concepts can constantly collide and spawn innovations. Such organizations constantly enrich our society so that organizations from all sectors may prosper.

Conclusion

Mr. Keating, Robin Williams's character in the movie *Dead Poets Society*, took a creative approach to his teaching. Once, he had his students stand on their desks, telling them, "You must constantly look at things in different ways."

Expressive behavior for direct gratification is part of our human nature, and we have formed organizations for expressive purposes since prehistoric times. Though current studies and organizational planning tend to ignore or discount expressive behavior, we need to recognize expression as natural, legitimate, and potent in achieving a wide range of ends. The more we understand expressive behavior and apply this understanding, the more effective will be our nonprofit leadership and our nonprofit organizations.

Needs for Further Research

I suggest that the independent sector's most profound need is to incorporate the expressive dimension into current theory. Researchers working with a specific organization or in a discrete field might track management practices from the end of World War II to the present to identify any changes in emphasis favoring either expressive or instrumental outputs. Finally, someone could serve us all by doing what I did not do—discovering a better name for expressive behavior.

Actions for Practitioners

My recommendations for leaders and managers will generally concern organizations with a paid staff. (All-volunteer groups tend to generate profound expressive outputs almost by definition.) However, if all-volunteer groups or organizations with small numbers of paid staff wish to enhance their expressive dimensions, I suggest that they implement the broad-brush-stroke recommendations to practitioners that are given at the end of each chapter. For example, if I could recommend only one thing to practitioners at this point, I would suggest that they talk about the expressive output concept with their inner circles or boards. They might ask: "To what degree do we, as individuals, benefit from the expressive outputs of this organization?" "How important was expressive activity to our founders?" "In what direction is our organization moving, toward more expressive or more instrumental behavior?" "Is that current direction our best course?" "Could we benefit by openly acknowledging our expressive dimension?"

As you read these chapters, especially Chapters Five through Ten, which build the foundation on which leaders and managers can expand and enhance organizational effectiveness through expressive motivations, I would remind you that this is a time for an attitude of openness and expectancy. Develop a new paradigm. Stop thinking of expressive behavior as parasitic and begin thinking of it as both a legitimate output and as a means toward instrumental ends. Sometimes, we must remember the six blind men who were studying an elephant. The first touched a tusk and decided the animal was like a spear. Holding a leg, the second described it as like a tree. The third felt its side and said it was like a wall, and the fourth felt its trunk and said it was like a snake. The fifth, holding the elephant's ear, thought it like a fan; and the sixth, holding the tail, said it was more like a rope. Like the six blind men, we need to expand our points of view. "To improve in major ways," Stephen Covey tells us, "I mean dramatic, revolutionary, transforming ways, quantum improvements, change your frame of reference. Change how you see the world, how you think about people, how you view management and leadership. Change your paradigm. . . . [Talk about] purposes that lift [people], ennoble them, and bring them to their highest selves. . . . [Use] values, ideas, ideals, norms, and teaching that uplift, ennoble, fulfill, empower, and inspire, . . . make work challenging and fulfilling, . . . talk about vision and mission, roles, and goals. [Talk about making] a meaningful contribution" (1991, pp. 173–180).

Finally, this book emphasizes the forest rather than the trees. While I admit that there are exceptions to everything, I have not qualified each observation I make. The voluntary nonprofit sector is broad, with overlapping and gaping classifications. There are virtually no universally valid statements that include every organization in this diverse sector. So I ask the reader to excuse any occasional imprecisions in the interest of focusing on pervasive principles. For example, instead of specifying "an expressive mutual-benefit voluntary nonprofit corporation," I will say "organization." Instead of writing, "an organization in which expressive behavior by participants predominates," I will write, "expressive organization."

In this introductory chapter, I have argued that legitimate expressive outputs need to be recognized and that they not only meet many human needs but also produce energy for organizations. While this book spotlights the nonprofit sector, its concepts have broader application. The next chapter looks at the general topic of uncovering and harnessing expressive energy.

Chapter Two

Uncovering and Harnessing Expressive Energy

This chapter covers several preliminary considerations. It describes how what should be obvious to everyone has been covered from view and how all voluntary nonprofit organizations generate expressive outputs, although the magnitude of expressive (and instrumental) outputs varies with the organization. This chapter also suggests that leading an organization toward optimum expressive outputs may be more art than science but that management skills can enhance the art. And it discusses the combination instrumental-expressive organizational model that I use in later chapters as the model from which we can learn the most.

The Veils

When what should be obvious to everyone is hidden from many, it is probably because a veil is blocking the view. For example, the Englishman known as Lawrence of Arabia became a leader of Arabs by seeing their world as they saw it. He moved all obstructions aside. He adopted the Bedouin perspective by learning Bedouin history and values, wearing Bedouin clothes, speaking Arabic, and adapting to the desert culture. According to a legendary story, Lawrence and an Arab comrade once conversed by a dying fire under the starry desert sky and reminisced about shared experiences of days past and their hopes for the Arabs in the days ahead. When the conversation lagged, the Arab politely inquired about the Englishman's boyhood home. Lawrence answered far beyond the interest of the questioner. He rambled on about the glades and brooks of home, about lush vegetation, stately ivy-covered estates, undulating green lawns, meadows of grazing sheep, golden wheat, ancient trees, singing birds, and familiar roads and paths. He suddenly realized he was describing a land he believed to have everything the desert lacked. Embarrassed by his bragging, he fell silent. Seeing that his friend was finally through, the Arab, with an unmistakable tone of compassion, exclaimed, "But you had no place for your camels!"

Years before, Lawrence had shifted perspectives in order to understand the Arab mind-set. However, his Bedouin friend, who had never visited the British Isles or tried to shift perspectives, was unable to step out of his habitual value system. He did not visualize England from the point of view of one who valued its topography.

Our world is one of grass *and* sand, islands *and* deserts. A realistic perspective sees the whole and adapts to each segment as necessary.

As mentioned in Chapter One, people who run organizations and theoretical scholars do not always share the same priorities. Decades ago, Chester I. Barnard, a successful manager and president of the New Jersey Bell Telephone Company, wrote a trailblazing management treatise in which he noted that management scholars excluded realistic social factors from their theories (1938). (Since then, Douglas McGregor and others have brought business theory more into line with the practical reality of the human side of enterprise.) Likewise, many students of the voluntary and nonprofit sector have tended to exclude expressive behavior from their theories. At the least, they have minimized its importance. It is as if a series of veils has covered the importance of the expressive dimension, hiding it from those who need to see it most. If we do not lift these veils, we may allow a vital ingredient to fade from the life of some organizations. We should consider the inner veil, the veil of measurement difficulty, the veil of sector youth, the veil of religious institutions, and the veil of objections.

Inner Veil

Nonprofit insiders put up inner veils to hide the expressive dimension. Some do so innocently, while others do so in a calculated movement toward increased professionalization and instrumentality. Those who drape these veils unintentionally hide reality by taking expressive behavior for granted. They want their work to appear utilitarian to conform to prevailing cultural values. They apply expressive motivation in problem solving and decision making, but they rarely talk about it openly. Some of them discourage the presence of unpaid participants in general and in decision-making positions specifically because they lack the confidence to lead volunteers in an ambiguous expressive milieu. They constrain their ultimate effectiveness when they become obsessed with an inner need to control all aspects of direct service to clients by personally making every decision within their sphere of responsibility.

Our utilitarian, materialistic scientific culture encourages participants to speak in terms common to science rather than art, to speak of instrumental outputs rather than fun and adult "play." Interviewed about her motives, a relief worker in Somalia will more likely say, "I'm here to feed the thousands of starving people," than, "I enjoy feeling needed and involved in something important." How self-centered to discuss the fun, the satisfaction, the feeling of importance, and the transcending "highs"!

In short, the inner veil disguises the expressive aspect from those who should value it most.

Measurement Difficulty

A second veil is measurement difficulty. Since the 1960s, several factors have put nonprofits under pressure to be more accountable for their instrumental results. One factor has been a growing emphasis on management and measurement in general. A business-oriented culture places a premium on the financial bottom line, and materialistic values shout to us with every commercial and advertisement. Another factor was Lyndon Johnson's War on Poverty and the new Office of Economic Opportunity. The War on Poverty funneled federal funds into the nonprofit sector for instrumental application toward solving many of the causes and results of poverty. Recipient organizations, many for the first time, had to account to outsiders for the results of their funded programs. (Although my experience in those early days was that the appropriateness and accuracy of the measurements was not nearly as important to the recipients as the full utilization of all the blanks in the report forms.) A third factor was the culmination of a decade of Wright Patman hearings and the 1969 Tax Reform Act requiring foundations to be more transparent. Since foundations had to be more accountable, they rightfully passed on more stringent requirements for instrumental expenditure accountability to the organizations they funded.

The accountability emphasis has done many good things. It has replaced much pabulum with beefsteak. Funding sources want to hear about more than good intentions. Recipients need to show that money given to solve social problems has gone toward some social benefit—preferably that X dollars produced Y instrumental output. How impressive to say, "Your $38,000 helped us to feed 317 homeless people for a week, provide each of them a change of clothing and a blanket, and place 17 of them in permanent jobs." However, even legitimate demands for accountability minimize concern for effective expressive aspects except as such aspects contribute to instrumental ends. Unfortunately, the emphasis on numerically measurable instrumental outputs has, to a great degree, obscured profound values because no government, foundation, or corporation asks about them. Nonprofit leaders today do not include the relatively unmeasurable expressive dimension in their financial reports to the board or in statistical reports to regulators or funders.

The incorporation of more evaluation and performance measures into programs and/or funding proposals has also profoundly affected the attitudes of nonprofit employees and the selection and training of new paid staff. Current reporting styles influence many leaders to hire professionals to do what expressive volunteers can do, and to increase earned income to replace expressive donations.

How does one measure expressive values and outputs? We all know that many vital things defy measurement. It was a poet not a scientist who took a stab at measuring love, and even Elizabeth Barrett Browning fell short when she wrote, "How do I love thee? Let me count the ways." She may have counted, but she did not assign a magnitude to each way. The more scholars think of themselves as scientists, the more they dismiss what they cannot measure, while pressures to produce measurements often result in selecting the wrong items to measure. But lack of measurability is endemic to the nonprofit sector, and lack of measurability is not lack of worth (Mason, 1984a, p. 29). As yet unmeasurable things such as love, fun, satisfaction, play, and joy are still good reasons for living. A nonprofit is no more accurately measured by its income than a symphony by the speed with which it is performed, a bank by its height, people by their weight, or a university by its altitude above sea level. We can measure these things, but that measure is unrelated to the quality or value of the entity. Beware all efforts to confine truth to what is readily available and easily measured.

Sector Youth

A third veil that falls between current scholarship and reality is the youth of the sector. To a degree, scholarship is still isolated within the older professional fields of the sector, such as religion, education, and health care. Scholars in these fields have studied churches, schools, and hospitals for centuries, but only recently have scholars in established academic disciplines like sociology and economics started to analyze the nonprofit phenomenon as a "sector." We must begin to blend the best understanding from the practical fields with the best from the academic disciplines.

A growing number of scholars and writers have discovered voluntary and nonprofit organizations in recent decades. Why would those whose experience lies in other fields be drawn to this sector? Perhaps because it is a huge, suddenly available market. Writers and consultants find that new journals and periodicals give them access to a tremendous market that they perceive as receptive and accommodating to their expertise. Consultants and publishers can change a few words in an old brochure designed for business prospects, add a fundraising or volunteer recruiting seminar, and have a go at the do-gooders hungry for management knowledge. One would not expect from these efforts anything but a cosmetic adaptation of an offering initially designed for business. They would, of course, omit essential components and would teach a new generation that what the authors leave out must not be important.

The new commentators tend to start with a template of assumptions gleaned from disciplines other than nonprofit studies. Given these assumptions, it is not surprising that some nonprofit researchers are reluctant to include within their purview a subcategory of expressive activities and expressive organizations that is not only extensive but also difficult to place within their basic conceptual frameworks. Instead, they proceed somewhat as their ancestors did when they named Native Americans "Indians" because they were looking for India. Now, there is absolutely nothing illegal about studying, say, a ruin of an ancient Greek temple from a physics perspective—aesthetics aside. There is nothing immoral about analyzing Renaissance paintings from the perspective of the chemistry of pigments—aesthetics aside. But one grossly errs if one seeks an aesthetic understanding of art solely through the eyes of physicists or chemists.

The impact of science on the culture of higher education has been to exclude almost all expressive perspectives from academic life because they are seen as lacking scientific credentials. To paraphrase Edmund Burke: In the groves of their academy, at the end of every vista, one sees nothing but the measurable bottom line. On the principles of this mechanic philosophy our institutions can never be embodied in persons to create in us love, veneration, admiration, or attachment. In a similar vein, David Horton Smith observes that "discipline-bound scholarship, suffering from over-compartmentalization with little or no synthesis across the compartments, insisting on professionally established variables, concepts, and research methods, is functional for orderliness, but dysfunctional for full understanding" (1980, pp. 1–13). And Theodore Hershberg complains that, "the social sciences in our universities are organized by departments and dominated by discipline-based research paradigms that make collaborative and interdisciplinary research exceedingly difficult" (1989, p. 75). It is important for us to be aware of the limitations of current scholarship and to encourage mature scholarship that focuses more on the reality of nonprofit institutions.

Religious Institutions

A fourth veil hides half of the nonprofit sector. It is the veil draped over expressive congregations and other religious institutions. The neglect of religious institutions by nonprofit scholars is especially unfortunate because congregations and other religious organizations have long been, and remain today, at the heart of a range of sector activities. Studies in the United States and Western Europe, for example, cite close links between individuals' adherence to a religion and their propensity to engage in voluntary action. Emerging evidence from Eastern and Central Europe suggests that churches and church-related aid agencies play a key role in the building and rebuilding of independent sector civil societies (Mason and Harris, 1994).

Besides being central to nonprofit sector activity, religion is central to the everyday lives of many individuals in the United States. In polls taken in March 1994, 93 percent of respondents said they believed in God, 59 percent said religion was very important in their lives, 29 percent called religion fairly important to them, and only 11 percent said it was unimportant (Peterson, 1994, p. 1; Sheler, 1994, p. 50). In Western Europe, approximately three-fifths of the population regard themselves as religious. As Nelson points out in a discussion of the neglect of churches by scholars of organizational and international management, "By generally ignoring churches, organization theorists neglect a significant proportion of all organizations, both nationally and cross-nationally" (1993, p. 655).

It is surely inappropriate to marginalize the importance of religious institutions within the nonprofit field. Margaret Harris of the London School of Economics and I attribute the existing "embarrassed silence" to technical and methodological challenges; to current definitions of sectorial boundaries; and to the secular culture, the academic and religious culture, and the traditions of the social sciences, that is, to points of view that narrow people's vision (Mason and Harris, 1994, p. 3).

As I have argued elsewhere, synagogues and churches are the organizational prototypes of today's typical nonprofit organization (Mason, 1995). We have inherited our cultural template of what a voluntary organization looks like, most of our nonprofit sector values, and many specific nonprofit "industries" from these institutions. Discussing nonprofits while ignoring their religious roots is like walking down Seventh Avenue in New York and believing you are seeing all of midtown Manhattan.

Objections

Commentators on the practical rather than the theoretical aspects of nonprofits may cover the expressive dimension with a veil of objections, viewing expressive aspects as dysfunctional glitches in otherwise worthy organizations. The following list contains four-teen liabilities that some believe plague nonprofit organizations. In comparison to organizations in other sectors, nonprofits are considered to be

1. *Less responsive to familiar management procedures.* The more famil-iar managers and scholars are with effective business princi-ples, the more frustrated they may become with a nonprofit entity. Typically impatient with the nonprofit culture's priori-ties and lack of numerical indicators, businesspeople confuse "businesslike" management with effective management.

2. *Incrementally inefficient.* Paid professionals in a production unit responsible for an instrumental output are more likely to reach their objectives faster than the same number of volunteers. Paid employees will probably start on time, spend less time relating to each other, produce neater reports, and require less guidance than a more expressive group.

3. *Tolerant of sloppy accounting.* The outputs of most nonprofits are less responsive to market pressures than are the products of other organizations (Mason, 1984a, p. 26). Comprehensive accurate accounting of donated time and expertise and of qualitative and objective outputs can easily cost more than the results are worth.

4. *Less responsive to autocratic control.* The coercive power of a mili-tary commander and the exchange power of an industrial man-ager can mandate immediate compliance from a subordinate. Voluntary enterprises get compliance by slower normative means. Many volunteer middle managers may not readily respond to top management's wishes because expressive expe-rience is a more potent motivation than a share of the alloca-tion of resources.

5. *Cumbersomely complex.* Nonprofit and voluntary organizations have both paid and unpaid staff, both instrumental and expres-sive purposes, multiple classes of stakeholders, and one system for service provision and another for revenue production. The best managers often require a professional education in the field of service the organization provides in addition to their management expertise (Mason, 1984a, p. 13).

6. *Unnecessarily archaic.* Some nonprofits cling to organizational

poverty as a badge of honor in what has been called the "servant syndrome" (Handy, 1988, pp. 7–8). A few eschew state-of-the-art technology, professional management, specific objectives, and realistic priorities.

7. *Tedious in decision making.* Choosing courses of action in expressive organizations can be slow and subjective and may be based on internal politics, social attitudes, and feelings rather than on rational decision-making procedures. In many organizations, there are two or even three management hierarchies—the professionals, the administrators, and the hierarchy of voluntary and/or elected leadership.

8. *Dominated by process and politics.* The priority of the process often overrides that of the product, and internal political considerations permeate every transaction. One must expect this when participants seek intrinsic rewards from their participation in the process itself, with the highest reward for work being given more rewarding work to do. The democratic nature of expressive organizations places a premium on political and diplomatic skills and means that leaders must develop a political base of power and influence.

9. *Rife with relationship problems.* Personnel burn many hours of off-duty and on-duty time in gossip, self-counseling, and the juggling of interpersonal relations. Seminars on board-staff relations and staff-volunteer relations are an industry. Problems at the interfaces of paid and unpaid domains are more often than not the clash of an instrumental and an expressive culture.

10. *Beset with funding limitations.* Funders are more likely to support instrumental than expressive activity (more likely to provide food for the homeless than to enable volunteer cooks). Outsiders become less likely to contribute as the expressive output increases in relation to the instrumental output because members are more likely to seek contributions for their charitable projects than for membership activities. (An exception occurs when expression has an ultimate instrumental result, like midnight basketball to keep youths out of trouble).

11. *Slow paced.* Business people often object to the slow pace of nonprofits. Democracy, cumbersome decision making, volunteer labor, complexity, internal politics, and imprecise goals

combine to gum up organizational machinery. The slow pace stresses the more industrious participants.

12. *Imprecise about their destinations.* Organizations with significant expressive components tend to have complex overlapping fuzzy goals and blurred objectives. A bias among the rank and file against management methodology may dominate. In spite of statements citing lofty transcending purposes, participants often find it difficult to define precisely where the total organization is really trying to go.

13. *Full of fanaticism.* For some participants, striving for the cause is much more important to them than the organization. They resist spending the energy necessary for organizational survival or legitimate self-interest. Nonfanatics frustrate impatient fanatics. Results and reason often count for little among fanatics. Their bad words are "success," "structure," "professionalism," and "management," and some tend to make a virtue out of failure (Handy, 1988, pp. 8–9). Anybody who ever differed with a "true believer" knows how difficult it is to deal with fanatics' behavior (Etzioni, 1988, p. 106).

14. *Beset by personal-organizational goal conflict.* Incongruent activities occur when the little personal arrows point toward different targets than the big organizational arrow. Activity that a business employer pays for but that does not contribute to the output of the business is indeed dysfunctional. One respected business scholar calls such work toward one's personal objectives without reference to organizational objectives "bureaupathology" (Thompson, 1961, p. 153).

A belief that these behaviors are liabilities in nonprofits because they are liabilities in business is a veil that has obscured much of the good of the expressive dimension, just as have the inner veil, and the veils of measurement difficulty, sector youth, and religious institutions.

Range of Nonprofit Organizations

To meet their diverse needs, human beings have constructed a wide range of organizations. The primary goal of a business is to be instrumental in making money. The goal of a government is to be instrumental in governing. Nonprofits take their generic name not from their goals but from the fact that distributing profits is not one of their goals. The potpourri of organizations that we call the voluntary nonprofit sector has the general attributes of being not-for-profit, nongovernmental, voluntary, and values-expressive. Nonprofit organizations are usually self-governed by local representative boards that achieve compliance by normative means rather than by exchange of wages for work or by coercion, are supported by contributions for member or public benefit, and have instrumental and/or expressive purposes. However, within this general pattern, there are many models, and even when organizations specialize in the same field, the model that works for one may be completely inappropriate for another. Nonprofit organizations span a tremendous range. Some are indistinguishable from businesses, while others are virtual governments. They vary in size from a neighborhood card club to the Catholic Church. I do not advocate the modification of these different formats to conform to a one-format-fits-all absurdity. The ideal is to adopt appropriate formats for different needs.

Nonprofit enterprises have been classified in various ways. Smith contrasts "established" nonprofit organizations that make wide use of paid staff to "volunteer" groups in which membership and volunteer staff predominate. He also contrasts organizations that are primarily "self-serving" in that they focus on member interests to organizations that are "other-serving" in that their goals involve improvement of some aspect of the larger society (1980, pp. 1–1 to 1–15). Amitai Etzioni classifies organizations according to their means of exacting compliance: coercive, utilitarian, or normative. He includes most of the nonprofit sector in the normative category: religious organizations, political organizations that have a strong ideological program, hospitals, universities, and voluntary associations that rely mainly on social commitments. Less typical are schools and therapeutic mental institutions in which coercion plays an important secondary role and professional organizations in which remuneration plays an important part (1975, pp. 40–41).

If we focus on expressive aspects of nonprofit organizations, I suggest that we can see a range of four types along an expressive-instrumental continuum (adapted from a 1957 typology by Jacoby and Babchuk; see Chapter Three for more detail).

- *Expressive.* Both the stated purposes and activities of purely expressive organizations involve the doing of the action itself. Examples are chess clubs, fraternities, and the Masonic Lodge.
- *Expressive-instrumental.* Expressive-instrumental organizations combine the purposes and activities of organizations at the extreme ends of the present continuum, but overt expressive values predominate. Examples are civic clubs, charismatic congregations, and Safari Club International.
- *Instrumental-expressive.* Instrumental-expressive organizations combine the purposes and activities of organizations at the extreme ends of the present continuum, but instrumental production activities predominate. Examples are hospital auxiliaries, parent-teacher associations, and the Literacy Volunteers of America.
- *Instrumental.* The purposes and activities of the purely instrumental nonprofit organization focus on producing something of value for people outside the organization, and any expressive aspect is incidental or distractive. Examples are nursing homes, private schools, and the American Automobile Association.

Rather than attempt to adapt each point in this book to each of the four types, I have focused on describing the instrumental-expressive model throughout. It is in the middle of the continuum, and it provides balanced benefits to both participants and society. The discussion of it covers managing and leading both the expressive and instrumental sides of a group; therefore, readers can select the information they need for their specific organizations.

In addition, I assume a national social service organization with regional offices and local chapters. The various units are iterative, each responsible for the same fundraising and service-providing activities as the others, but at a different level and location. An example is a literacy council in a major city. It is governed by a volunteer board and is managed by a CEO with a small support staff. It raises its operating funds through an annual drive, supplemented by small grants and the United Way. A corps of volunteer tutors works in small groups or one-on-one with functionally illiterate adults and teenagers. The literacy council is affiliated with a state coordinating committee and a national organization to which it contributes nominal dues based on its membership. A charismatic woman founded the local council, and the organization has waxed and waned in size over the years. The council has two principle outputs: it teaches people to read (instrumental), and it provides a richly satisfying service opportunity for its tutors (expressive).

Range of Personnel

Consider the denizens of voluntary nonprofit organizations, the people who operate them. I identify the following classifications for salaried staff and unpaid volunteers.

Many *paid staff members* enjoy their jobs for the sake of the work itself, and their ideal reward is more work with more responsibility. They enjoy a collegial environment and gain satisfaction from their work. They tend to be better educated than their business counterparts and think of their work as being more important than any material rewards. They compare their pay with that of others in their field to meter how well they are doing. The big salaries of business impress them, but they consider manufacturing soft drinks or selling cars or keeping track of other people's money as unworthy of someone with their higher calling.

Paid staff members traditionally serve under considerable stress, accomplishing more with fewer resources, trying to make their segment of the world better by stretching limited dollars. They meet several important needs even in small volunteer-rich organizations. These needs include control, continuity, and a predetermined amount of staff time devoted to a predetermined schedule (Ellis, 1986, p. 9).

Nonprofit *founders* tend to be persistently influential, even after death. Nonprofit organizations do not form spontaneously or accidentally. They evolve from founders' goals and specific purposes. More often than not, founders are charismatic individuals who see their fledgling causes as instrumental means but are themselves fiercely expressive (Mason, 1992). The founder then attracts a core group that shares a common vision and is willing to join the founder's quest for a near-impossible dream. Members of the core begin to create an organization as other individuals are incorporated. They begin building a common history. "Founders will typically have their own notion, based on their own cultural history and personality, of how to get the idea fulfilled. Founders have strong assumptions about the nature of the world, the role that organizations play in that world, the nature of human nature and relationships, and how truth is arrived at" (Schein, 1985, p. 15).

Managers are a class of leaders (discussed in much more detail in later chapters). They are specifically charged with running the organization. Their motives tend to combine concern for the instrumental outputs by which many judge their success, and achievement of the expressive satisfactions that first enticed them into the field. Many enjoy leadership activities for the sake of leading and making important things happen. These leaders tend to make less money and are more committed to their organizations than are many of their business counterparts. Often the *chief executive officers* of nonprofit organizations began as professionals and moved into administrative functions. They can be sensitive to the needs and attitudes of professionals and accepted as members of their fraternity. They have rarely been formally educated as managers, and they often maintain the orientation of their base profession toward management and managers.

Managers who come from the outside or who would score high on task orientation on the Blake-Mouton scale (Blake and Mouton, 1964, p. 11) are likely to clash with constituents oriented toward the expressive pole. Many outside managers do not like the charismatic style of leadership combined with laissez-faire management that is often seen in nonprofits. They expect stricter accountability and quicker response to authority. They manage each aspect of an organization by its contribution to profit and loss, through unambiguous goals, and through personnel who respond to financial incentives, who accept unpleasant activities and demands as part of the territory, and who know nothing of numerically unmeasurable objectives or achieving compliance through organizational norms.

Managers who stress relationships over task accomplishment tend to be more popular with their constituents than are task-oriented managers. Typically, they are well-educated professionals with a firm commitment to the cause for which the organization exists; in some cases, their commitment to the cause may transcend their commitment to their employer. Managers who lead voluntary enterprises tend to need affiliation more than power or achievement (McClelland, Constantian, Regalado, and Stone, 1978). They do not place as much value on wealth and security as do managers in the business sector. They show greater concern for status, personal relations, and social recognition (Rawls, Ullrich, and Nelson, 1973). Many people in the field find that nonprofit personnel have less recognition than businesspeople that they need aggressiveness to succeed. As Max Wortman observed, "Managers work for voluntary organizations because of the possibility of close personal relationships, and close personal relationships tend to be the glue that holds such voluntary organizations together" (1980, p. 65).

Professionals and other executives and specialists, such as educators, social workers, and clergy, are often the key people in nonprofit organizations. As mentioned earlier, professionals who manage organizations usually derive their primary values and expectations from their commitment to a cause or to their profession rather than to their organization. The professional well-educated specialists who are not managers tend to be highly committed to a field because of their interest in its substantive subject matter and/or the environment it provides for the practice of their specialty: teachers teach in schools, physicians heal in hospitals, clergy minister in churches, curators work in museums, musicians perform in orchestras, and social workers help in welfare agencies. Professionals often rank expressive satisfaction above their employer's instrumental goals.

Besides professionals, other types of knowledge workers make up a high proportion of nonprofit personnel. Knowledge work is, of course, more intangible than is physical work and less precise in measurement or sequence. It must, by its nature, be designed by the worker himself or herself. The output of both knowledge workers and professionals is more subject to the influence of morale, mood, human relations, and character than that of manual workers.

Most nonprofits, and virtually all those with a significant expressive component, operate two distinct systems. One provides the services, and the other generates the resources. I will refer to people in service areas as *program personnel* and people who generate resources as *development personnel,* or *fundraisers.* Program personnel interested in certain specialties are drawn to organizations in their fields of interest. Fundraisers may have evolved into their function from another specialty because they are effective at getting money. An individual who is respected as a professional in the organization's basic competency and who is also a good fundraiser may become its CEO. Development personnel are also recruited from the ranks of volunteers or from outside the organization. Fundraisers are the nonprofit organization's sales personnel, and unlike most program people, fundraisers show a direct relationship between their performance and their tangible results—in their case, the funding they bring in. All else being equal, development people may be paid in relationship to the amount of money they raise. Competition among organizations for their talents and their exposure to the outside community may generate a higher turnover for them than for program people.

Support staff are those who file, drive, type, keep books, operate computers, clean, and attend to other technical or administrative details, much as do their business counterparts. They may or may not exhibit strong commitment, and their pay and work are often quite similar to that in comparable business positions.

Volunteers are unpaid participants who often identify themselves not by the generic tag "volunteer" but by their roles as members of a certain committee, as fundraisers who helped to raise a specific sum, as planners or helpers for an annual banquet, or as participants in some other specific function. The expressive aspects of participation are important. The volunteers get together with friends in the organization. They enjoy making things happen. They like to feel needed. They find the rich intrinsic rewards gratifying. Volunteers are usually committed to the cause and tell their friends about it, contribute to it, and build the image of the organization in the community. As a group, they contribute more money than do uninvolved outsiders and are strongly influenced by the expressive component.

Individuals who determine expressive ends tend to dominate those concerned with instrumental means. A premium is placed on the volunteer's commitment to an ideal or on her or his personal charisma, status, character, and ability to facilitate good human relations. Idealists and persons with a strong dedication to a cause tend to gravitate to appropriate nonprofit organizations. The fact that the principal tool of nonprofit organizations is voluntarism influences the organizational culture. With their need to cultivate volunteers and voluntary contributors, nonprofit organizations emphasize relationship-oriented behavior. Amiability, inoffensiveness, persuasiveness, and a cooperative spirit are highly prized.

Susan Ellis, a consultant to volunteer programs, suggests that nonprofit organizations prefer unpaid personnel because they have credibility and are seen as objective and sincere. They make a difference to recipients of services, are effective policy makers, have freedom to criticize, work under less pressure and stress, have a private citizen status (important because of their flexibility and freedom to act on behalf of the organization in cutting through red tape, lobbying, and advocating its interests), and enjoy latitude to experiment and innovate. Ellis adds that volunteers are often more serious than employees, provide diversity, possess augmenting skills, have access to the community, stimulate good public relations, bring an intensive focus on particular issues or clients, and contribute financially (1986, pp. 6–8). I would add that their utilization enables an organization to generate high levels of work during peak periods.

Some unpaid volunteer participants are first-rate professionals, businesspersons, or high-level governmental figures who find in the voluntary organization something not found elsewhere. Such volunteers are virtually confined to this sector. Many are no less managers than paid department heads and no less professionals than paid teachers or accountants.

Volunteers range across an infinite span, but for the sake of convenience, I will use three general levels: board members, unpaid staff, and direct service and administrative volunteers.

Board members sanction the organization on behalf of the society, organizational members, or other constituencies. They hire and fire the CEO, and their actions constitute organizational policy. In many cases, they rise through lower internal volunteer ranks or are selected externally owing to their community leadership coupled with their interest in the organization's instrumental outputs. Some volunteer because society or family tradition expects persons in their position to contribute to the community. Some serve for prestige, contacts, a sense of religious fulfillment, a quid pro quo return on a favor, or to avoid other obligations. In addition to assuming responsibility for instrumental outputs, many board members work for expressive satisfactions. For example, Mr. B. is a wealthy entrepreneur investing primarily in oil and real estate. He can do what he wants with his time due to the nature of his work. He is an idea man and adviser on seven boards. He will neglect his business if he is needed by his church, if he has a responsibility for running a training institute in civic leadership for upwardly mobile young people, or if he is teaching a course in entrepreneurship at a local university. These instrumental-expressive organizations tap his wisdom, energy, and wealth to a degree not possible without his enjoying an expressive outlet.

Volunteers who function as *unpaid staff* play key roles in many effective organizations. Though their activities are usually part-time, they are decision makers, advisers, and/or providers of the service for which the organization was chartered. Like sergeants in the army, unpaid staff run the operations, and in many cases, the paid staff exist to facilitate their work. They are the scoutmasters, church school teachers, and Little League coaches. They usually work for an organization's instrumental outputs with a major expressive motivation. Drucker estimates that perhaps 10 percent of the volunteer population falls into this growing category. He believes unpaid staff should be given all the responsibility they can handle, encouraged to set their own performance goals, and allowed to participate in decision making. "They expect opportunities for advancement, that is, a chance to take on more demanding assignments and more responsibility as their performance warrants" (1989b, p. 92).

Mr. C., for example, owns several companies, and hobnobs with a member of the British Royal family. His companies combined do not meet his desire to shape the values of his community. Though he serves on two boards, he prefers hands-on unpaid management work. He applies his management skills to an artistically successful but financially troubled symphony orchestra and works at both the local and national level for his church. The expressive aspects of these organizations reward him in a way his relatively anonymous business ventures do not.

The original reason for establishing many nonprofits was to provide meaningful participation for a group of persons. Many organizations serve as an extended family or a community for an individual. As a community, the organization can use norms to exert a strong persuasive influence over the adherents. People choose their roles in organizations as much or more for normative and affective (social and emotional) reasons as for calculated rational reasons. If all expressive aspects were squeezed out of nonprofit volunteers' help, they and others like them would be squeezed out, too.

Direct service and administrative volunteers may overlap with unpaid staff in that these volunteers are often frontline, entry-level personnel interacting with clients and others who are recipients of instrumental outputs. They volunteer for many reasons: to have interesting social interaction, to fulfill religious or societal expectations, to obtain work experience or credit for academic courses, and so on. Members of this class are distinguished from other volunteers by having rare or very limited decision-making authority. They may work as refreshment providers and servers, transporters of senior citizens, friendly visitors, baby-sitters, tutors, Candy Stripers, docents, house-to-house canvassers, teaching assistants, and office volunteers, including the proverbial envelope stuffers. In time, many move up in the volunteer ranks or are hired as staff. They are often motivated by an organization's expressive opportunities and would not serve an unworthy cause. For example, not all of Dr. A.'s needs are met by the industrial medicine clinic she heads, so she is active in her yacht club and in her group of physicians who travel together to underdeveloped nations each year, contributing their expertise to save, extend, or improve human lives in areas where physicians are scarce. The yacht club is unabashedly expressive, providing for some of her recreational and ego needs, while the overseas service organization is primarily instrumental; however, without the service organization's expressive opportunity, I doubt if she would participate in it.

Clients are the persons who benefit from a nonprofit organization's instrumental outputs: patients, students, parishioners, audiences, or simply, "the next one in line." For most clients, the organization is instrumental, meeting their needs for health, education, welfare, culture, entertainment, advocacy, or whatever. Moreover, clients are not the same thing as customers. Service providers in organizations with significant expressive components tend to tailor the services to conform to client needs as perceived by those providing the services. The balance of power is toward the provider and away from the client in many cases (Ackroyd, Hughes, and Soothill, 1989, p. 608).

Rank-and-file members are usually the largest group in membership organizations. Of course, not all organizations are membership organizations, so many entities do not call their participants members. In others, all classes are also members. In others, only unpaid personnel are members. Clearly, there can be much overlapping between this category and other categories. In this book, *members* refers to all residual participants, those without an office, title, or other designation.

Contributors give money, often in addition to their time. Ideally, people in all the classes of participants listed so far are also financial contributors at some time and to some degree. However, governments, businesses, foundations, and unaffiliated individuals also can and do support organizations, primarily public-benefit ones. As a rule, contributions are earmarked for an organization's instrumental objectives, but the individual contributor's act of giving itself may be expressively motivated. Outsiders who contribute typically do so because someone they like, respect, or want to impress asks them to. They rarely know the cost effectiveness of the organization's output but give when asked because of an emotional affinity with the appeal. Receiving a certificate or seeing their name in the paper is a plus.

Is the Expressive Dimension Subject to Management?

Managing a voluntary organization has been likened to herding cats (Mason, 1992). Metaphors tap into our complex memory banks and turn on more of our senses than can the mere sight of sterile letters or the hearing of abstract sounds, so I ask you to visualize this process.

Cats must all be volunteers, since they can neither be coerced nor made to work in exchange for compensation. My studies have shown that cats primarily focus on self-centered expressive behavior resulting from intrinsic motivation. My resulting hypothesis is that cats may be herded, one at a time, utilizing an outsized corral with eleven-foot, five-inch high slippery sides, and the herders must have the assistance of 2.6 skilled canines per cat. But the costs in frustration, claw marks, and disabled canines will be great (283 percent of benefits). It will be more feasible to locate a site where cats congregate and build a corral around it, organizing them on an expressive basis. If an instrumental basis is given or if the corral location is fixed, the most cost-effective approach will be to offer something cats find appealing, place it in the corral, and open wide the gates. My conclusion is that cats are more easily enticed than pushed. Therefore, if managing nonprofits is like herding cats, better to lead than to manage. Find what cats like to do and give them a boost.

To what degree can expressive organizations be led? While employees in business are rarely able to choose among alternative instrumental tasks, volunteers, like cats, have much more latitude and will more likely persist if they can choose alternative expressive tasks. If these tasks contribute to an instrumental goal, then one stone kills two birds.

Once leaders identify their organization's expressive outputs, they can enhance a culture that nurtures the organizational components that contribute to expressive behavior, and thus, they can increase both the quantity and quality of the expressive output. The business sector has no more monopoly on effectiveness than the government has on bureaucracy or the voluntary sector has on good intentions. All organizations are simply vehicles we assemble to get us to where we think we want to go. Effective leadership and management in any sector consists of making those thoughts and desires happen.

Voluntary nonprofit organizations have the ability to satisfy many expressive needs. This, in turn, vitalizes participants and endows them with the motive power to achieve the instrumental objectives of their mission. Therefore, managing voluntary organizations without understanding their expressive aspects is as frustrating as reading mystery novels with the closing pages ripped out. Examine the Venus de Milo from a physics perspective, aesthetics aside; examine the family from an economic perspective, love aside; and examine voluntary nonprofit organizations from a business perspective, expressive motivations aside. Such studies produce knowledge—but not understanding.

Effective management for expressive outputs tends to be a combination of tight and loose control—tighter control for the work and looser control for the people. The methodology is based primarily on adapting the structures, the decision-making process, and the specialized concurrent functions detailed in Chapter Eight. When leaders match potential participants' intrinsic motivation and/or drives and/or needs and/or personality characteristics with appealing tasks, the participants work with a will.

Managers can create an environment that releases what Handy calls the "E" forces: "excitement, energy, enthusiasm, and effort" (1988, p. 27). Handy further suggests that when organizational expectations and the energy contributed are balanced, they produce a psychological contract that often rewards participants with more autonomy or more responsibility.

The voluntary not-for-profit sector is indispensable to our way of life. If it disappeared today, we would recreate it tomorrow. We must openly appreciate the power of organizations that offer us expressive satisfaction. Volunteers, people working together for the work's sake, are much more than cheap labor. The voluntary spirit flavors our society, nourishes the sector's constituents, and spices the lives of millions of individuals. Yet its present posture is nothing compared with the power to enrich that lies latent within it. Like Gulliver bound to the ground by the many ropes of the Lilliputians, the voluntary sector lives, breathes, and stirs within its bonds. In my opinion, it yearns for the unleashing of motivations that only the right quality of leadership and management will provide.

Conclusion

Though expressive behavior is ancient, natural, legitimate, and all about us, our view of it and its importance has been obstructed for various reasons. Some nonprofit organizations are purely expressive, and others are instrumental, with expressive-instrumental and instrumental-expressive organizations ranging between. The impact of expressive outputs on organizational participants varies across the range of personnel, according to whether a participant is paid or unpaid and also according to an individual's function.

Leading an organization with an expressive component may be more art than science, but specialized management skills can be applied to the process, and managers can effectively enhance expressive outputs.

Needs for Further Research

Scholars might enrich and expand earlier research on the range of expressive organizations. Should the veils that hide the importance of the expressive dimension be lifted? Should the list of veils that I have suggested be tested empirically? We need more interfacing between generic sector scholars and those who work in and study a sector field or industry such as health, religion, or education.

More interchange among scholars, practitioners, and industry should teach us much about expressive behavior in the real world. An organization such as ARNOVA (Association for Research on Nonprofit Organizations and Voluntary Action) might conduct a conference for this purpose. Also, I know of no one catalogue of all the scholarly journals and relevant periodicals in the various industries that comprise the sector.

We need more research into the interplay between the expressive and instrumental cultures within individual organizations. Researchers studying a specific organization or field might explore the degree of expressive motivations among classes of organization participants. Are there inherent expressive values in an organization that relies on financial support from its own constituency, as does the typical religious organization?

Actions for Practitioners

Leaders and managers should benefit by analyzing the degree of expressive behavior at different personnel levels in their organization. They might compare their organization's position on the typology continuum to the positions of organizations they consider similar to theirs. They should consider where their organization should be on the scale and whether or not they are managing for optimum expressive outputs. Purely instrumental organizations might consider profitizing—moving into the business sector or creating a for-profit subsidiary.

At this point, practitioners should concern themselves more with examining their own motives and attitudes than with taking any action in their service-providing or resource-developing systems. Leaders might consider stepping up a tier in their management so that they are managing the internal organizational environment—not directing operations as much as setting the stage for what the participants choose to do and motivating them toward doing it.

This chapter discussed some veils that must be lifted to uncover the benefits of expressive outputs, how the degree of expressive outputs varies from organization to organization and from participant to participant, and the potential for management to contribute to optimum expressive behavior. Chapter One and this chapter have cleared the underbrush and prepared a foundation for what will follow. The next chapter reviews scholarly investigation into the expressive phenomenon.

Chapter Three

Understanding the Varieties of Expressive Behavior

We wrest control from a phenomenon when we learn its name. When I first heard of the expressive-instrumental continuum, I gained a degree of control over what I had already sensed of its form in the dark. It now had a face. I could recognize it and call it by name when I met it again. That name is often misunderstood, and it does not fully describe the rich brocade of action available for expressive gratification, but knowing it gives us a handle to hold.

This chapter will look at some underlying ideas that scholars have previously explored, putting names to them. My purpose in this chapter is not to pass judgment on what the explorers have found but simply to assemble information on expressive behavior for the reader. We will find that writers have identified empirical expressive behaviors—the existential realities of involuntary and voluntary expressive behavior—and also individual and collective expressive behavior. We will see that most of the many human needs that experts describe are expressive—especially the "higher" ones. The literature substantiates the inherent naturalness of expressive behavior, underlines its legitimacy as a subject worthy of continued serious investigation, and points to its underlying ubiquitous presence in organizations. Finally, this chapter will consolidate three typologies to classify nonprofit organizations.

What difference does it make that an organization's expressive outputs are natural, legitimate, and ubiquitous in meeting human needs? It is important for observers to better understand intrinsic human motivation and for leaders to harness its power in shaping organizations. If even a dead armadillo can move with the current of a river, how much more headway can an Olympic swimmer make by going with the flow? Policy and practice based on a positive natural phenomenon that leaders thoroughly understand are likely to develop effective processes and fulfill profound purposes.

Involuntary and Voluntary Behavior

To express means to directly and firmly "press out." Expressive behavior presses out into action certain cognitive, emotional, or normative motivational states, including deep-seated beliefs and personality attributes. As I have already noted, expressive activity is directly gratifying action for the sake of the action itself. Expressive behavior is an old concept, and established scholars have investigated it from several points of view.

Expression may be either involuntary or voluntary, and we will see that the term *expressive behavior* is used by biologists and psychologists on the one hand and by social scientists on the other hand to mean, respectively, the involuntary and voluntary sides of the same coin. Involuntary expressive behavior is a basic human attribute, recognized as such by eminent founders of both modern biology and psychology. One may express spontaneously, involuntarily, and even unconsciously by direct manifestation of an inner state into facial expressions, gestures, nervous activity, and other muscular and vocal discharges. However, one may also manifest one's will expressively in conscious voluntary speech and conscious intentional action.

For example, consider this brief scenario: a well-dressed man knocks on Mrs. Slater's door, addresses her by name, and introduces himself as Chaplain Balnicky. Noting his furrowed brow, she senses something is wrong as he clears his throat, shifts his shoulders, and rubs the side of his nose. She responds quickly with an anxious, "Yes?" "Your child was in a serious accident," he says. She gasps, covers her mouth, and her knees begin to give way. Both the bearer of bad news and Mrs. Slater are spontaneously and involuntarily expressing their inner emotional states. An observer could read their emotions by their nonverbal expressions.

Consider another scenario: Balnicky voluntarily enrolls in a cabinet-making class at the community college and joins the Lions

Club. Now, the chaplain is consciously expressing his desire to expend physical energy working with his hands and to enjoy the lighthearted fellowship of similar people for whom he has no special responsibility. True, his cabinets have utilitarian value, and the Lions perform valuable community services; however, Balnicky's joy is in the working with wood and in the weekly comradeship. Mrs. Slater, too, has enjoyed singing in a choral group for years. After her child's accident, she works vigorously with Mothers Against Drunk Driving (MADD). She expresses her singing talent in the chorus and her rage over the disfigurement of her son through MADD. These are examples of voluntary expressive activity—actions of conscious intentional choice.

Though outward spontaneous involuntary squeezing out of inner motivational states is of only limited interest in itself for our present purpose, a further review of primary or involuntary expression will facilitate our exploration of voluntary expressive behavior as manifested in organizations.

We typically think of involuntary expression as an individual behavior. "Expression is to passion what language is to thought," wrote Sir John Bell in 1865 (p. 198). "The passions or emotions have also a corresponding organ. . . . The bodily frame, though secondary and inferior, comes in aid of the mind; and the faculties owe their development as much to the operation of the instruments of expression as to the impressions of the outward senses. . . . [E]xpression appears to precede the intellectual operations" (p. 167). Charles Darwin had also observed that expressions are universal and innate manifestations of emotions in both animals and human beings. Darwin's study included questionnaires mailed to scholars worldwide, and he believed expression was part of our nature as mammals and people (1872, p. 4). Infants exhibit a repertory of reactions including crying, excitement, startle responses, and facial expressions of disgust. People in all cultures express joy by laughter and distress by crying. Some see this phenomenon as innate and biological since babies born blind exhibit physical expressive activity.

Freud wrote of expression as a manifestation of our nurture as well as our nature. He shared his insight that internalized moral values in the superego were a component of individual personality. He also identified three points of reference for expression—

the needs of the organism, the external situation, and the patterns of culture. Freud established the notion that individuals unconsciously act out of deep-seated motivations more than they consciously act after careful cognitive calculation (1914). Durkheim argued that morality is society's system of rules and values embedded in the individual and acting as an internal constraining influence on that individual (Etzioni, 1988, p. 7). He also wrote of the power of moral authority as opposed to external coercion and the way that moral authority depends on the internalizing of value patterns as part of personality (Durkheim, 1938, p. 73).

Ethologists have expanded our understanding of involuntary expressive behavior to include animal and human physical displays and full-body activities (Tinbergen, 1952; Van-Hoof, 1963; Lorenz, 1966; Morris, 1969). Those of us who observe animal behavior are aware of involuntary interspecies expression that enables animals and humans to interact with each other as they encode and decode information about primary emotions. A number of scholars early in this century quietly examined this field, establishing that innate expressive behavior is a fundamental and universal component of human personality. This type of expressive phenomenon has lent itself to relatively precise study and experiments with quantifiable results. In the mid 1960s, the nonverbal communication aspects of involuntary expression became a prevalent topic in the popular media and the term *body language* was popularized.

Individuals express themselves involuntarily when they are components of audiences, crowds, and mobs, often acting in unison. Experienced performers and speakers know how the size and compactness of an audience can facilitate or diminish the response to a presentation. Individuals will express their anger as part of a mob to a degree they would not consider in isolation. Hence, we see the basic naturalness of expression as an integral human characteristic, both when we act individually and when we are in groups.

In addition to our natural expression of emotions unconsciously and involuntarily, we voluntarily choose to satisfy intrinsic needs with complex expressive behavior. In both involuntary and voluntary activities, we can see the profundity of the expressive action in which we engage for the sake of the action itself. No wonder we form organizations to facilitate such necessary satisfying action, and no wonder efforts to eliminate it are futile and ill advised.

The literature on voluntary expressive activity is sparse (perhaps because the typically ambiguous milieu of voluntary expression does not lend itself to precise and clearly quantifiable study) but informative. In passing, we must recognize that individuals often experience voluntary expression in isolation, while, for example, jogging along a country road, singing in the shower, fashioning a vase on a potter's wheel, collecting butterflies on a Saturday afternoon, writing a book in the evenings, or building wooden toys for homeless children before Christmas. However, the discussion here concentrates on the expressive dimension of organizations, that is, individuals voluntarily expressing themselves in concert with other organizational members.

Expressive Needs

The more those who determine the direction of a nonprofit organization understand ubiquitous expressive needs, the more likely they are to enable the organization to satisfy those needs. The more effectively the organization meets expressive needs, the more successful it will be. But when we attempt to identify those needs, we find that social scientists are waging big battles on this very territory. David Bouchier comments, "Nobody knows for sure what all 'people need.' We have ideas, based on our own viewpoint, but they are not universals. What a Rwandan refugee 'needs' and what a middle-class person from Iowa 'needs' are a million miles apart. If we knew the universal human needs we would know 'human nature,' and all our important problems would be solved" (personal correspondence, August 20, 1994).

Nevertheless, students of human personality have suggested at least a range of needs. An overwhelming preponderance of these needs can satisfy themselves in expressive organizational behavior. Thus, understanding needs is more than a theoretical exercise—it adds arrows to the quiver of those organizations that want to appeal to more people at a deeper level.

Freud wrote of needs rooted in the sex drive. Jung believed we needed energy for satisfying biological and instinctual needs. Adler believed we are constantly striving toward "the fullest, most complete differentiation and harmonious blending of all aspects of man's total personality" (Ader, 1959, p. 17). Fromm thought we all create our own personality out of the raw material of heredity and experience, and he cited five needs that arise from the conditions of each individual's existence: (1) relatedness, (2) transcendence, (3) rootedness, (4) identity, and (5) frame of reference (1968). Voluntary expressive participation in organizations can satisfy each one of these five.

Ardrey identified the three basic needs of identity, security, and stimulation (1966). Allport (1955), Cattell (1946), Lewin (1948), and Murray (1938) acknowledged the multiplicity of human needs and motivations. Of special interest are the attributes of group membership that Adler (1925), Fromm (1968), Horney (1950), Rogers (1961), and Sullivan (1940) recognized. In all these findings, financial needs (the needs of homo economicus) are not dominant; instead, intrinsic needs are dominant. Deci defined intrinsically motivated activities as those "for which there is no apparent reward except the activity itself . . . [T]he person is deriving enjoyment from the activity. . . . [I]ntrinsically motivated behavior is behavior that is motivated by one's need for feeling competent and self-determining" (1975, pp. 23, 62). If relatively few human needs are material, as all these observers of human nature believe, how can so many other observers describe organized activity as an exclusively economic or instrumental endeavor?

Maslow visualized a pragmatic way of looking at the multiplicity of human needs when he proposed a hierarchy in which various needs are stated to follow a predetermined, ascending order (1965, pp. 122–144). The principles governing this order are these:

1. Everyone wants, and wants more than he or she has. Wants depend on what one already has. When a person satisfies one need, another moves into its position.
2. Satisfied needs do not motivate. Only unsatisfied needs motivate.
3. Needs exist in a hierarchy. Lower-level needs are dominant until satisfied. After lower-level needs are met, those at the next higher level demand satisfaction.

Maslow's hierarchy begins with a foundation of physiological needs. Above that foundation lie safety needs; above that, social needs; and above that needs for esteem. At the peak of the pyramid are self-actualization needs. One need not agree with all of Maslow's theory in order to benefit from his basic idea that needs form a hierarchy. His broad brush strokes have helped us see that our highest needs are expressive and that our priorities change as we satisfy various levels of need.

Maccoby lists eight value drives, or needs, in the workplace: survival, relatedness, pleasure, information, mastery, play, dignity, and meaning. He finds that "we feel the most productive energy when there is an opportunity to satisfy these needs through a balance of work and play" (1988, pp. 57–58). Again, the expressive value drives predominate.

Expressive needs that humans choose to satisfy voluntarily vary in kind and intensity to such a degree that we are not yet able to catalogue them all. Yet I believe that organizations with an expressive dimension provide a range of activities that satisfy many basic needs. Let me suggest examples that satisfy some of the more common needs, beginning with our need for play and including our needs for social relatedness, esteem, physical activity, achievement, creativity, charismatic experiences, fulfillment of duty, and caring.

All of us seek *playful fun*. Purely expressive organizations dedicate themselves to such needs. These organizations include choirs for singers, theaters for actors, and teams for athletes. We not only enjoy play ourselves but also enjoy watching other mature adults play. People form a range of clubs and associations for expressing the passions of amateurs of all classes. In addition to the opportunities offered by such avowedly expressive member-benefit groups, most public-benefit organizations committed to instrumental purposes concurrently provide expressive activity for their participants.

Organizations are a *social* environment for expressing *relatedness*. People need to associate with others and especially to interact with colleagues with common interests. Social activity gives participants affiliation, joy, and camaraderie as part of a community. It satisfies the expressive need for a variety of interactions. It supplies an audience for each person's charm, wit, personality, and pride of association. Social expression is a major motivation for volunteers. As one volunteer expressed it, "I love the human contact—real moments of authenticity." Even an informal group effort can produce joy and exhilaration. Kenyans use the Swahili word "Harambee" when people work together spontaneously. When they lift a heavy log from a jungle trail, they utter "Harambee" as they strain their backs in effort. The word now carries a strong association with other such positive workgroup efforts, and that connotation allowed Kenyan leaders to employ the word to generate energy for their independence movement.

Nonprofit organizations probably best express *values*—whether those responding to the values be paid professionals or volunteers. Jeavons has observed that "the values-expressive character of many private, nonprofit organizations is what distinguishes them from business and government organizations." And he agrees that many organizations "come into being and exist primarily to give expression to the social, philosophical, moral, or religious values of their founders and supporters" (1992, pp. 403–404). The instrumental purpose of the organization may be to advocate a particular position, but participants' primary motivation is often the opportunity to express their feelings about their values. Whether they love ideas, art, baseball, principles, persons, places, things, Harley-Davidson bikes, music, humanity, country, or God, they find whole classes of local and national nonprofit organizations to facilitate the expression of the values they feel.

Participation in voluntary nonprofit organizations, particularly at leadership levels, meets the need for *esteem*. We need something to feel important about. When people find themselves with nothing important to do, they fill the vacuum and make whatever they do seem important. Their action may be motivated by the need to either strengthen their self-image or to enjoy the admiration and approbation of others. The permeable boundaries in nonprofits and the rapid upward mobility for dependable and energetic workers result in an excellent climate to satisfy the need for esteem and to enjoy the influence and even power it may provide. Many nonprofit leaders pour tremendous energy into their work simply because, as they will often say, they "love" running their organizations. Satisfaction in the work itself has been an avenue for many to "show their stuff," find themselves, develop a sense of individual identity as a significant person, and enhance self-worth. Meeting the expressive need for esteem can build a more favorable self-image and decrease feelings of powerlessness and isolation (see Erbe, 1964, p. 198; Aberback, 1969, p. 86).

Rogers stresses the balance that exists between the dual needs for self-regard, or esteem, and positive regard (1961, pp. 223–224). Madden continues this theme in his idea of our need to be "blessed" by significant others. He further believes that as we in turn affirm others, we enhance our own authenticity (1988, p. 3).

Mothers and elementary school teachers will affirm (especially on a rainy day) that small human beings need to burn up energy. Oliver Wendell Holmes said, "I find the great thing in this world is not so much where we stand, as in what direction we are moving. . . . [W]e must sail sometimes with the wind and sometimes against it, but we must sail, and not drift, nor lie at anchor" (*Correct Quotes*, 1991). A need for *activity* persists throughout our lifetimes for many of us and is satisfied through organizations, among other means. If activity is worthwhile, healthy, and fun, so much the better—but staying busy in itself can be a means of satisfying the need for activity. Ubiquitous voluntary organizations offer easily available tasks and roles, often with modest responsibility, for persons who simply need something to do.

People thirst for *achievement*. McClelland, scanning a wide range of cultures, identified three primary needs—affiliation, power, and achievement (1961, p. 36). Handy observed that although "high need for power by itself will often lead to unconstructive authoritarianism," when "combined with, in particular, need for achievement it can lead to productive and satisfying results. . . . [A] high need for affiliation *alone* will tend to be more concerned with developing and maintaining relationships than with decision-making. These sort of people are often seen as ineffective helpers, probably because they are not task-oriented enough. . . . [A high scorer] on this need [for achievement] will like personal responsibility, moderate and calculated risks, feedback on how he is doing. . . . [However,] the high need achiever may tend to become too individualistic" (Handy, 1985, p. 36).

There is an intangible feeling of achievement in working for the sake of the work that is more expressive than instrumental. We can feel a sense of achievement in exploring opportunities or acquiring knowledge, wisdom, or understanding. Closely akin is our thirst for *creative expression,* especially in the process of *meeting a challenge*. Management guru Peter Drucker reports that when he asks business executives why they volunteer for nonprofit tasks, many say, "Because there isn't enough challenge in my job"

(1989b, p. 93). Voluntary nonprofit organizations have a way of exposing challenging opportunities for achievement. The psychological makeup of many who respond to the challenge is like that of Sir Edmund Hillary. When asked why he climbed Mt. Everest, Hillary responded, "Because it is there."

People need *charismatic experiences.* Experiencing a Julio Iglesias, Jimmy Swaggart, Joe Montana, or Barbra Streisand performance; seeing Nelson Mandela parade down Fifth Avenue; or witnessing Boris Yeltsin atop a Russian tank stirs a collective effervescence in the audience. Charismatic personalities themselves are usually motivated by needs for affection, esteem, and self-actualization. They want and need an audience, and an audience needs them (Burns, 1978, p. 246).

Society places a cloak of *duty* around our shoulders, which we experience as an expressive need to be met. Theodore Roosevelt spoke of "the happiness which comes only with labor and effort and self-sacrifice, and those whose joy in life springs in part from power of work and sense of duty" (*Correct Quotes,* 1991).

Many persons need *caring.* Whether it arises out of a sense of duty or a stewardship orientation or as an expression of a deep concern for the survival of our species, the need to offer care bears both on the persistence of nonprofit organizations and the relationship between the rational and emotional bases of human organizations. The word *caring* transcends expressive feelings and instrumental labor, encompassing both "concern for" and "taking charge of" the welfare of others, embracing both love and work.

Western thought has tended to treat emotional expressiveness and rational instrumentality as mutually exclusive, labeling the former as primarily feminine and the latter as primarily masculine (Weber, 1966, p. 197; Waerness, 1984, p. 34). Institutions committed to both compassionate and rationally effective caring confront this notion that expressiveness and instrumentality are mutually exclusive. They challenge the distinction between rationality and compassion. Nonprofit practitioners tend to believe that labor translates love into results. The nonprofit sector, pervaded by such emotionally laden concerns as values and caring, recognizes an equilibrium between "head" and "heart." Hochschild suggests the image of sentient actors for nonprofits. Sentient actors are more than blind emotionalists or bloodless calculators, more than either mere conscious cognitive actors or mere unconscious feeling actors (Waerness, 1984, p. 197).

This discussion of needs has touched on enough personality theories to demonstrate that human beings seek more than physical and material benefits. It is a wonder that many leaders fail to construct organizations that avowedly and intentionally meet people's ubiquitous expressive needs.

Evolving Theory

If a variety of needs are intrinsic and expressive in nature, it is reasonable to assume that people would have joined together early in order to satisfy some of them. And we have evidence that they did.

Sorokin has noted that early philosophers observed two contrasting mentalities that manifested themselves in two types of relationships, foreshadowing Tönnies's gemeinschaft-gesellschaft (community-association) dichotomy (Sorokin, 1957, p. ix). We can see the roots of the instrumental-expressive dichotomy in Sorokin's observation that in the *Republic* and the *Laws,* Plato portrayed two types of society and two types of human personality: "His ideal republic, especially the personality and social regime of the Guardians, is clearly and definitely of the Gemeinschaft type, while his detailed picture of the oligarchic or capitalistic society and man is a conspicuous example of the Gesellschaft type" (Sorokin, 1957, p. ix). Aristotle and Cicero also described the contrasting types, and Sorokin noted that "the same types are found running through the works of the Church fathers, especially those of St. Augustine. Here the theory of the Church and the 'City of God' as the *corpus mysticum* of Gemeinschaft type is contrasted to the 'society of man' depicted along the lines of the Gesellschaft type" (p. ix). The dichotomy persists in the work of medieval thinkers like Joachim de Fiore, Albertus Magnus, St. Thomas Aquinas, and Nicolaus Causanus. It is the central theme of the great Arabian thinker, Ibn Khaldun in his *History of Berbers* and in his *Prolegomenes to the Universal History.* Hegel's expressive Family-Society and instrumental Civic Society are also early prototypes (p. x).

Gemeinschaft and Gesellschaft

Perhaps the most complete modern prototype of our subject comes from the work of German sociologist Ferdinand Tönnies. He spent the better part of his life developing his complex fundamental concepts of gesellschaft and gemeinschaft ([1887] 1957, pp. 18–30). Scholars have largely continued to use his untranslatable German terms to differentiate two types of society. Their English approximations are "association" (gesellschaft) and "community" (gemeinschaft). The expressive organization fits Tönnies's idea of gemeinschaft like a glove fits a hand.

Tönnies built his theories in levels, or concentric spheres. He moved from explaining natural and rational will to a theory of relationships, then to social norms, to social values, and finally, to the larger systems of human endeavor. He saw each level as reflecting two contrasting ways of thinking and relating socially. He initially distinguished between two types of will: the natural individual will and the rational social will—the first concerning relationships between individuals and the second concerning relationships between the larger collectives of society. Tönnies looked at basic "social entities" like kinship, neighborhood, friendship, barter, and contract and then inquired into human will as it relates to human interaction. Next, he saw humans as, by nature, social beings unfolding their essence only by living in communities of kinship, space, and spirit. He posited that rules of conduct express individual relationships based on natural will, in the same way as customs, ethics, and laws express the rational will of larger associations.

Gemeinschaft describes individuals of a similar mind coming together in collectives. They provide services benefiting their own collectivity or the society. The collectives correspond roughly with traditional groupings based on personal and diffuse ties. Tönnies identified gemeinschaft as all kinds of interaction in which natural will predominates, with commonwealth and friendship willed naturally because individuals value those relationships in and of themselves, based on faith. He illustrated with examples of collectives and described the pivotal role of the church as the point of origin. Tönnies summed up Confucius's theory of the five fundamental relationships of father and son, elder and younger brother, husband and wife, ruler and subject, and friend and friend as a reflection of natural constructs in contrast to more instrumental relationships. As another writer has expressed it, "The search for community is the search for roots, place, and belonging—for a group of people in which significant relationships of sharing and caring can take place. . . . [Individuals are] not simply searching for contracts; they are searching for covenant . . . searching for people with whom they can live out life together" (Callahan, 1983, p. 35).

Conversely, Tönnies applied the term gesellschaft to all those associations that form, and are conditioned by, rational will—organizations that are based on contractual relations and that sharply differentiate between means and ends. These associations concern the instrumental appropriation of wealth, barter, exchange, and other activities based around money. The contrasting modes are in common currency in Germany today: *Gemeinschaft* designating a unified community, and *Gesellschaft* designating business relationships.

As time passed, other dichotomous sociological typologies echoed Tönnies's synthesis. Durkheim (1938) differentiated society into the mechanically solidary society in which belief and conduct operate uniformly in tandem and the organically solidary society in which interdependent components unify the society.

Cooley differed with Durkheim's view that the group had primacy over the individual; he also disagreed with Spencer, who saw the group as no more than the sum of its individual constituents. Cooley (1906) emphasized the mirror-like interaction and mutual influence between the group and individuals. He stressed the role of primary groups like families, neighborhoods, and children's play groups. McKinney (1957, p. 15) contrasted a rural with an urban society. The isolated rural group is homogeneous and solidary and has no more members than can know each other well. The economically independent rural group has little division of labor other than between the sexes, and its technology is simple. Behavior is spontaneous, personal, and traditional. Kinship is central, and tradition is unquestioned. Group members see all activity as an end in itself. Compliance is by normative means. The urban group has the opposite characteristics.

Becker (1960) elaborated on the sacred-secular dichotomy.

The sacred society's attributes are isolation, fixed habits, and in-group and out-group attitudes. Secular societies are accessible, rationality is dominant, and a scientific mind-set is predominant. Secular societies encourage innovation, and change equals progress. Legal contracts are the rule. Sorokin delineated familistic and contractual relationships that corresponded to Tönnies's categories. Love, sharing, sacrifice, and devotion characterize familial relations, fusing the ego with the "we" feeling. Norms mandate unlimited embracing, forgiving, and giving. Contractual relationships, such as employer-employee and buyer-seller relationships, are specific and constrained, relating only to the involved parties. These relationships are usually time limited, and each participant typically seeks to maximize his or her benefit and minimize his or her contribution (McKinney, 1957, pp. 16–18).

Weber contrasted a traditional approach with a rational approach. Traditional action rests on the habit of long practice. Traditional means may become ends in themselves or at least rank as high as ends. The rational approach takes the expectations of an individual as the means to some value: the individual weighs each alternative against the other and selects the most expedient action (Tönnies, 1957, p. x).

All these dual views of our relationships suggest why we find both instrumental and expressive purposes in our organizations.

The Expressive-Instrumental Continuum

Humans are not only expressive beings, but they also make and use tools. Tools (implements) are intermediary means or agents for getting what we cannot get (or cannot get as well) without them. One of our most effective and adaptive implements is the organization. External scholars and internal leaders, managers, and specialists have devoted quality time to understanding organizations, how they work, and how to help them become even better implements. A few, very few, of these experts have put the ideas of expression and instrumentality together.

Scholars who have differentiated expressive needs and actions from other needs and actions have given us a more well-rounded and precise understanding. Among the most helpful have been Robert F. Bales and Talcott Parsons of Harvard University. Specifically, we are indebted to Bales for his small-group experiments and to Parsons for his leadership of the team that formulated the Theory of Action.

Bales experimented extensively with interactions of individuals within small groups. He observed activities in a social-emotional category and a task category. The social-emotional area included positive expressions of liking, enjoyment, solidarity, tension release, and agreement, and negative expressions of disliking, disagreement, tension, and antagonism. The task area showed the actions of suggestions, opinions, orientation, and requests for opinions and suggestions. Bales concluded that in small groups, the instrumental and the expressive systems are typically segregated, with one task leader and a different social leader. In rare cases, a "great man" might play both roles. Bales also acknowledged that task-oriented groups might display expressive behavior (1953, pp. 111–161).

Bales deals with interactions pertinent to the expressive dimension. He views an act as primarily expressive when it is "steered by cognitive orientation primarily to the past, or if it is felt to be caused in a nonmeaningful manner by some existing state of emotion or motivational tension in the self, and if the results which follow it are . . . not . . . specifically anticipated by symbolic manipulation." Conversely, he wrote that if the act is "steered by a cognitive orientation to the future as well as the past and [is] caused in part by the anticipation of future consequences, . . . the act is instrumental. This distinction is recognized in our everyday habits of speech in what we have called primarily expressive activity. The individual is said to act 'because' of some immediate pressure, tension, or emotion. In the instrumental act, the individual is said to act 'in order to' realize certain ends" (Bales, 1950, p. 51).

Bales's idea of "phase movement" functions is also of interest. He developed a concept of four phases through which a system moves over time. The first phase consists of *adaptive instrumental activity* in which individuals implement needs and desires as organized personalities and biological organisms. Bales notes, "This instrumental process of activity, once initiated in a situation, immediately involves the second class of functional problems." The second phase involves *expressive instrumental activity*. This phase involves adaptation of activities to the external situation—outside the group. Once this modification begins, a third class of functional problems immediately arises, precipitating another phase. The next phase consists of *integrative expressive activity,* which Bales describes as "the integration of activities within the social system itself." As before, when this modification process is initiated, the fourth class of functional problems is triggered. The next phase, *symbolic expressive activity,* consists of "the expression of emotional tensions created within the personality by changes in the situation, the social system, and its culture." When this expressive phase begins, it automatically "re-involves the class of instrumental problems" (1976, p. 27).

Concerning these phases, Bales observed, "When attention is given to the task, strains are created in the social and emotional relations of the members of the group, and attention then turns to the solution of these problems. So long as the group devotes its activity simply to social-emotional activity, however, the task is not getting done, and attention would be expected to turn again to the task area" (1950, p. 8).

Bales also posited that "the social system in an organization . . . tends to swing or falter intermittently back and forth between these two theoretical poles: optimum adaptation to the outer situation at the cost of internal malintegration, or optimum internal integration at the cost of maladaptation to the outer situation" (1955, p. 128).

Parsons, leading a group of four psychologists, three sociologists, and two anthropologists, spearheaded the challenging task of developing a Theory of Action. A major aspect of the work was the idea that human action takes four forms (Parsons and Edward, 1962):

Instrumental Functions

1. Input
2 Allocation

Expressive Functions

3. Social integration
4. Normative integration

The considerable research on extrinsic and intrinsic motivations and rewards is also significant. I see a direct correlation between expressive activity and intrinsic rewards. Of special interest to us is psychologist Edward Deci's finding (1975) that an extrinsic reward will reduce a preexisting intrinsic satisfaction. If this finding is true, the phenomenon has a bearing on reward structures in the sector. Though some criticize Deci's view, my own experience with volunteers in the 1960s bears him out. Diligent volunteer workers "turned off" when they were offered government-funded paychecks for the work they had been performing for free. The majority quit the project. The phenomenon seems to relate to human beings' resistance to control, even when the manipulations produce a positive result. Viewed another way, one can experience a means as less desirable than it would have been as an end in itself.

So far, we have seen that researchers have differentiated two types of expression. The first is involuntary (unconscious) expression, in which our bodies and faces reflect an inner emotional state, and the second is voluntary (conscious) expression, in which we choose certain behaviors. Researchers have noted individual and collective expressions. Their work has illustrated a variety of approaches to defining human needs, concluding that many are expressive, yet they cannot settle on any one comprehensive catalogue. They have found a relationship between expressive and instrumental action, and a correlation between expressive needs and intrinsic rewards. In short, we have seen that scholars have established that expressive behavior is a natural and important aspect of human nature—a legitimate end in itself.

The Concept of Expressive Behavior in the Voluntary Sector

A handful of scholars has applied the concept of expressive activity specifically to voluntary nonprofit organizations. Some of the earliest scholars to work in this area were Eduard C. Lindeman, George Lundberg, Louis Wirth, and Arnold Rose. As early as 1921, Lindeman wrote, "Vital-interest groups provide the means of self-expression which have regard for like-mindedness and special capabilities of individuals. Such groups have come to be the vital, functioning parts of modern communities. The individual's relationship to such a group, or groups, need not be minimized in order to relate him organically and democratically to the larger community. He must be brought into the community process through the expression of his most vital interests" (1921, p. 174). In 1934, Lundberg and his associates used the term "instrumental organization," contrasting it with "leisure organization." He defined the latter as groups in which activities were ends in themselves, while the instrumental groups were means to reaching goals (pp. 126–127).

In 1938, Wirth published a paper on growing urbanization. He cited the diminishing role of the farm, manor, and village, the cumulative accentuation of the modes of life associated with the urban scene, and the social consequences thereof. He commented, "Characteristically, urbanites meet one another in highly segmented roles. . . . [They are] dependent upon more people for the satisfaction of their life-needs . . . thus are associated with a greater number of organized groups." Though subsequent studies do not support all his observations, Wirth wrote of the city dweller's relative lack of intimate personal relationships. Urban relationships, said Wirth, tended to be anonymous, superficial, and transitory. Wirth described the urban dweller's substitution of secondary for primary contacts, the deterioration of family and other kinship bonds, and the quest for the means for creative self-expression and group association. He made the point that "being reduced to a stage of virtual impotence as an individual, the urbanite is bound to exert himself by joining with others of similar interest into organized groups to obtain his ends. This results in the enormous multiplication of voluntary organizations directed toward as great a variety as there are human needs and interests" (1938, pp. 20–22). Social integration provided by the home, the extended family, the neighborhood, and the local community seems to be inversely related to modern urbanization and industrial development. Voluntary association based on common values and interests can foster such integration. Without a society rich in organizations that satisfy the human need for affiliation and expression, citizens would suffer even more alienation and psychological trauma than they do now.

Arnold Rose believed that the voluntary sector consisted of only two organizational types: the expressive and the social influence type. The first includes scientific societies, avocation groups, and sports associations that express or satisfy interests in relation

to themselves. The latter focuses on changing some limited segment of the social order (1954, pp. 62–66). Other sociologists also
described the expressive category, contrasting it with the instrumental classification (Smith, 1972, p. 5).

In their quest to develop a systematic theory of pluralism, Rose
and William Kornhauser incidentally advanced our understanding
of voluntary expressive organizations. While they were more concerned with the social influence organization, which sought to
modify some aspect of the social system, they also acknowledged
"expressive" organizations that satisfied members' interests. They
cited three ways organizations strengthened American democracy.
Organizations (1) distribute power over social life among a large
proportion of the people; (2) encourage a sense of satisfaction with
democratic processes through helping the individual see how these
processes function in limited circumstances of direct interest to
himself or herself, rather than grind away in a distant, impersonal,
and incompressible fashion; and (3) provide a social mechanism
for "continually instituting social changes" (Rose, 1954, p. 51).

In *The Power Structure,* Rose expanded his earlier work, adding
that voluntary associations also functioned to (4) "tie society
together and to minimize the disintegrating effects of conflict";
(5) give the individual a feeling of identification with a smaller
group that he or she can fully understand and can influence, thus
helping to give meaning and purpose to the individual's life; and
(6) enhance an individual's social status (1967, pp. 250–251). He
suggested that in an urban society, voluntary associations may be a
replacement for a weakened church, community, and family in
providing for the individual's security and "self-expression" and for
"satisfaction of his or her interests." As summarized by Smith and
Freedman, Rose posited, "If this is the case, the voluntary association would tend to contribute to the democratic character of American society, since strong family systems, churches, and
communities tend to be totalitarian in their influences over the
individual, whereas voluntary associations distribute and diversify
power and influence" (Rose, 1967, p. 59; Smith and Freedman,
1972, p. 45).

Nicholas Babchuk and his associates devoted special attention
to the expressive dimension by applying the concept specifically to
the voluntary sector (Gordon and Babchuk, 1959; Babchuk and

Booth, 1969; Jacoby and Babchuk, 1957). They examined assumptions concerning voluntary associations on an expressive-instrumental scale and demonstrated the validity of the concept as a way of understanding the voluntary sector.

A 1959 paper by Gordon and Babchuk about organizations in a Rochester, New York, slum began with the hypothesis that individuals join organizations because they are recruited through others' personal influence. Gordon and Babchuk found that people were more likely to join expressive groups through personal influence than they were to join instrumental groups. Arthur Jacoby and Nicholas Babchuk posited that since the two classes of organizations served different needs and produced different kinds of satisfactions, their members would exhibit different personality and social characteristics (Jacoby and Babchuk, 1957, pp. 76–86; Smith, 1972, p. 39).

Voluntary organizations are an environment for expressive activity and an emotional support structure for the pursuit of a variety of personal values and needs. They are a means for short- and long-term gratification. Jacoby and Babchuk, very significantly, added, "Instrumental-expressive associations provide a framework which links deliberately and self-consciously instrumental and expressive functions" (1957, p. 77). Gordon and Babchuk found that "the apparent expressive character of any organization is consistent with the view in organizational theory that activities and sentiments tend to develop above and beyond the requirements of the formal system. Hence, whatever the purpose of the organization, it will incorporate expressive characteristics for its maintenance and provide a framework for personal gratification" (1959, p. 63).

Jacoby used the expressive-instrumental dichotomy as a means of exploring organizations' attraction for different kinds of persons. Among other things, he believed that those people who join organizations for their instrumental functions are concerned with long-range goals at the expense of immediate satisfaction and with other people only as a means to their personal goals. He found that expressively oriented association members have more friends than instrumentally oriented members, indicating to him a greater need for and/or ability to maintain personal relationships. Expressively oriented members were also more likely to exercise personal influence in an attempt to get their friends to join the associations to which they belonged. Jacoby saw these characteristics as part of a syndrome, with some persons having a general expressive orientation, reflected in their organization behavior (summarized by Smith and Freedman, 1972, p. 143).

On the basis of a study of sixty organizations, out of seven hundred identified in a community of 30,000 people, Warriner and Prather grouped all organizations into four types, according to the consequences of activity relevant to the organization as a unit or common to its members (1965, p. 140; Warner and Associates, 1949, p. 7; Smith, 1972, p. 4). Note that the first three in the list are expressive, and only the final one is instrumental.

1. Organizations that provide the members with "pleasure in the performance itself"
2. Organizations that act as vehicles for communion among members
3. Organizations that use symbols or signs that evoke and reaffirm a valued belief system
4. Organizations that produce goods or services or cause a change in some object or objects

Testing the applicability of the expressive-instrumental dichotomy, Joan Moore studied women serving on Chicago hospital boards. She found she had to differentiate between organizational type and personal motivation. For example, on the one hand, she found that "middle-class women belonged to more expressive organizations than instrumental ones but that the women stressed instrumental factors, such as the importance of hospital board goals, when asked why they retained their membership. On the other hand, upper-class women emphasized personal gratification, although they belonged to predominantly instrumental associations" (1961, p. 592; Smith, 1972, p. 6).

Some scholars correctly observe differences in the stated and unstated purposes of some organizations (Warner and Associates, 1949, p. 24). For example, civic clubs professing instrumental community problem-solving purposes really relied on social interaction and other expressive motivations. However, Smith and Freedman warned against the tendency of sociologists to dismiss members' definitions of organizational goals as incorrect. In this case, the women viewed their organizations as service groups. Smith and Freedman felt that the members' view seemed as important as scholars' classifications (1972, p. 6). Gordon and Babchuk's instrumental-expressive classification also addressed the overlapping and/or ambiguity of purposes.

James Ashbrook's detailed 1963 to 1967 investigation of the relations of 534 members to 120 Protestant churches and their ministers looked at expressive-instrumental activity in an unambiguous nonprofit voluntary setting (1966). He specifically measured expressive and instrumental activity with members of low-intensity calculative involvement or high-intensity moral commitment. He wrote, "Expressive activity has no utilitarian intent beyond that of giving expression to what constitutes the purpose of the organization . . . Instrumental activities . . . create and maintain the organization and are means . . . designed to sustain the organization in order that it may achieve its general purpose through specific activities" (p. 400).

Amitai Etzioni accepted the Harvard (Parsons, Bales, and others) small-group dual-leadership model, combined it with his understanding of Mayo's informal and formal dichotomy and with insights into leadership styles of the "Michigan line of inquiry," and applied the composite model to complex organizations (1975, p. 156). He also developed the valuable concept that the three forms of eliciting compliance are coercive, utilitarian, and normative, the latter being characteristic of voluntary sector organizations and closely correlated with their expressive aspects. Ashbrook's studies strengthen Etzioni's proposition that "in normative organizations expressive leadership and related tasks will take preference over instrumental ones" (Etzioni, 1975, p. 199).

David Adams compared voluntary actions to activities such as work, play, and love and said that voluntary actions are a distinct authentic mode of behavior. He cited survey data collected from volunteers in 1988 that showed "fun" motives often ranking first or second in motive frequency (1990). Earlier, he wrote, "Voluntary action is fun. . . . [T]he undeniable fun of voluntary action seems to me to be a characteristic of this phenomenon almost entirely overlooked in the literature" (1981, p. 1). He suggested (1976, p. 4) that the phenomenon of voluntary action, like play, is

1. A legitimate existential category for behavior, a type of action different from other types of action.
2. An end in itself; voluntary associations are often goal-oriented social groups.
3. An action given freely. In common with much human action, it is norm governed, but it differs from other forms of human action because, in it, the actor freely agrees to follow its norms. That is, voluntary acts are voluntarily performed.

Adams posits that volunteering derives from a desire for the simultaneous experience of the two modes of behavior—play and work. He describes play as an expressive, intrinsically rewarding activity that we no longer designate as play if it becomes an extrinsically rewarding instrumental activity, a means to some other end. He suggested that freely chosen action can have either an intrinsic or extrinsic purpose. When the purpose of the free activity is intrinsic, it is play, and when the purpose is extrinsic, it is volunteering; "this helps to account for the fun of volunteering" (1981, p. 7). Adams also observes that "perhaps the 'betwixt-and-between' quality of volunteering also contributes to its fun: Volunteering is not work—one doesn't get paid for it—but it's not play either—it is, after all, serious; it's playful work, on the one hand, and serious play, on the other" (1990, p. 3). And he suggests that volunteering has evolved into a significant "contemporary ritual of American society which contributes to a general and sacred social order" (1984, p. 3).

Smith also comments on the work/play interchange, saying, "To speak of the play element here is not to speak of something trivial and unimportant. As society becomes increasingly complex, and as work activity is increasingly structured in terms of large bureaucracies, people's unsatisfied needs for play, novelty, new experience, and all manner of recreation tend to increase. The kind of easy interchange and blending of play and work that could be present in more traditional economies tends to be lost." Smith indicates that voluntary nonprofit groups often provide "variety and intrinsic satisfaction in an otherwise rather boring or at least psychically fatiguing world of work and responsibility. . . . Partly through directly 'expressive' nonprofit groups, whose aims are explicitly to provide fellowship, sociability, and mutual companionship, and partly through the sociability aspects of all other kinds of collective and interpersonal forms of voluntary action, the voluntary sector helps in a very basic way to satisfy some of the human needs for affiliation, approval, and so on" (1973, p. 116).

Daniel Yankelovich's *New Rules: Searching for Self-Fulfillment in a World Turned Upside Down* (1981) carries with it the author's access to a lifetime of poll taking and social analysis. He comments on the shifting instrumental-expressive balance in the changing cultural environment influenced by the post–World War II generation. While not specifically addressing the voluntary sector, he observes a new shared meaning: "the assumption that it is wrong to subordinate the sacred/expressive side has an awesome power to change our lives. By wrong, people mean three things: it is no longer necessary; it is not worth it; and it is destructive. . . . [B]y the mid-seventies a majority of the American people had reached a conclusion comparable to that reached by intellectual critics of industrial civilization in earlier years, namely, that our civilization is unbalanced, with excessive emphasis on the instrumental, and insufficient concern with the values of community, expressiveness, caring and with the domain of the sacred" (p. 232).

Robert Wuthnow's *Acts of Compassion: Caring for Others and Helping Ourselves* (1991) is a significant recent contribution to the expressive-instrumental debate. He contrasts the utilitarian motivation with the motive driven by desire or will. His survey reveals many expressive motivations on the part of caregivers who want to do something useful. He emphasizes the role of choice in volunteering and shows that voluntary action is one way we express our individuality. He suggests that the voluntary sector may be a secular acting out of the religious teaching of the parable of the Good Samaritan, and says, "For many people, voluntarism symbolizes what has been good about America in the past—the free spirit, the lack of coercion, the camaraderie of the small town, the personal touch one experiences among friends" (p. 267).

Though the writings that apply the expressive-instrumental scale specifically to the voluntary sector are few, those cited above attest to a persistent, if intermittent, interest in the subject. As we proceed, we will see that what these writers said can enrich our application of expressive motivation to today's organizations.

An Organizational Typology

As mentioned earlier, Gordon and Babchuk (1959) prepared an organizational typology consisting of expressive, instrumental-expressive, and instrumental organizations. Warner and Associates' analytical typology (1949) consisted of four value functions: plea-sure in performance, sociability, ideological symbolism, and pro-duction. Palisi and Jacobson (1977) synthesized these two typologies and were the first to classify the first three Warriner and Prather categories as expressive and the final one as instrumental. They added two actions of their own to the instrumental category: production for others and production for self.

As discussed briefly in Chapter Two, I have subdivided Gordon and Babchuk's combination instrumental-expressive category into two categories—one in which expression predominates and another in which instrumentality predominates. Below is a fuller description of all four categories in my synthesis of the existing typologies.

Expressive Organizations

Both the stated purposes and the routine activities of purely expressive organizations involve the doing of the thing of interest itself. These organizations include social clubs that socialize, yacht clubs that sail, fraternal organizations that fraternize, bowling leagues that bowl, and other collectivities that help people who enjoy doing the same things to do them better together. Clubs of horseback riders, bridge players, square dancers, golfers, musicians, softball players, and collectors of all hues may be 100 percent expressive. "Organizations which exist primarily for their members, and consume their own products, are much to do with just being there" (Handy, 1988, p. 13). This expressive type includes many mutual benefit membership groups that consume their own ser-vices. It includes mutual support organizations, which Handy describes as "those organizations that are created in order to put people with a particular problem or enthusiasm in touch with others like themselves who can give them understanding, advice, support and encouragement" (1988, p. 12).

Robert Stebbins's book on collective amateurism (1979) details a class of people who blossomed with the shortening of the work week and whose activities are often highly expressive. Expressive amateur astronomers, athletes, artists, and photographers, for example, are often quite serious about their activities and occasionally outperform their professional counterparts. (I believe that amateurs are less familiar than professionals with the impossible and therefore conquer it more often.) These individuals love a particular activity and pursue serious leisure. Stebbins's work covers theater groups and other organizations on the expressive end of the scale. He describes leisure that is characterized by the search for a state of satisfaction as an end in itself (p. 261) and observes people pursuing amateur activities for the expressive motives of self-actualization, self-expression, enhanced self-conception, self-gratification, self-enrichment, re-creation, and sociable interaction as well as for group effort or accomplishment (p. 265).

Expressive aspects of organizations also meet affiliation needs. They provide friendship, recreation, status, self-help, and opportunities for advancement and self-aggrandizement for participants. The values of expressive organization members lie in such things as enjoyment, status, camaraderie, business interaction, and/or "the good life." Measures of success for these organizations are often the quality of their members; the comfort and beauty of their property; their ability to provide information, status, or business or social contacts; and/or how well they stand in relation to competitive groups.

The expressive category can be subdivided further by Warriner and Prather's three expressive value functions: pleasure in performance, sociability, and ideological symbolism.

1. *Expressive, with pleasure in performance.* These organizations are purely expressive in providing pleasurable activities to be performed by members. Examples are hobby clubs, sports clubs, dance clubs, and golf clubs.
2. *Expressive, with sociability.* These groups provide activities that bring people together for social purposes. Examples are birthday clubs, social clubs, fraternities.

3. *Expressive, with ideological symbolism.* These entities provide activities evoking or reaffirming a valued belief system. Examples are churches, lodges, and the Daughters of the American Revolution.

Mutual-support expressive groups can prosper with a minimum of organization and management since the participants eagerly set their own objectives, communicate spontaneously, and initiate activities.

Expressive-Instrumental Organizations

Expressive-instrumental organizations combine elements of both purely expressive and instrumental organizations. Civic clubs, choral groups, art societies, and charismatic churches may serve expressive needs with some instrumental outputs. Overt expressive values and activities predominate though the organizations spend some of their energies for instrumental purposes. Initially, they may have been founded with either an expressive or an instrumental aim. For example, members attend civic clubs for the friendship building, but they periodically contribute to or work on a community project. These groups may start out as exclusively expressive, but "when . . . members get frightened of their own aggression or begin to feel dissatisfied with doing nothing except being together, they will seek a task to do" (Klein, 1956, p. 151). In our utilitarian culture, it is difficult for many people to persist in purely expressive activity. We have a cultural tendency to direct expressive behavior toward some personal or societal instrumentality. As children, many of us learn to be industrious instead of lazy, productive instead of idle, and altruistic instead of egoistic. The best of us, yes, those who contribute the most to the society, have a mental Calvinistic tape playing in the background. If nothing else, purely expressive groups will undertake instrumental projects to benefit themselves—redecorating and painting the clubhouse, for example. Individual members who are aware of a neighbor's problem might discuss the need with the expressive group, and the group will take up a collection or undertake an instrumental caring project. "Enduring social contact, even when the object is exclusively social, seems generally impossible without activity. . . . [People] seem impelled to *do something*" (Barnard, 1938, p. 117).

Organizations can be instrumental and expressive simultaneously. They are instrumental when they are producing an output to their external environment. They are expressive when participants meet their own needs through the organizations' processes. Thus, the processes may produce an instrumental output to the organization and an expressive input to the individual. Civic clubs, choral groups, art societies, and charismatic churches may serve expressive needs while producing some instrumental outputs.

Cognitive dissonance may cause purely expressive organizations to evolve into entities with instrumental components. Festinger's cognitive dissonance theory (1957) posits that when an individual holds two conflicting cognitions, he or she will seek to act to reduce the discomfort caused by the dissonance. I suggest that persons are uncomfortable when engaging in purely expressive activities in an organization when the larger society prioritizes instrumental outputs. Inevitably, internal and/or external pressures bear on the purely expressive organization to contribute toward solving some societal need. Participants then reduce their dissonance by adopting some degree of instrumental activity. This nation's Judeo-Christian values of self-discipline, stewardship, and delayed gratification, particularly as embodied in the Protestant work ethic, emphasize instrumental activity. They tend to influence participants in many otherwise purely expressive organizations to undertake instrumental activities and projects.

Instrumental-Expressive Organizations

Instrumental-expressive organizations also combine elements of the groups at the extreme ends of the typology but with instrumental production activities predominating. Board members, committee workers, fund drive solicitors, and service providers would not participate were it not for their organization's instrumental services; but once involved, they are intrinsically motivated and expressively fulfilled. Typically, in these organizations, activities are instrumental for the organization but expressive for the participants. The Scouts build youths into adults of character while the scout leaders have as much fun as the youths. Advocacy (or campaigning, as the British say) groups consist of many participants who vehemently espouse the organizational cause and exult in a vigorous expression of their views. People start hospital auxiliaries, trade associations, and volunteer fire departments for instrumental purposes, but these organizations retain their workers through their expressive activities.

In some organizations, the stated instrumental purpose is a well-intended guise for expressive activity. One Tuesday, I visited a women's club, the members of which had met weekly for decades. Their purpose was to sew and assemble layettes for infants born in New Orleans' towering Charity Hospital, once the nation's largest hospital. Two days later at a Rotary luncheon, I sat beside a manufacturer of infants' and children's clothing. I discreetly inquired about what his factory did with its "seconds." Then, with visions of officiating at a serendipitous wedding made in heaven, with the manufacturer getting a tax deduction and the women a wealth of resources, I asked to meet again with the women the following week. I shared my idea and sought permission to complete the arrangement with my Rotary friend. Expressions of dismay and confusion rather than joy and anticipation met my idea. The club president thanked me for thinking about the club members and promised to get back to me. Even as I drove back to my office, I knew the club would leave the groom at the altar. The instrumental purpose of providing layettes was a valid one, but the expressive activity of getting together and sewing tiny garments would carry the day.

Work is an autonomous human activity. When a person undertakes voluntary action in the form of work, regardless of whether he or she enjoys it, it is for an instrumental end. Regardless of whether we classify an organization as expressive or instrumental, the individual in that organization can have both motivations personally. When an organization by its instrumental objectives attracts someone who finds self-expression and fulfillment in the contribution he or she makes, that participant engages in a multiply rewarding activity. A major reason why the benefit of voluntary action is so great and why it can be such a significant tool is its ability to motivate participants toward instrumental ends while the participants enjoy expressive rewards. As Richard Cornuelle and Robert Finch wrote, "Nothing can melt human and social problems faster than the willingness of one individual to involve himself voluntarily in helping another individual overcome his problem" (1968, p. 7).

Instrumental Organizations

The purposes and activities of the purely instrumental nonprofit organization focus on its producing something of value for others outside the organization, and any expressive aspect is distractive. The National Geographic Society, the American Automobile Association, and many "commercial" nonprofits are almost indistinguishable from businesses. Cooperatives and many nursing homes and hospitals are also at the instrumental end of the scale.

Instrumental organizations can be further divided according to the subcategories that Palisi and Jacobson added to Warriner and Prather's categories: production for others and production for self.

1. *Instrumental, with production for self.* Semivoluntary in that they are concerned with economic advancement or protective functions, these organizations seek to influence nonmembers for the benefit of the members, and they may show defensive behavior with outsiders. They may establish codes to protect their own interests. Examples are unions, professional associations, and trade associations. Many of these organizations serve as both ends and means, helping people achieve goals indirectly while simultaneously providing direct gratification. For example, an organization that collects and disposes of garbage is instrumental for most participants. A Thursday morning bridge club is expressive for its members. However, a swimming club in which parents rotate the task of instructing their children in water safety is both a means of saving lives and a way of having fun in the process.

2. *Instrumental, with production for others.* Concerned with influencing outsiders for the benefit of those outsiders or the recipients of their services, these organizations tend to have a cooperative orientation and do not treat outsiders with suspicion or antagonism. Since the expansion of third-party payments for health care, with the institution of Medicare and Medicaid in 1965, nonprofit hospitals have become less dependent on charitable contributions, and profitable proprietary hospitals have become possible, so hospitals are increasingly instrumental.

In my view, the most interesting of the four types of organizations are those that can be arenas for both expressive and instrumental activities, and especially the avowedly instrumental organization with a significant expressive output. They are the most challenging to manage, and the potential benefits to those who learn about their interactions are potentially profound.

This fourfold typology becomes more complex when the possible incongruence between the motivations of professionals and the motivations of unpaid workers is considered. For example, as described in Chapter One, the staff of an expressive group may have instrumental goals and enjoy extrinsic rewards. University faculty may be finding expressive fulfillment while the school's administrative and clerical personnel look for extrinsic rewards for meeting instrumental needs. Nonprofit organizations' paid personnel are largely motivated by opportunities for expressive behavior.

Conclusion

In 1981, social analyst Daniel Yankelovich found that his polls were showing a shift in our society, including our workplaces, from an instrumental to a more sacred/expressive view. He noted that the former predominance of an instrumental view implied that people were working in order to generate the income to do what they really wanted. The shift to a predominantly sacred/expressive view implies that people are beginning to see work apart from its instrumentality, as something valued for itself. Yankelovich cited many surveys and described many cases of people who changed their lives in search of more sacred/expressive opportunities. It appears that the voluntary sector's current yearning for more instrumentality is running counter to society's attitudinal swing toward more expressiveness. A winning strategy would be for voluntary nonprofit organizations to grasp expressive outputs as a legitimate purpose and to use people's hungers for expression to attain instrumental ends.

Involuntary expressive behavior is a basic human attribute, recognized as such by eminent founders of both modern biology and psychology. Though less spontaneous, voluntary expressive activity is also natural and intrinsic to human nature. In fact, of the many human needs that experts have identified, most are expressive especially, the "higher" ones.

Expressive behavior is an old concept, and established scholars have investigated it from several points of view. While managers apply it in practice in the voluntary sector, economic concepts in the emerging body of organizational theory have tended to overshadow it. A few scholars have noted the expressive dimension of organizations, particularly in various kinds of voluntary associations. Though scholars have not explored the subject of expressive behavior extensively, they have established its naturalness in human experience, its legitimacy, and its pervasiveness in organizations.

Needs for Further Research

Expressive behavior is a legitimate subject of scholarly inquiry, and it presents a vast territory for further exploration. Researchers can contribute to human satisfaction and organizational life by pushing back the bounds of ignorance on the subject. To what degree have scholars in the various segments of the voluntary sector acknowledged expressive outputs? This chapter posited that the term *expressive* as used primarily by biologists and psychologists and the same term as used primarily by social scientists to describe both involuntary and voluntary aspects of behavior point to the same thing. Is this true?

Is there a pattern of gradual gravitation of organizations toward the instrumental end of the organizational continuum? Or is the movement in the opposite direction? If there is movement, why? Scholars could look at prominent current theories and test them against the expressive output concept. They might test organizations according to my proposed typology. Can all nonprofit organizations covered by the International Classification of Nonprofit Organizations, the National Taxonomy of Exempt Entities, and all appropriate categories in the Standard Industrial Classifications system fit into our typology? Scholars might contrast transforming and failing organizations for expressive output implications. They might project the work led by Parsons and Bales and apply the Theory of Action specifically to the voluntary sector.

Researchers working within a discrete field might survey scholarship in that field for work on the expressive dimension.

Do the trends in their field coincide with the Yankelovich findings about the growth of expressive behavior in our culture? How does the trend away from collective action toward more individualism as reported by Robert Putnam (1995) relate to the expressive dimension?

Actions for Practitioners

Organizational leaders might conduct more internal research on expressive behavior. (ARNOVA could recommend researchers who specialize in leaders' particular interests.) Boards of directors would benefit from a retreat in which board members identify their organizational values and attempt to rank them into a hierarchy of importance. If I could recommend only one thing to managers at this point, I would suggest they identify where their organization should be on the expressive-instrumental scale in order to better accomplish its goals. They might classify the successful and less successful organizations in their community or field in relation to the typology shared here.

One of the most important ways to increase expressive outputs in an organization is to include direct service participants in planning. This requires greater leadership skill than planning that includes only the few at the top, but leaders' confidence in participative planning can grow with successful experience. It has more to do with changing attitudes than anything else, changing to move toward intentional planning and toward including expressive outputs when thinking about an organization's future. Initially, it may require more time to involve a larger number of people in planning and organizing; however, their inclusion will ultimately accelerate goal achievement, and staff members at all levels will have increased their competency and the size of their domains. The more and higher the involvement of participants, the greater their commitment to their organization's success in developing resources and in providing service. The better one understands a unit's objectives, the less inefficient, noncontributing activity there will be and the greater the unit's purposeful accomplishment will be. Including all participants in the early stages of fund drives should produce more funds and greater commitment to success.

This chapter looked at involuntary and voluntary, individual and collective expressive behavior, demonstrating that most human needs are expressive. The literature substantiates the inherent naturalness of expressive behavior, underlines its legitimacy as a subject worthy of continued serious investigation, and points to its underlying ubiquitous presence in organizations.

Chapter Four

Contrasting Attitudes Toward Management and Organizations

Winston Churchill once observed that the difference between American and Russian strategy was the difference between football and chess. We frequently use images and metaphors as conceptual shorthand, as Churchill did in the preceding observation, and they shape the way we understand things. We change our behavior when we act on the basis of one metaphor rather than another. A person who sees life as a mountain to climb will not make the same decisions as one who sees life as a performance or as a feast prepared for her or his personal enjoyment. Images access our emotional memory banks. Root metaphors and cognitive paradigms are more evocative, memorable, and influential than wooden generic descriptions.

In his book *Imaginization* (1993), Canadian management guru Gareth Morgan suggests that images create shared understandings among people seeking to align their activities in organized ways (p. xxix). If this is so, a nonprofit organization's guiding metaphors must legitimate expressive outcomes and enable expressive behavior to flower. An organization that characterizes its participants as "cogs in a machine" will constrict individual expression while an organization that pictures people as "teammates" will stimulate expressive behavior. (Though not all of the contrasting ways of thinking about organizations that this chapter covers are metaphors, many of them are, and we need to appreciate the power of cognitive paradigms.)

The *extended family* is a common example of the type of image that encourages expressive relations among participants in all organizations. I hosted a television program for a decade. For several years, I included a segment in which I interviewed guests from a different church each week. One of my standard questions was, "How is your church different?" Invariably, the answer included the family metaphor. Every church, it seemed, was different because it was "like one big happy family." Approaching his retirement from the army, General Colin Powell told how he would miss the Army "family": "Soldering is about people in the same value systems, the same cultural system. You go from one Army post to another, you might as well have been at the last one. You immediately fit in" (*U.S. News & World Report,* September 20, 1993, p. 51).

The *military* itself has given rise to several familiar organizational metaphors. The generation of American leaders currently phasing out of power were shaped in the crucible of World War II. Military philosophy permeated their formative years and pervaded most of the rest of their careers. In the army, all soldiers and units must be interchangeable because of the high potential for loss of life. Esprit de corps and unit cohesion are vital for survival. The chain of command, span of control, outflanking maneuvers, reserve forces, and other military concepts—especially those of responsible leadership—colored the way the World War II generation spoke of and structured and managed civilian organizations. Eisenhower used a powerful metaphor for the final phase of World War II when he combined a military with a religious metaphor to call for a "Crusade in Europe."

Images from *religion* are prevalent in the independent sector, especially in idealistic nonprofits. Secular associations use church-related terminology when they speak of mission, vision, spreading the word, quoting chapter and verse, or when they refer to their manual as their bible.

Sports and games have given us many organizational images. One Fortune 500 CEO, a former football great, sprinkles virtually every "huddle" with such metaphors as home run, hold the line, end run, challenge, fourth down and goal to go, punt, out of bounds, score, and the ball is in our court. People who like the outdoors may speak of setting the hook, getting one's ducks in a row, or being a straight shooter, or they may turn down a notion by saying, "that dog won't hunt." The competitive spirit links games with careers in seeing circumscribed, usually symbolic conflict in careers (Zaleznik, 1989, p. 198).

This chapter is about organizational concepts at the ends of the expressive-instrumental continuum, or typology. The location of an organization's self-image along that continuum strongly influences the degree to which the organization is able to produce expressive outputs. Reviewing these concepts should stimulate leaders to reflect on their habitual way of thinking about their organization and its management. When organizational leaders shift the metaphors and concepts they use to think and talk about their organization, the compliance (or resistance) of other participants can profoundly affect the organization's direction.

Conceptual Continua

This section examines a number of contrasting concepts that are commonly used in discussing and managing organizations: head and heart, patriarchy and matriarchy, Machiavellian and Pauline models, rational and natural structures, machine and organism, formal and informal organizations, economies and social systems, Theory X and Theory Y, extrinsic and intrinsic motivation, self-contained units and open systems, tasks and people, jungle fighter and craftsman, and transformational and transactional leadership. There is merit on each end of most of the dyads, but I will suggest that one view, in some cases a blend of the contrasting positions, is preferable for enhancing expressive outputs.

Head and Heart

Ancient folk wisdom has it that people may be torn between listening to their heads or to their hearts. Even today, the head symbolizes our rational thoughts, and the heart symbolizes our feelings and emotions—the ancient Greek philosophical ideas of *logos* and *pathos,* respectively.

In 1840, William Ellery Channing, essayist and clergyman, noted that people unite in voluntary associations that elicit energy: "Men not only accumulate power by union, but gain warmth and earnestness. The heart is kindled." He also wrote that the "creative

principle calls forth new forces, and gives the mind a consciousness of powers, which would otherwise have been unknown" (pp.
283–284). Most of us realize that though our hearts may beat more
noticeably in the presence of fear or joy, they have more to do with
pumping blood than with being the seat of our emotions; nevertheless, the contrast between warm emotion and cold calculation
persists in our language and in our thought.

In recent years, the more scientific left-brain and right-brain
theory has somewhat supplanted traditional head and heart
imagery. Henry Mintzberg hypothesizes that while formal planning
uses processes like those identified with the brain's left hemisphere, "important policy processes of managing an organization
rely to a considerable extent on the faculties identified with the
brain's right hemisphere" (1976, p. 53). The right hemisphere specializes in the "heart" functions of emotion, images, wholes, relationships, synthesis, and simultaneous and holistic thinking, and
is time free (we may also think of these functions as "feminine").
The left hemisphere specializes in the "head" functions of words,
specifics, analysis, sequential and incremental thinking, and goals,
and has a distinct sense of time (we may think of these functions
as "masculine"). Moving this image into the organizational sphere,
we can see that some organizations are all instrumental head; they
have great systems but are weak in expressive caring and heart
motivations. Others have heart and are weak in systems, structures,
and controls.

Patriarchy and Matriarchy

Expanding the extended family image, Gareth Morgan goes so far
as to differentiate the family analogy into contrasting patriarchal
and matriarchal models. He says that formal organizations tend to
build on characteristics associated with maleness in Western society, which males have historically dominated. "One person defers
to the authority of another exactly as the child defers to parental
rule. The prolonged dependency of the child on the parents facilitates the kind of dependency institutionalized in the relationship
between leaders and followers, and in the practice where people
look to others to initiate action in response to problematic
issues. . . . Key organizational members also often cultivate fatherly

roles by acting as mentors to those in need of help and protection" (1986, p. 211).

Thus, a patriarchal organization would be more instrumental than expressive, emphasizing tasks over relationships. Management would be authoritative, rational, judgmental, objective, and technologically oriented. The manager's relationship with subordinates would stress challenging tasks to test and improve workers' skills and their ability to function independently. Management might involve harsh discipline and impatience with deviations from rigid standards. Organizational tone would lean toward hardness rather than softness, would be demanding and aggressive, and would address both opportunities and problems on a discrete, incremental basis.

Matriarchal values, says Morgan, emphasize unconditional love; the qualities of optimism, trust, and compassion; and a capacity for intuition, creativity, and happiness. "Under the influence of matriarchal values, organizational life would be far less hierarchical, be more compassionate and holistic, value ends over means, and be far more tolerant of diversity and open to creativity. Many of these traditionally female values are evident in nonbureaucratic forms of organization where nurturing and networking replace authority and hierarchy as the dominant modes of integration" (1986, p. 212).

A matriarchal organization would emphasize expressive relationships over instrumental tasks. There would be a caring, nurturing, forgiving, accommodating, permissive, forbearing, sensitive, and protective attitude toward all participants. Decision making would be relatively subjective, intuitive, and emotional. It would address problems and opportunities globally, and it would foster a soft, supportive workplace. A good organization, like a good family, needs a judicious balance between patriarchal and matriarchal influences.

Machiavellian and Pauline

Machiavelli saw humans as rebellious and uncooperative, requiring strict and ruthless coercion and/or manipulation if they were to produce what their leaders required ([1513] 1958, p. 31). Some organizations, especially governments and organizations with megalomaniac leaders, practice Machiavelli's view of power, the view that a prince must strictly and ruthlessly control other human beings because of their rebelliousness and uncooperative behavior (Knowles and Saxberg, 1971, p. 103). In its day, the Machiavellian model produced strong states that dominated their less disciplined neighbors. Writing from the perspective of the ruler, Machiavelli viewed a society as a stratified system with the ruler competing rather than cooperating with his subjects. The king or prince must master, and ultimately exploit, his subjects for his personal benefit.

Conversely, writing to the early Christian church in Corinth (1 Corinthians), the apostle Paul outlined an idealized interdependent democratic organizational system that would be analogous to the human body, to a system of organs. He wrote, "For the body is not one member, but many" (1 Cor. 12:14). (As far as I know, this is the earliest description of an *organ*ization.) Assuming a human capacity for cooperative action, he wrote that the eye has one function, the ear another, and the hand and foot another. Each needs the other and must voluntarily respect the other's role. "And whether one member suffer, all the members suffer with it; or one member be honored, all the members rejoice with it" (1 Cor. 12:26). For the early church, Paul pictured a cooperative instrumental-expressive system characterized by sharing, mutual concern, and connected community—in Greek, a *koinonia*.

Paul's analogy stressed diversity within unity. The body needs all of its organs and is diminished if any of its parts suffers. Its success is due to the diversity of its functions. Each part vitally relates to the whole, and all serve each other. No part should assume the rightful function of another. The more exalted parts should not look down on the humble parts, but each appreciates the others' own essential functions as part of the whole body. Paul, like Jesus, saw leaders as facilitating servants, encouraging and edifying the whole for the benefit of the whole body and its superordinate cause. Expressive outputs obviously flourish under the Pauline model.

Rational and Natural

The idea of organizations as rational, economic, technological, and efficient instruments goes back to roots in the work of such social theorists as Hobbes and Lenin (Wolin, 1960, p. 352). Simon defined rationality as the "selection of preferred behavior alternatives with some system of values whereby the consequences of behavior can be evaluated" (1976, p. 75). The rational paradigm focuses on management as entirely instrumental, with expressive behavior reserved for the people at the top. Rational management structures are associated specifically with Henri Fayol and Frederick Winslow Taylor. Taylor based his *Principles of Scientific Management* (1911) on the rational principle that specializing, standardizing, and simplifying the tasks of low-level participants maximizes productivity. Under scientific management, each employee works on only a small segment of a product. Every action in a task is studied to determine the best way of doing it. Employees are a constant in the production equation, and managers are the only people expected to think, coordinate, and control (Lawler, 1992, p. 26). Taylor viewed employees as adjuncts of machines and prone to inefficiency unless properly programmed. He saw workers as naturally lazy, concerned only with self-interest. In this view, managers must tightly control, and extrinsically motivate, workers to overcome their propensity to avoid work (Knowles and Saxberg, 1971, pp. 107–108). Kenichi Ohmae has suggested that the resulting "separation of muscle from brain may well be a root cause of the vicious cycle of the decline in production and loss of international competitiveness in which U.S. industry seems to be caught" (1982, p. 226).

The contrast to the rational structure is the spontaneous natural social structure. The natural system theorists acknowledge that organizations have certain distinguishing rational characteristics, but say that these characteristics are not their only attributes (Gouldner, 1959, p. 406). Natural groups, they say, have always included nonlogical aspects. Selznick cites two major nonrational features within rationally ordered organizations. First, individuals are wholes. They do not work only in terms of their formal vocational roles. They bring social characteristics with them and develop commitments that restrict their capacity for totally rational action. Second, formal organizational structures include complex informal systems linking participants with one another and with others outside official boundaries (1957).

The natural model encourages expressive behavior and focuses on commonalties among organizations and other natural social

systems. Theorists in this area recognize that while individual organizations have distinctive features, generic systems and processes
overshadow these features (Scott, 1987, p. 72). One can trace the
natural view of organizations as communitarian, arational, and
organic systems to the social theories of Rousseau, Proudhon,
Burke, and Durkheim, who were the intellectual ancestors of Mayo,
Barnard, Selznick, and Parsons (Wolin, 1960, pp. 352–434). Many
organizational images subsequently grew out of this rational-
natural continuum, such as the metaphors of organizations as
machines or organisms.

Machine and Organism

A dyad of metaphors parallel to the rational-natural dyad is that of
the machine and the organism, the instrumental machine being
rationally designed and the expressive organism developing
according to natural processes. The comparisons go as far back as
Sir Isaac Newton for the machine and the Bible for the organism.
Newton compared the universe to a celestial machine, and
Descartes viewed plants and animals as superior forms of machines
(Morgan, 1986, p. 347), while Paul, as we saw, compared the organization of the early church to the body. Jesus' metaphorical use
of the vine and its branches to represent his relationship to his followers also applies here.

Influential proponents of the machine model include Fayol
(1949), Mooney and Reiley (1931), and Gulick and Urwick (1937).
For each of them, "the idea that the organization is a machine sets
the basis for the idea that it ought to be run like a machine" (Morgan, 1986, p. 76). To a degree and for some time, this approach
worked like clockwork. It conceived organizations as made up of
impersonal interlocking cogs, shafts, and slots that were uniform
and capable of being made perfect. In many quarters, the machine
analogy remains an automatic response and the one best way to
think of organizations.

Technology is central in rational machines. The assembly line
(first used in a slaughterhouse and later perfected in manufacturing automobiles) is the prime exhibit of persons filling slots in the
larger machine. Today, many of us can see rational technical systems as limiting rather than mobilizing human capacities. The

mechanical view is a highly formalized instrumental model with almost exclusive emphasis on quantifiable goals. Management specifies all interrelations, and results are predictable. The construct emphasizes a value-free rational scientific appearance (Kramer and Specht, 1975, p. 509). The machine model may work well where machines work, but it is not adaptive, able to learn, or innovative. A machine operates uncritically and unquestioningly and is unable to anticipate undesirable consequences.

In the 1950s, British researchers Burns and Stalker urged a return to an organic model. They believed it possible to identify a continuum ranging from the mechanistic to the organic. They noted that "in mechanistic systems, the problems and tasks facing the concern as a whole are broken down into specialisms. Each individual pursues his task as something distinct from the real tasks of the concern as a whole, as if it were the subject of a subcontract. Somebody at the top is responsible for seeing to its relevance. The technical methods, duties, and powers attached to each functional role are precisely designed. Interaction within management tends to be vertical" (Knowles and Saxberg, 1971, pp. 107–108).

In contrast, Burns and Stalker recommended a more organic model. When changing technology and new market conditions present new challenges, managers should adopt more open and flexible management and organization styles. The more organic organizations shape themselves to adapt to changing needs. They tend to encourage open communication, many meetings, and alternative channels for identifying problems and exchanging information. Personnel are selected for their general competence and encouraged to discover their own best way of contributing to the total effort.

The organic metaphor stresses process over an arrangement of parts. Management concerns itself with processes in relation with other internal processes and the environment. The organization improves to the degree to which it satisfies needs in a continuing struggle to survive. There are always ranges of options, with innovation as a priority (Morgan, 1986, pp. 71–75). The organic model owes much to the work of Spencer (1966), Durkheim, (1938, 1951), and Radcliffe-Brown (1952) (Morgan, 1986, p. 352). Most nonprofit organizations conform to the organic model, which is user-friendly to expressive behavior.

Formal and Informal

Weber described the ideal formal organization as a bureaucracy—an organization of positions with strict division of responsibilities, clear lines of authority and accountability, a homogeneous outlook, written rules, and a separation of the rights and duties of office from the personal resources of individual officials. He argued that bureaucracy would dominate modern society because of "its purely technical superiority over any other form of organization. Precision, speed, unambiguity, knowledge of the files, continuity, discretion, unity, strict subordination, reduction of friction and of material and personal costs—these are raised to the optimum point in the strictly bureaucratic administration" (1947, p. 214). Chester Barnard, however, observed that interpersonal ties create a condition of communion. We have all seen interpersonal ties spontaneously evolve into informal organizations in the face of opportunities or problems. They provide mutual support, and as Barnard noted, "the opportunity for commandership" (1938, p. 148). Many of these informal organizations, in turn, evolve into formal organizations, while others dissolve as the opportunity or the problem that precipitated them fades. We associate the informal mode more with brief, intermittent, small, local, or start-up circumstances, and the formal mode with longer-term, persistent, large, or widespread activity. Both modes occur in voluntary organizations, government, and businesses. Both formats have their advantages, according to differing circumstances.

An idealized image of the formal organization had persisted until someone discovered that underneath it, between its formal units, inside the cracks, and in fact, over all this orderly structure, there were disorderly social groups within the formal organizational boundaries. And they had been there all along! Within every formal organization, an informal structure develops its own processes that modify goals (Barnard, 1938, p. 224). Participants within formal organizations generate their own communication networks, sociometric structures, working arrangements, norms and behavior patterns, and status systems (Scott, 1987, p. 54). The characteristics of individuals shape these informal groups, which Barnard saw as maintaining feelings of personal integrity, self-respect, and independence (1938, p. 122).

The landmark investigations by Elton Mayo in the 1930s at the Hawthorne plant of the Western Electric Company documented the role of social factors in functions of small, informal groups. Mayo found an influential informal network inside the formal one. Such expressive informal structures facilitate communication, strengthen cohesion, correct inadequacies of the formal systems, and undergird commitment and stability.

Economies and Social Systems

Following the industrial revolution, theorists viewed human beings as rational economic beings who made deliberate decisions based on their instrumental economic needs. Later experts saw workers more as expressive social beings identified through their relationships on the job. They viewed external controls and manipulations as constraining autonomy and limiting motivation. Today, we recognize that human beings are complex beings who move through one psychological stage of development to another as motivations overlap and wax and wane in importance. Management, then, focuses on creating opportunities for the complex evolving personality by providing a social environment for productive work.

Selznick noted that "any concrete organizational system is an economy; at the same time, it is an adaptive social structure" (1957, p. 25). An extreme instrumental economic model will produce an organization quite different from an adaptive social system with its rich expressive interaction. An organization is a social system, with grapevines, status systems, and rituals. It mixes logical, nonlogical, and illogical behavior (Hicks and Gullett, 1972, p. 374).

Douglas North, the 1993 Nobel prize winning economist, says that economic choices are a function of how people see the world, and that people have subjective mental models and act on the basis of ideologies and religious views. He thinks some economists' thinking has focused too much on mathematics and not enough on human behavior to explain the real world and that what people believe is as important—or more important—than what they exchange (remarks at the Chautauqua Institution, July 28, 1944). Even the economists' patron saint, Adam Smith, observes that people relate not only through exchange relations but also through seeking the approval of others, behaviors that in turn concern not only enhancing wealth but also acting morally. Adam Smith writes, "How selfish so ever man may be supposed, there are evidently some principles in his nature, which interest him in the fortune of others, and render their happiness necessary to him" ([1759] 1981, p. 8).

Etzioni recently argued persuasively that the application of neoclassical economics distorts reality. Though he did not slant his appeal in *A New Morality* toward organizations in the nonprofit world, that 1988 book concerns the nonprofit area more than others. Etzioni details the profound influence of emotions and society on human choices (p. 25), and he contends that "in contradiction to the neoclassical assumption that work is a pain, and leisure a pleasure, . . . most people prefer a mix of work and leisure over leisure alone, and that work has great intrinsic rewards. . . . [M]ost people feel they ought to keep some kind of balance between their private take and their public contribution (charity, voluntary work, help to neighbors, and so on). People divide their time and moneys between the two" (p. 84).

Theory X and Theory Y

Many supervisors assume that people dislike work too much to move the gears in the rational machine models on their own. A good boss is required who knows how to make them do it. These supervisors act as if workers were lazy good-for-nothings, lacking ambition, avoiding responsibility, and requiring firm direction and close supervision. In these circumstances, "All of the planning is done by superiors, and the workers simply do what they are told to do, when and how they are told to do it" (Deci, 1975, pp. 221–222).

Douglas McGregor took another view of workers' attitudes. In 1960, he challenged the old models when he said: "If employees are lazy, indifferent, unwilling to take responsibility, intransigent, uncreative, uncooperative, this is due to the traditional assumptions and methods of organization and control" (McGregor, 1960, p. 48). McGregor called the old way Theory X. He proposed Theory Y, in which people are admirable, like to work, and want to do a good job. A good boss is one who enables subordinates to do that good job.

Theory Y, which is compatible with expressive behavior, makes these assumptions: (1) Work is as natural as play or rest. The average person does not inherently dislike work. Work may be satisfying (and will be voluntarily performed) or punishing (and will be avoided if possible). (2) Workers will exercise self-direction and self-control for goals to which they are committed. (3) Commitment to goals results from rewards associated with their achievement. Effort directed toward organizational objectives may produce expressive gratification, the most significant reward. (4) The average human being seeks responsibility. Avoidance of responsibility, lack of ambition, and emphasis on security are generally consequences of experience, not inherent human characteristics. (5) The capacity to exercise imagination, ingenuity, and creativity in the solution of organizational problems is widely distributed in the population. (6) Modern industrial life only partially uses the intellectual potentialities of the average human being (McGregor, 1960, pp. 33–35).

Theory Y, unlike the old scientific management approach, integrates planning and doing. Operations people have greater freedom to decide how best to do the job. Given broad objectives, they have substantial discretion to determine how to achieve those objectives (Deci, 1975, p. 222). (For detailed descriptions of Theory Y management, also see Likert, 1961; Argyris, 1957; Maslow, 1965; Marrow, Bowers, and Seashore, 1967.)

Inevitably, theorists have recognized that appropriate organizing and managing depend on the kinds of people, tasks, or environments involved. Alternative management styles achieve different appropriate mixes to get results, and different environments need different types of organization. This contingency approach to organization and management is now a dominant perspective in modern organizational analysis (Morgan, 1986, pp. 48–49). The keys to the contingency approach are the manager's ability to represent the values of the organization and the employees' acceptance of their role along with their consent to the organizational values. The manager has maximum flexibility in responding to each situation by encompassing parts of both Theory X and Theory Y (Mink, Shultz, and Mink, 1979, p. 30).

Extrinsic and Intrinsic Rewards

Organizations meet some of a participant's needs in exchange for work. Some rewards are extrinsic, and some are intrinsic. The questions that arise about rewards are these: Are extrinsic or intrinsic motivations the most potent? Who desires which? What is the proper mix of motivators? What is the optimum, most economical amount of motivation needed to get results?

Rationally, an employer expects to exchange something tangible in return for an employee's production on the employer's behalf. What is exchanged might be money, fringe benefits, stock options, or other extrinsic compensation for the time and energy expended or the expertise shared. Extrinsic rewards, which are part of the package business employers offer, depend on the organization's ability to discriminate among differences in performance, its capacity to reward, and its willingness to reward. Intrinsic rewards may also constitute part of business compensation, but it is in voluntary organizations that they are the paramount offering. The Theory Y approach is that while equity may require compensation, the task accomplishment itself is a valuable outcome for the worker. According to this view, the redesign of the task by enlargement or enrichment becomes an employer's priority—making the task more expressively satisfying and, therefore, more motivating for the worker. The intrinsic theorists, like McGregor and Likert, assume higher-order needs (à la Maslow) are prevalent in modern workers and that individuals seek expressive satisfaction from the activity itself, provided they have some freedom in defining how to do the job. This approach says that genuine involvement and participation will tend to increase motivation. Handy contends that "rewards tend to lie in the task itself or in the individual's relations with his group. The ideal is to create conditions where effective performance is a goal in itself rather than a means to a further goal. The manager is a colleague, consultant and resource, rather than a boss" (1985, p. 31). Put another way, the opportunity for expressive satisfaction motivates.

Early ideas on the motivation of workers assumed that the more satisfied the worker, the more productive the worker. This commonsense idea gave way to the idea that people will work harder if they get specific rewards or if their good performance is reinforced. Theories of intrinsic motivation then stepped in with the idea that the worker will be more productive if given a worthwhile job and enabled to pursue it—that is, the reward comes from the expressive satisfaction of the work itself.

Workers do enjoy environmental factors like attractive workplaces, coffee breaks, long vacations, air-conditioning, recognition and rewards, handy watercoolers, new paint on the walls, good lighting, and other pleasant fringe benefits. Therefore, many assumed that such factors would motivate workers to produce more and better. Then, Herzberg did the research that grouped workers' needs into "hygiene factors" and "motivating factors." He found that the factors that actually affect performance are on the high end of Maslow's pyramid (power, competence, autonomy, and so on) and are met by the factors he called motivators. They include the work itself, recognition, advancement, possibility of growth, responsibility, and the opportunity for creativity and influence. Their presence can cause increased production; however, their presence or absence does not necessarily affect job satisfaction (1966, p. 27).

Hygiene or maintenance factors, like the environmental enhancements listed above, meet needs at the lower end of Maslow's hierarchy. These are the factors that relate to job satisfaction. They do not motivate, but when they fall below an adequate level, they become *de*motivators. While their presence or absence determines job satisfaction, it is unrelated to job performance. Other scholars have supported Herzberg's theory that a satisfied worker is not necessarily a good performer.

Self-Contained Units and Open Systems

The self-contained unit concept goes back to the rational machine models. Self-contained organizations operate as if every functional department works in compartmentalized isolation. Higher authority specifies a unit's work, then fits its output into the work of other units, like discrete pieces of a jigsaw puzzle. Authoritarian managers move the organization down the track with precision.

The open-systems approach evolved from dissatisfaction with older approaches. A system is a set of related elements. Everything in it affects everything else. Its components interact with each other and the environment, creating a synergistic whole greater than the sum of its parts. The systems approach recognizes that like other organisms, organizations depend heavily on interactions with their environment. According to systems theory, we cannot analyze, manage, or evaluate the performance of any one element in a system as a discrete entity (See Georgopoulos and Tannenbaum, 1957, p. 535).

Ludwig von Bertalanffy contributed considerably to this idea with his writings on general systems theory, which he extrapolated from studying biological systems. He viewed organizations as open systems interacting with their environments for resources and being constrained by environmental influences. Each system's common purpose holds it together, and its hierarchies of subsystems provide the functions required to achieve the total system purpose. Organizations conceived as open systems see themselves as a "bounded group of individuals harnessed together by incentives and commitments . . . open to new pressures from the environment as it both obtains and gives back resources to that environment and, simultaneously, attempts to affect its internal constituent parts and its environment" (Zald and McCarthy, 1987, p. 80).

Many of the problems that arise in dealing with systems lie in the failure of managers, planners, analysts, and administrators to differentiate between *systems improvement* and *systems design*. Van Gigch wrote *General Systems Theory* to emphasize the differences in intent, scope, methodology, and results between improvement and design. The concept of improvement assumes that the design of the system is set, that norms for its operation have been established, and that one can bring the system closer to some standard operating condition. Systems design, however, is a creative process that "questions the assumptions on which old forms have been built. It demands a completely new outlook and approach in order to produce innovative solutions" (Van Gigch, 1974, p. 2). I believe that in order to structure expressive outputs into an organization's systems, leaders must think in terms of system design.

Tasks and People

The traditional view holds that the task is everything and that the efficient manager applies all the resources at her or his disposal to the job at hand. In contrast, the human relations school of thought holds that relationships are everything and that the managers who keep their people satisfied will get the best results in the long run. Robert Blake and Jane Mouton's *Managerial Grid* graphically illustrates that optimum results come from task management and human relations skills working in tandem. I think optimum results flourish with a mix of expressive and instrumental outputs. Blake and Mouton have a similar view. They developed tests that determine where a manager falls along the two axes of a grid. One axis relates to concern for people, the other to concern for production. Blake and Mouton contend that the best managers are those who are both production *and* people oriented. When a manager emphasizes tasks without regard to the human side of enterprise, the results are poor. Likewise, results are poor when the manager stresses relationships almost to the exclusion of production concerns, in a "country club" atmosphere. Therefore, the effective managers are those with a balanced orientation toward both production and the producers (1964, p. 134).

Blake and Mouton later expanded their grid into a full-blown system designed to increase organizational productivity and individual effectiveness. They remind us: "People are people regardless of the context in which the work takes place. . . . [A]ccountability for results based upon trust and obedience or sympathy, understanding, and support of another person facing adversity also reflect concern for people. . . . [D]epending on the character of concern, subordinates may respond with enthusiasm or resentment, involvement or apathy, innovative or dull thinking, commitment or indifference, and eagerness or resistance to change" (1968, p. 37).

Jungle Fighter, Craftsman, and Others

Maccoby's extensive in-depth interviews with 250 male executives led him to define four distinctive executive personality types: gamesman, company man, jungle fighter, and craftsman. Each type has its own set of drives, needs, and preferences. Each is effective in its own way, and each has a distinctive approach to work. While the characterizations do not distinguish among different organizational philosophies, I describe these four types because of the unusually thorough psychiatric interviews that led to them. One of the types, the intrinsically motivated craftsman, fits the expressive model precisely. The craftsman focuses almost exclusively on the task at hand. He is motivated by the process of producing high-quality work and something of value. The craftsman is a self-contained and exacting individual who performs his own function well but who does not typically develop the organizational skills necessary for cooperative teamwork.

The jungle fighter needs power. He may see himself as leading the righteous in a battle for survival. He is brave and protective to his "family" and ruthless toward competitors. The company man has balanced judgment. He focuses on service and institution building, concerned with the human side of the company and committed to maintaining corporate integrity. He can sometimes sustain an atmosphere of cooperation and a sense of service. The gamesman is Maccoby's hero. He takes calculated risks, and new methods fascinate him. He thrives on competition and communicates his enthusiasm, energizing his peers and subordinates like the quarterback on a football team. He seeks fame, glory, and the exhilaration of victory (Maccoby, 1976, p. 76).

Transactional and Transformational Organizations

Transactional organizations may know exactly where they are going and produce many worthwhile outputs, but their participants emerge from its organizational process relatively unchanged. In contrast, transformational organizational processes change participants, and the organization itself may grow in unanticipated directions in the process of producing worthwhile outputs. Advocacy of the potent transformational leader-follower relationship is one of the most widely discussed recent management trends (Inkson and Moss, 1993).

Though both transformational and transactional leader-follower relations have been around for a long time, James McGregor Burns is credited with first publishing the difference between the two. From his perspective as a professor of government, Burns wrote:

> *Transactional* leaders approach followers with an eye to exchanging one thing for another: jobs for votes, or subsidies for campaign contributions. Such transactions comprise the bulk of the relation-

ships among leaders and followers, especially in groups, legislatures, and parties. *Transforming* leadership, while more complex, is more potent. The transforming leader recognizes and exploits an existing need or demand of a potential follower. But, beyond that, the transforming leader looks for potential motives in followers, seeks to satisfy higher needs, and engages the full person of the follower. The result of transforming leadership is a relationship of mutual stimulation and elevation that converts followers into leaders and may convert leaders into moral agents [1978, p. 4].

Handy (1985, p. 104) likens transforming leaders to ternary as opposed to binary thinkers—tripods as opposed to bipods. The bipod thinks of life and success in terms of his or her relationship to other people. The tripod (transformational leader) considers a third corner—the task or purpose. He or she is concerned more with "What is it for?" than with "Shall I win?"

One can see that a transactional or transformational relationship between leaders and followers translates into transactional or transformational organizations. Whereas the transactional model has been common in business and government, the transformational mode has been the traditional norm among religious and value-based nonprofits. Burns noted that transforming leadership "ultimately becomes *moral* in that it raises the level of human conduct and ethical aspiration of both leader and led, and thus it has a transforming effect on both. . . . Leaders address themselves to followers' wants, needs, and other motivations, as well as to their own, and thus they serve as an *independent force in changing the makeup of the followers' motive base through gratifying their motives*" (1978, p. 20).

Adapting for Expressive Outputs

Organizations have operated on a wide range of premises, including the images and concepts described above. Some of these paradigms and operating styles are more appropriate for enhancing expressive outputs than others. They have more to do with attitudes, with modes of thinking, and with perspectives than with specific behaviors, yet the effect of one attitude over another can have a tremendous impact on the full gamut of organizational activities.

Selecting the alternatives that are most likely to enhance expressive outputs from the dyads reviewed here presents an illuminating profile. We begin with the image of an extended family of intertwining, mutually supportive relationships. Charismatic patriarchs or matriarchs are the founders of most nonprofits. The family is neither exclusively patriarchal nor matriarchal but retains the father's instrumentality and holds on to the mother's care for every member, regardless of accomplishment, and her facilitation of expressiveness.

The full range of voluntary nonprofit entities will not reject the head but will incorporate the heart. These organizations will reject the egoistical Machiavellian model and shape themselves according to the Pauline admonitions. They will guard against sliding from the higher level into the megalomaniacal abyss as did the followers of Jim Jones and David Koresh. Dictators rule because some organizations have preferred to defer to a charismatic leader rather than go it alone, but these organizations may want to shift to democracy. The expressive dimension tends to flower with increased freedom, the most propitious time for a transition being when the current leader steps down. Rather than hailing the successor with, "The King is dead. Long live the King," they will proclaim, "The King is dead. Power to the people." The elective model is definitely more functional, and it can begin with the second generation after the founder or other highly controlling leader.

Natural structures represent a source of energy for the expressive nonprofit. With rare exceptions, when a natural body encompasses a rational structure, the natural organic model is superior to the mechanical alternative. Expression is organic by nature, and organic models enhance it. Instrumental organizations are extremely important, but we must also retain effective expressive outputs that enrich organizations with instrumental purposes and strong expressive components. The informal expressive entities that form within an instrumental context do so naturally because of the expressive purposes they fulfill. Expression is the function of informal groups, and the more harmonious the relation between the formal and informal entities, the better the whole will be.

Certainly, there are economic aspects to voluntary and nonprofit institutions, but they are not the organizations' reason for being. They are means only in what is primarily a social system.

People, not money, are the ends. When confronted with any competing demands between the individual and the group, the individual relinquishes some of her or his autonomy for the good of a community. In turn, the community provides for the individual something she or he cannot enjoy in isolation. Individuals may exchange energy for expressive opportunities, an exchange that may enhance instrumental outputs whose processes are expressive to those who work on them.

The spirit of most volunteer organizations is on the far end of the Theory Y side of the scale. If people were all recalcitrant and unwilling to work, there would be no volunteers. McGregor would probably have never identified Theory X if all organizations were voluntary. Intrinsic motivation is the pull toward expressive behavior. Intrinsic rewards are what individuals look for in volunteering for expressive ends, and intrinsic rewards will predominate over extrinsic ones in a healthy sector. Moreover, satisfaction need not always equal production for that satisfaction to be good for nonprofit participants. Expressive voluntary and nonprofit organizations always need to retain participants. Therefore, hygiene factors are essential in nonprofits.

We should see things from the systems perspective: first, because it represents reality and, second, because voluntary organizations are all about interacting relationships. Boundary permeability and open systems can be compatible with highly effective voluntary organizations. Participative decision making and shared responsibility enrich intrinsic rewards in an expressive organization.

Conclusion

Shakespeare reminds us, in *The Merchant of Venice*, "If to do were as easy as to know what were good to do, chapels had been churches, and poor men's cottages princes' palaces." One must adapt theory to policy and then put it into practice for anything to happen. On one end of a scale representing the work people do and the people who do the work are routine tasks that are specifiable, predictable, and long-term. At the other extreme are one-of-a-kind tasks that are not specifiable and are unpredictable. At the routine end of the scale are the traditional "smokestack" manufacturers, and at the other, many of the organizations in the voluntary sector, where most of the people who do the work are either volunteers or professionals motivated to serve. The more we go toward that end of the scale, the more acceptable to management are expressive motives and activities. The extent to which such intrinsic rewards are obtainable in the work situation will depend primarily on the way in which the job and tasks are structured by the organization. Sometimes the individual will give himself or herself an intrinsic reward even though others do not give him or her extrinsic rewards (Porter and Lawler, 1968, p. 36).

Needs for Further Research

Scholars might compare characteristic metaphors and concepts across sectors. They might investigate metaphors and categorizing ideas typically used by boards, managers, volunteers, and staff in a class of organizations. If images are not congruent, is the difference appropriate or a symptom of problems? This chapter is rich in potential topics for researchers working within a specific organization. Common metaphors and organizational theories employed in an organization, or by different factions of that organization, can be symptomatic of conflicting attitudes and behaviors. Researchers might test Morgan's suggestion that metaphors are good tools for organizational change (1993).

Actions for Practitioners

Managers might identify the images and concepts they typically use and compare them with the images and concepts used by persons with whom they differ. They should also benefit by identifying the most appropriate metaphors for describing their organization's desired future. At a minimum level, any leader should benefit by becoming more sensitive to metaphors and the terminology of particular theories as indicators of various mind-sets.

This chapter described a number of organizational concepts to stimulate leaders to reflect on their habitual way of thinking about an organization and its management, because the compliance (or resistance) of participants to leadership perspectives can profoundly affect organizational direction.

To this point, I have discussed the concept of expressive behavior as it relates to leading and managing nonprofit organizations and have cited what others have said on the subject. In the chapters that follow, I will discuss how leaders and managers may infuse more and better expressive participation into their organizations, tapping into the often hidden source of human energy and power. The following "how to" suggestions should also provide additional insights into the concept of expressive outputs. As in learning to ride a bicycle, the relationship between balance and momentum is best understood when one is actually in motion.

Chapter Five

The Role of Culture in Steering Nonprofit Organizations

When the American Cancer Society (ACS) began its search for a new CEO in September 1991, there were 825 applicants for the job. ACS computerized selection criteria shrank the candidates to 90. A committee cut the 90 to 15. Personal interviews reduced this number to 4. One candidate withdrew as the committee scrutinized backgrounds and visited each applicant's work site. The time finally came for the crucial last interview to select the leader of one of the world's major nonprofit corporations. The interview began with the following three questions:

1. What is the difference between the culture of nonprofit and for-profit organizations?
2. How has your organization's culture affected you?
3. What effects have you had on your organization's culture?

Did the American Cancer Society know something that most organizations do not? It knew that governmental entities like prisons and armies use *coercion* to get participants to respond to organizational directions. Government also achieves compliance from the diversity of citizens through its potential for coercion in the form, for example, of agencies such as the Internal Revenue Service. ACS knew that business entities use *exchange* for acquiring inputs and producing outputs. They purchase goods and services (inputs), exchange money for the work needed to turn those inputs into outputs, and market those outputs in exchange for the customers' money. However, ACS also knew that expressive organizations use the *expectations of their cultures* to get things done and achieve organizational purposes. Participants are affected by and comply with what the organization expects them to believe, to do, and to refrain from doing. They act in accordance with their group's established standards.

This chapter uncovers some of what is known about organizational culture, normative compliance, the role of values, and what leaders can do to nudge a culture in a desired direction. An organization is usually a group of smaller groups. It is in these smaller groups that a culture resides, and this chapter will also describe the important functions of these small groups.

Culture is to an organization of people what personality is to one person. At the outset of this chapter, I want to make it clear that though an organizational culture can be changed, it is no easier to change than an individual's personality. Also like an individual, the older it is, the harder it is to change. Change may be influenced by outside forces, but real change must be internally motivated. While I suggest some ways of cultural transformation that have worked in the past and can work again, I am not saying the process is either fast or easy. However, organizations are continuously adding participants, and leaders will find they can effect change more readily in these newcomers than in the participants already socialized into the traditional culture.

A culture is a group's integrated system of beliefs, values, and behaviors, including its concepts, communications, and actions. A culture consists of patterns of values that give the organization meaning and give members the organization's behavioral rules. The values are transmitted from one generation to the next through participants who personify them, rituals that symbolize them, and a network by which they are reinforced (Deal and Kennedy, 1982). An organization's culture is an amalgamation of all the factors that elicit compliance from its participants: its beliefs, values, purposes, norms, knowledge, customs, stories, and rituals. Kroeber and Kluckhohn (1952) have identified almost three hundred definitions of culture. I have an ambition neither to expand their list nor to reproduce it; but by examining several aspects of culture, I will expand our understanding of ways we can enhance the desired mix of expressive behavior in our organizations.

What does culture have to do with expressive outputs? A purely expressive culture, one that encourages participants by saying, "If it feels good, do it," will produce expressive outputs for a while, but it will remain undisciplined and weak. An instrumental culture, one that focuses exclusively on the financial bottom line, may increase instrumental outputs for a time but will ultimately crash. One way leaders produce an optimum instrumental-expressive mix is by slowly steering an organization's cultural expectations toward the mix of outputs that organization desires.

Cultural change requires an intentional commitment by top leaders to concentrate more on their processes than their products for a time. They may need to focus on the attitudes and behavior of the people who raise the money and provide the service. Leaders must see the organization and its participants as the leaders' responsibility and look on what the organization produces as the participants' responsibility. If leaders can produce the right culture, the culture will produce the right mix of outputs. The process is like getting warm on an icy winter day. One could apply heat directly to one's body, but it is more effective to heat the house and let the house keep everyone warm. This is the organizational view that I believe is essential for normative organizations like most voluntary groups and nonprofits. They are "cultural *systems* of *values* with shared symbols and shared cognitive schemes which tie people together and form a common organizational culture." Therefore, "change comes about by altering the norms and cognitive schemes of the members of the organization" (Tichy, 1983, p. 197).

Normative, of course, means relating to the norms, or "ought-to" customs, of a culture. Norms vary in their nature and importance from organization to organization, but nonprofit organizations in particular are normative because they emphasize conformance to norms. Norms are long-established behavior patterns and common practices, so habitual to a particular culture that they help define it. Norms are authoritative binding principles that have evolved over time; patterns of action that have consistently solved a group's problems and given it a sense of security. They are the shared expectations about what is acceptable that have survived and become integrated into the culture. An organization's norms are supported by a broad consensus, including rewards for compliance and sanctions for violations. Because norms are accepted and internalized, they are a powerful force, inducing conformity and increasing cultural unity.

"One of the most important and most difficult tasks of top management is to decide the content of the organization's culture, that is, to determine what values should be shared, what objectives are worth striving for, what beliefs the employees should be committed to, and what interpretations of past events and current pronouncements would be most beneficial for the firm" (Tichy, 1983, p. 10). Once an organization's leaders decide they want to produce optimum expressive outputs and begin to think and talk with images that encourage expressive behavior, they need to make certain they have cultural norms that value activity for the sake of direct gratification.

Organizations with a potent expressive dimension will come down heavily on the side of a human relations emphasis in their norms. Maccoby's "craftsman" abounds in the expressive atmosphere of the nonprofit organization. Many of this type find voluntary organizations a refuge from some of the constraints of other kinds of entities. The better organizations in the nonprofit sector have always been transformational rather than transactional, and the business sector can learn more about the vital model of transformational leadership from our sector.

Many expressive organizations, especially religious ones, have long been aware of the behavioral patterns that set them apart. Daniel was thrown into the lions' den and Shadrach, Meshach, and Abednego were thrown into the fiery furnace because they were unwilling to violate their cultural norms. In the last two decades, businesses, too, have begun to recognize the behaviors of their members as corporate cultures. Terrence Deal and Allan Kennedy have explained that "every business—in fact every organization—has a culture. . . . [I]t affects practically everything—from who gets promoted and what decisions are made to how employees dress and what sports they play" (1982, p. 4). *Fortune* magazine carried a cover story on corporate culture in its October 17, 1983, issue. The 1990s brought the recognition that an organization's culture is pervasive, important to corporate success, and difficult to change.

In any culture, participants are rewarded for conforming to "normal" expectations with smiles, recognition, appreciation, and popularity. Participants who violate norms are punished by scowls, scorn, avoidance, and ostracism. (Pottery was as common in ancient Greece as is plastic in modern California. Broken bits and pieces of pottery, called *ostraca*, lay on streets and public places like pebbles on country roads. One way community members punished an offending person was to pick up *ostraca* and throw them at the offender, "ostracizing" him or her.) Rejection, shunning, or expulsion of those who disregard or violate common values is one of the most universal practices of religious, scientific, artistic, and other commons (Lohmann, 1992, p. 257).

Norms may defy reason. I know of no rational reason why I should eat a pig or an oyster but not a cat. My cultural norms also mandate against eating dogs, but if a Chinese family invites me to stay for chow, I may get Chow. Sometimes, my wife wears skirts. At other times, she wears shorts or trousers. I wear only trousers or shorts. I could wear a skirt, I guess. No, I could not wear a skirt! However, if I played a bagpipe, lived in Scotland, and belonged to a marching band, I guess I could on special occasions.

Primitive, mechanical assumptions about organizations saw participants as responding directly to the directions of their supervisors, as if their lives in the workplace were isolated from the rest of their lives. The contemporary sophisticated assumption sees that participants in the workplace are whole persons who base their decisions on more than rationality. All people are strongly influenced by their cultural expectations and their individual feelings. They do not choose most courses of action by logic. Most of their decisions, including economic choices, are based on cultural and emotional considerations regarding means as well as ends. Both emotional forces and cultural pressures are primary influences that often preclude or override rational decision making. Also, even when the paramount considerations are logical and empirical, they are themselves defined by "factors that legitimate and otherwise motivate such decision-making" (Etzioni, 1988, p. 93). Berelson and Steiner (1964, p. 5) point out that the more people are emotionally committed to their beliefs, the harder they are to change through a logical appeal (see also Beer and others, 1985; Walton and Lawrence, 1985).

Values

Leaders who encourage a culture that values expressive behavior can expect the culture to produce expressive outputs. The most potent forces in this effort are the organizations and coalitions with distinctive norms, seeking to establish their normative dominance. A voluntary nonprofit organization's values are its power base and energy source. There is no greater social power than the normative influence of a group over its committed adherents. We can identify both the kinds of values that most nonprofits hold and the importance of understanding the particular values of one's own organization.

All organizations typically start with a founder with an idea. The founder attracts a core group whose members share a common vision. Members of the core create an organization as they incorporate more individuals into the group and begin building a history of common experiences. If the group remains stable and shares learning experiences, it will gradually develop assumptions about itself, its environment, and how to do things to survive and grow—it will develop a culture (Schein, 1985, p. 15). The core group first creates a culture; then, as the culture matures, the culture creates the organization.

When faced with a crisis of understanding, leaders should go to the organization's roots and ask: What did the founder and the founder's inner circle think was important enough for them to invest the blood, sweat, toil, tears, and dollars to establish and maintain this organization in the first place? Did they want to enjoy themselves? Did they want to save, protect, help, honor, or improve something or someone? Answer these questions and reveal the organization's root values. If these values generated sufficient energy to move the entity forward in the first place, they can probably still propel it forward today.

An organization's cultural philosophy and values should deeply affect everyday behavior and organizational strategy. Stanley M. Davis, who played an important role in marketing the concept of corporate culture, defines cultural philosophy as *guiding beliefs* and behavior as *daily beliefs*. Guiding beliefs are the roots from which the daily beliefs grow (Davis, 1984, p. 4). Philosophy, values, and guiding beliefs deal with *why* the organization does such and so. The behavior of people in an organization, their daily beliefs, and the organizational strategy have to do with the *how* of cultural life. It is vital that philosophy and everyday behavior be congruent. If they are not, the organization is at best hypocritical and at worst schizophrenic.

While it may be extremely difficult to change a culture, bringing an organization's behavior and strategy into line with its philosophy is a manageable, though challenging, task. That task begins with a clear definition and understanding of the organization's real purpose and philosophy and its underlying core values. Then, organizational leaders must articulate and exemplify their expectations to the rank and file. Kouzes and Posner (1987) carefully examined the relationship between individual and organizational values of over 2,300 U.S. managers representing all types of organizations and all levels in the organizations. Their findings showed that leaders' clarification and articulation of their personal values pays off significantly for both leaders and their organizations. Shared values foster strong feelings of personal effectiveness, promote high levels of loyalty, facilitate consensus about key organization goals and stakeholders, encourage ethical behavior, promote strong norms about working hard and caring, and reduce levels of job stress and tension. Without such shared values, study participants felt they were wasting energy trying to figure out what they were supposed to be doing (p. 193).

A preponderance of organizations in the voluntary nonprofit sector generally hold these ten core values: *accountability, caring, citizenship, excellence, fairness, honesty, integrity, loyalty, promise keeping,* and *respect* (Barry, 1979, p. 5; Beauchamp and Bowie, 1979, p. 17; Guy, 1990, p. 34; Solomon and Hanson, 1985, p. 7).

The Josephson Institute, which pioneered the study of nonprofit ethics, endorses the ten values above and enlarges the list by adding *fidelity* and *safeguarding the public trust* (Josephson, 1986). Mason (1969, 1990a) endorses all of the above and adds seven others: *altruism, culture conformity, democracy, frugality, pluralism, stewardship,* and *voluntarism.* In its report "Obedience to the Unenforceable," the thirty-member Ethics Commission of the Independent Sector (1990) presented a list of values and ethical behaviors. Their list endorsed seven of the previously stated values: *accountability, honesty, citizenship, pluralism, public trust, respect, stewardship.* In addition to specifying appropriate values for the voluntary sector, the report defined an ethical motivation: "Commitment beyond the law, to obedience to the unenforceable, is the higher obligation of leaders of philanthropic and voluntary organizations" (p. 7).

Lohmann's creative approach defined several values specific to what he calls "the commons" (1992, pp. 259–268). In addition to *prudence,* he lists *proportion, contextualism, the asoka principle* (the monarch's obligation to support religion), *noblesse oblige, conservation, consensus,* and *community.*

Jeavons argues that the managers of nonprofit organizations need to create and maintain organizational cultures that "accept and honor in practice (as fundamental) a set of 'core values' that are in continuity with the historic philosophical and religious roots of the voluntary sector and that meet the public's current expectations" (1994, p. 186). He specifies that the five values that must permeate these organizations are *integrity, openness, accountability, service,* and *charity* (in the original sense of the term). Robert T. Golembiewski (1992) argued that organizations operating under Judeo-Christian values can achieve higher (instrumental) production, and (expressive) satisfaction than those that do not. A significant body of scholarly work has been built on his concept, and the same idea has always been a basic premise of religious bodies.

To this point, I have listed only positive values. They vary in weight, and different organizations at different times will rank them in different orders. But each positive value has its negative counterpart. For altruism, there is self-interest; for frugality, there is extravagance; for honesty, there is dishonesty and deceit, and on and on.

Organizations also have values that are ethically neutral. Among these might be growth, decentralization, a particular management philosophy, a certain aesthetic taste, or a political or geographical bias. These are also tenets strong enough to be adopted as the focus of group activity. For example, a literacy council holds the convictions that the ability to read is important to people's lives, that volunteer tutors can teach people to read, and that the tutors can benefit from the experience. Such defined convictions are specific and explicit in an organization's overt reason for being, deeply grounded in the psyche of participants. Values, however, are typically implicit rather than explicit in an organization's purpose.

As the basis of an organization's culture, values account for much of what distinguishes one organization from another. Both the NAACP and the Ku Klux Klan consider values important, but their values differ. The German Red Cross of 1939 and the

American Red Cross of the same era both valued obeying the law but disagreed on other values. Both the National Forest Farmers Association and Greenpeace value the health of trees, but their other values clash. An organization's attitudes are based on its values hierarchy of relative worth, which provides criteria for organizational decision making.

Convictions of particular interest to specific organizations might outrank the core values previously discussed. For example, the National Organization for Women (NOW) would rank women's rights at the top of its hierarchy. A parochial school's highest priority might be professing Catholic Christianity. The rights of animals would be high on several advocacy groups' hierarchies, and stewardship of the soil might rank high for the 4-H Club.

Given that a group's cultural values are at its core, any internal clash of competing cultures can crack the core and devastate the organization. Can there be competing cultures in one organization? Certainly, nonprofits typically have several cultures existing in equilibrium. While the cultures within the small units of any organization will be internally consistent, cultural conflicts often arise at the junctures between groups that do not share a typical way of doing things. There may be a contributor culture, a management culture, and a culture of volunteers. There may be a resource development culture and a service-providing culture. There may certainly be both an instrumental and an expressive culture. For example, Kouzes and Mico (1979, p. 449) suggest that human service organizations have three distinct domains: policy, management, and service. They believe that these domains operate with contrasting principles, success measures, structures, and work modes and that interactions among domains create conditions of disjunction and discordance. As long as an organization contains several cultures, a peaceful equilibrium is as good a situation as one can expect.

Businesses often have a management culture and a labor culture. For two years, I consulted with a major pharmaceutical company in New York State that had one culture among the research people who developed the drugs and another among the production people who manufactured them. I had to tailor my work to the differences between the two divisions more than I have had to adapt it to suit the differences among distinct companies. Governmental entities may have cultural bifurcation along party lines. Voluntary and nonprofit organizations may divide along staff-volunteer, developmental-program, liberal-conservative, or expressive-instrumental lines.

I deal with the expressive-instrumental bifurcation in more detail in later chapters, but very generally speaking, human relations problems occur and inhibit organizational progress when persons representing instrumental and expressive internal cultures collide. However, each can learn to accommodate to the other to each one's benefit. A frank, open approach, recognizing that there is a chasm to be bridged, is a first essential step toward the assimilation of either an instrumental or an expressive orientation into the existing culture of the organization.

A cultural clash is different from a difference of opinion on ends or means, which can be discussed objectively. Cultural differences tend to degenerate into criticism of personalities and other cultures as each individual involved becomes more and more polarized and each position is reinforced by the emotional statement and restatement of that position. In most cultural clashes, then, differences can be greatly reduced and much hostility defused if each side recognizes the clash as cultural and opens itself to an understanding and appreciation of where the other side is coming from. If each side can appreciate the other's history and experience, motivations and objectives, and find a ground of common agreement, both sides can then begin to move forward together.

Instrumental, task-oriented managers are accustomed to strict accountability, to quick response to authority, to unambiguous goals, as well as to personnel who respond to financial incentives, who accept unpleasant activities and demands as part of the territory, and who know little of objectives that cannot be measured numerically. Such managers are accustomed to resource allocation on more or less objective criteria. They are not familiar with the boundless resources available free to nonprofits, to the organizational energy that can be elicited and applied to objectives as a result of the nonrational appeal we call inspiration. Instrumental managers have been taught that resources are generated by the production of outputs on a quid pro quo basis, not appreciating that in most nonprofits, the resources are generated by a distinct fundraising system that does not necessarily relate directly to the service-providing system. They think that if you can dissect a financial statement, you can understand an organization's strengths and weaknesses, and they gain a great deal of comfort in numbers that can be added and subtracted, multiplied and divided.

Persons from instrumental cultures are unaccustomed to a social climate in which compliance is achieved by normative means. If the norms of an expressive organization have not yet gone through the process of assimilating a management orientation, they will clash with the behaviors of the instrumental constituency. In such a case, the managers can work with their charts, numbers, and objectives all they wish, but they will find themselves doing so out in left field while the expressive ball game goes on as usual. Alternatively, in a format suggested by Malcolm Walker, the forms, but not the substance, of instrumental management may perform ceremonial functions. Walker says, "What we may be seeing is the adoption of strategic management as ceremony at the institutionalized network level: shared concealment and impression management through the production of strategic statements, lists of goals, evaluation of 'studies,' and so on by particular organizations, and widespread participation in conferences at which the virtues of strategic management are celebrated" (1983, p. 51). Again, the instrumental orientation has not been assimilated by the expressive culture.

Groups

Many organizations are iterative, like cauliflowers. Their parts are self-similar; when the whole is broken into parts, each segment resembles the whole. Break the parts into still smaller parts, and a magnifying glass reveals that the parts of the parts also resemble the whole. One might compare most voluntary nonprofit organizations to a three-dimensional honeycomb of many small cells, fitting closely together to form the whole, or to a three-dimensional mosaic that appears solid at a distance but that is really many segments held together by a cohesive mortar. Leading with an eye on the vital role of these groups is essential in guiding the expressive aspects of an organization.

Small iterative subgroups are where an organization's culture resides and where most of its expressive activity takes place. They are profoundly important in understanding organizational culture, in understanding how an organization grows, and in understanding how the organization produces its outputs.

Groups have always been "carriers" of cultures. They are an inevitable and ubiquitous means for fulfilling human purposes. Malcolm Knowles points out that "first in the family, then the clan, the tribe, the guild, the community, and the state, groups have been used as instruments of government, work, fighting, worship, recreation, and education" (1973, p. 48) Leland Bradford argues that "the biological nature of man, his capacity to use language, and the nature of his environment which has been built into its present form over thousands of years require that man exist in groups" (Mason, 1988, p. 4).

Expressive groups, in particular, are essential for a democratic society. In 1951, Amy Loveman observed, "Our population is so immense that only by breaking it down into groups can we hope to make it a propelling force. . . . If we are to effect the purposes which alone will make for the survival of civilization it will be because each individual realizes his obligation. . . . [I]n the small group he can register opinion, and the sum of the small groups which make up those millions [of people] can become the motive power which directs society" (1951, p. 17).

In an organization, these small iterative subgroups collect people in social units of up to ten individuals who have interdependent roles and relationships and who work together as a team on some aspect of the larger organization. The limited size of these workgroups is determined by communication factors. When an assembly of people grows beyond seven to ten individuals, close face-to-face communication among individuals becomes difficult. As the number of members continues to increase, the group will tend to subdivide so that face-to-face communication remains possible.

There are many specific reasons why people form groups. Members of groups have strong positive feelings about each other. They like each other and want to participate with each other. Groups have a high esprit de corps, and the members are loyal to each other. Members' integration into a group involves acceptance of the group's norms and role structure and the distribution of member rights and responsibilities. That is, in exchange for the benefits the group has for the individuals, the group expects conformity to its values and norms. The group becomes an arena of activity in which members share information and can concentrate their many points of view on group challenges. Mutual expectations form the cement that holds the group together. Members regard themselves as a group and regularly interact. "The existence of all is utilized for the satisfaction of some needs of each" (Cattell, Saunders, and Stice, 1953, p. 336).

Members normally have common purposes or interests, are comfortable in each other's company, and may be good friends. They have shared experiences—some of them good and some of them not so good. These shared experiences, and the satisfaction group members have achieved through working with each other's help, form a bond that holds members together. Established groups develop their own beliefs, values and norms, customs, routines, and even rituals that regulate behavior, and they have worked out among themselves how their various duties will be handled (Mason, 1988, p. 18).

Individuals in these small groups normally communicate freely with each other. They exchange opinions, experiences, and expectations. They are not only interdependent when accomplishing their instrumental tasks, they are also interdependent because they give and receive expressive affection and appreciation. The outcome of their effort is a result of contributions made by everyone in the group. There is something at stake that the members need each other to achieve. Each benefits by the success of the mutual work or suffers when it fails. To a degree, each member participates in setting group objectives and assuming responsibility for achievements. The individual is responsible for decisions, and the group is responsible for supporting the individual member. Persons in the group have an overriding motive: to stand well with each other.

Most nonprofits consist of two overlapping types of small iterative groups: task groups and expressive affinity groups. Task groups are built around an instrumental objective and are usually formally designated and recognized. Affinity groups coalesce around an expressive objective and tend to form spontaneously and informally. Organizations utilize groups of both types for managing, distributing, and controlling work; problem solving and decision making; collecting and processing information and ideas; testing and ratifying decisions; coordinating and setting up liaisons; increasing commitment and involvement; negotiating and resolving conflicts; inquiring into the past; and building social cohesion and transmitting organizational culture (see Handy, 1985, pp. 155–156 for a further discussion of workgroups). *An ideal group is both instrumental and expressive;* it is either a task group whose members develop an expressive affinity with each other or an expressive group whose members undertake instrumental tasks. What a proverb says of the wolf, "The strength of the wolf is the pack, and the strength of the pack is the wolf," can be said of humanity: the strength of the individual is the group, and the strength of the group is the individual.

There are additional specific reasons why people find groups so attractive, and leaders need to be aware of all of them.

1.   Group members can accomplish tasks that single persons cannot do. Groups give an individual an opportunity for sharing and helping in a common activity or purpose. The individual both becomes and remains a member of a group because it helps him or her reach some personal objectives. Groups help a person in carrying out his or her particular objectives, which may or may not be the same as the organization's.

2.   Groups give one a sense of security and a sense of control over one's environment. Notable examples are street gangs of youths who do not feel accepted by the larger society, clubs for Latin Americans recently transplanted to the United States, and some fraternal orders. However, all groups provide a psychological home for the individual and are essential to organizational effectiveness because they are the cells within the honeycomb.

3.   Group membership helps the individual solve communication problems. Face-to-face communication is part of the purpose of the group. College and army bull sessions, for example, help freshmen and recruits get information and learn the expectations of an otherwise overwhelming new society.

4.   Group membership provides an individual an opportunity to participate in group planning and problem solving and to have

an influence on decisions that affect a part of his or her life. Conversations often revolve around humorous, difficult, or unsuccessful problem solving. Many retired executives so hunger for this kind of participation that they go back to work in nonprofit enterprises as volunteers to feed that hunger.

5.   A group perpetuates cultural values and preserves members' integrity as it relates to the group. Manner of dress is an easily observed manifestation of this group function. Groups enforce dress codes, whether the individuals in the group be lawyers, college women, jet-setters, or motorcyclists.

6.   Group membership is an opportunity for self-development and education. An inexperienced or uninformed individual can be assigned peripheral tasks while he or she learns from other members and begins climbing the ladder toward greater responsibility for the group's success. The learning process begins when an established member takes a newcomer under his or her wing and serves as a sponsor.

7.   Group membership meets people's need for affiliation and prevents alienation. Groups provide support in time of trouble and often give their members a system of values and behavioral norms. They provide certain social satisfactions and an excellent opportunity to relate to other individuals. Membership in a large organization does not guarantee immunity from alienation, however. When an individual goes off and forms a new group, it suggests that the larger group has not been meeting that individual's personal need for either recognition or sense of accomplishment. He or she may not be getting the kind of support needed. The group may not have been fulfilling its function of helping individuals feel that they belong to something and share in something.

8.   The feeling that one belongs to a group of people with shared problems can reduce anxiety over a situation. In a therapeutic community, for example, group membership gives the individual an established group of peers to help him or her deal with problems and an opportunity to express feelings without rejection.

9.   Groups give their members a functional identity. They offer a means of establishing a self-concept, for it is easier to define oneself in terms of a relationship to others than in isolation. In this way, the group not only provides services desired by society, but it also serves to tie individuals into the culture's pattern of interrela-

tionships. As individuals define themselves in relationship to others, they are given a cultural role. (Consider how often people base their image of an individual on the information they have concerning his or her group affiliations. I often try to imagine what the driver in the car ahead of me is like by reading his or her bumper stickers!)

10.   Group participation establishes reality. It provides consensus validation. An individual needs the group so that he or she will have an accepting body off of which to bounce personal views and against which to test perceptions of reality. This effect is easily observed in a person who changes group affiliation and begins to see the world from a different point of view.

11.   Group membership serves an individual's self-interest. Voluntary enterprises are notoriously political in their make-up, and group membership can provide an individual with a stronger power base than he or she had before.

Given our human propensity to form groups and benefit in many ways from them, organizations can usually reach their instrumental goals better through mobilizing the energy of groups than by other means. Groups are ideal ovens for baking the ingredients of expressive fulfillment. All the expressive needs that I have written about satisfying are facilitated by group participation. Nothing really changes until change happens in the affinity and task groups that comprise the larger entity. Unless and until we understand the role of small groups in organizational culture, our ideas will not be likely to translate into action.

Sweden's Volvo automobile company provides a classic example of a manufacturer that intentionally increased opportunities for expressive behavior in order to increase instrumental outputs. The company changed the factory culture by initiating self-managed workgroups, and their more satisfied workers efficiently produced a better product. Tichy notes that one principle underlying the Volvo success story is that "the core unit for improving employee satisfaction and performance is the work group, not the manager or the individual worker" (1983, p. 219).

As we have seen earlier, informal expressive groups form spontaneously in large organizations as opportunities for comradeship and mutual support. They are essential to the operation of the encompassing formal organization because much of our knowledge, our values, and our attitudes comes from experience in such groups.

A study of 109 welfare workers in small, medium, and large organizational units of a state welfare department, for example, found that there was more role consensus, greater breadth of role conception, higher ethical commitment, and better quality of work performance in smaller units (Thomas, 1959, p. 30). Groups, though producing fewer ideas in total than group members would on their own, produce better ideas than individuals do in the sense that group ideas are better evaluated, more thought through, and gain more commitment from group participants.

We most often think of groups as officially designated by an organization to perform some instrumental task. But why not have formal expressive affinity groups too?

Blau and Scott have noted:

> The exercise of power in informal groups is legitimate to the extent that there emerges a set of norms and beliefs among the members subordinate to the power wielder that the distribution and exercise of power is acceptable to them and is regarded as appropriate. The emergence of such norms significantly alters the control structure . . . : Given the development of social norms that certain orders of superiors ought to be obeyed, the members of the group will enforce compliance with these orders as part of their enforcement of conformity to group norms. The group's demand that orders of the superior be obeyed makes obedience partly independent of his coercive power or persuasive influence over individual subordinates and thus transforms these other kinds of social control into authority [1962, p. 29].

One of the benefits that individuals seek in joining an organization is this close relationship with a group striving toward the same goal. They become part of a social system, participation in which is satisfying in itself. In fact, many social scientists look on small primary groups (rather than the individual) as the basic unit of society.

As we recognize the importance of small groups in shaping organizational culture, we also need to become aware of some of the symptoms of sick group subcultures. Leaders must be particularly concerned about contagiously sick groups—groups with problems that may infect and injure the larger encompassing organization. Deal and Kennedy (1982, p. 138) list several such symptoms. Sick groups become ingrown—there are no transactions among their subgroups. Their differences surface; going beyond healthy rivalry, a sick group will publicly try to undermine or "show up" another group. Sick groups become exclusive; they arbitrarily exclude others or restrict access by others. Finally, sick groups preempt encompassing values; group members are taught that the group's own culture is superior to that of the encompassing organization.

Socialization and Institutionalization

How then does an organization that creates culture and is composed of norm-rich expressive groups maximize its benefits from this potent condition? It incorporates individuals into the organizational culture by socialization. Socialization is the process of integrating an individual's needs with the demands of an organization's culture through exposing the individual to a group and allowing him or her to learn about its culture; its values, attitudes, roles, and folkways; and his or her role in it—a learning process that continues as long as the relationship exists. To a degree, the participant accommodates to the norms of the group. In the process, he or she inhibits or otherwise moderates unacceptable behavior and moves from unacceptable actions to acceptable substitutes. The participant transfers from neutral or prohibited goals to approved goals and hence to automatic use of a large number of approved action patterns. Through such socialization, the participant learns and habitually applies many approved patterns and adapts to the culture's acceptable expectations (Murray and Kluckhohn, 1948, p. 45).

Since groups and organizations are systems in which everything affects everything else, the participant's own individuality also influences the norms of the group. The socialization process is like homemade yogurt. As long as the yogurt culture is present, added ingredients will become transformed into yogurt although they may also add some of their own flavor. Similarly, as an individual is socialized, she or he comes to want what the culture wants her or him to want.

Institutionalization is the process of infusing an organization with value beyond the demands of the instrumental task at hand (Selznick, 1957, p. 17). It involves developing an orderly system of relationships with stable norms of interaction based on formal rules, customs, and rituals; making social behavior predictable by defining its desired and legitimate values; and defining approved roles, including sanctions for deviant behavior.

Institutionalization links values with the social system; it legitimizes values. Statuses and situations are differentiated when values are thus institutionalized. Institutionalization attaches positive and negative differentiated and graduated sanctions. Or, as Parsons put it, "Conformity with different institutional expectations, and different degrees of conformity and infraction of the same ones, are ascribed to different categories of statuses and roles in the social system" (1960, pp. 177–178). (For further insights on the socializing and institutionalizing of culture in organizations, see Durkheim, 1938, Weber, 1947, Parsons, 1973, and Harris, 1979.)

Application

Tunstall and Tichy have suggested several additional points one should consider in steering organizational culture. Tunstall has postulated that management of cultural adaptation within any major corporation requires a three-step process.

1. Management must understand the meaning and impact of corporate culture and must ascertain, often through empirical methods, the elements of its own culture.
2. The "cultural wheat must be separated from the chaff." Decisions must be made about which elements support future goals and strategies, and thus must be retained, and which elements are no longer appropriate, and must be changed.
3. Appropriate actions must be taken to effect the required changes in a way that leaves the desirable elements unaffected (1983, p. 18).

Tichy, in *Managing Strategic Change,* cogently suggests that there are two critical issues in normative management: the content of the organizational culture and subcultures and the *process* for molding and shaping culture and for incorporating subcultures into the organization (1983, pp. 134, 269). Tichy follows Katz and Kahn (1966) who said that "a majority of the active organizational members should accept the beliefs, endorse the values, and abide by the norms [of the organization]; and . . . individual members should be made aware that the beliefs, values, and norms have collective support" (Tichy, 1983, p. 134). Tichy also describes two basic cultural transmission vehicles: "The first is interaction of people and is reflected in special jargon, stories, symbols, rituals, and the creation of role models. The second is reflected in, and reinforced by, management planning systems, information systems, and human resource systems" (p. 255). Finally, Tichy identifies three key functions through which an organization should shape its culture. One is the "human resource system." Shaping culture "starts with a selection process that sorts out cultural deviants at the door: Don't hire people who don't fit with the culture." Another area is the "socialization of development." And the third area comprises "the appraisal and reward processes which channel and reinforce cultural values" (p. 269).

All organizations develop cultures. A culture will evolve and coalesce on its own without any intentional action by a leader or a leadership group. Nevertheless, leaders can take calculated actions to influence cultural norms toward enhancing expressive outputs. Science has not yet isolated all of the components of normative change and is not likely do so. Yet religious leaders like Muhammad, Jesus, Joseph Smith, Elijah Muhammad, Martin Luther King, and even Jim Jones, have succeeded in changing culture to one degree or another. Political leaders like Adolf Hitler, V. I. Lenin, Nelson Mandela, Fidel Castro, Mao Tse-tung, Douglas MacArthur, and the Ayatollah Khomeini have met with mixed success. Thomas Alva Edison, Helen Gurley Brown, the Beatles, Betty Friedan, and Levi Strauss have had their impact. In most formal organizations, the founders have influenced culture more than anyone. Next in line are the charismatic transformational leaders who may have reinvented the organization. The current CEO is the person most likely to be able to modify the organization now, especially if he or she does so as soon as possible after taking office. A leader's values about what is important in an organization serve as the standards for others. Leaders can elicit tremendous energy when their personal values and the organizational values are in synch with one another.

Morgan states that "managers can influence the evolution of culture by being aware of the symbolic consequences of their actions and by attempting to foster desired values, but they can never control culture in the sense that many management writers advocate" (1986, p. 139). Leaders can modify a culture "by influencing the language, norms, folklore, ceremonies, and other social practices that communicate the key ideologies, values, and beliefs guiding action" (p. 135). However, leaders do not normally change a culture overnight. Short-term change caused by management can be expected only in smaller entities, and even then, it will be only of a superficial, cosmetic nature. Through normative means, leadership can have a profound lasting result, but the implementation of cultural change requires a committed long-term application.

Unless an organization has been waiting for a new leader who will precipitate dramatic change, a leader can steer a culture on a tangent to its original course but dares not try to reverse that course. In other words, a leader is more likely to succeed in modifying a culture by moving its participants toward expressive behaviors within the existing cultural milieu than by countering it head on.

The influence of leadership on organizational culture is discussed by Barnard (1938), Bennis and Nanus (1985), Peters (1978), Peters and Waterman (1982), Selznick (1957), Schein (1985), Smircich and Morgan (1982), and Morgan (1986). In brief, however, leaders may take the following steps to bring the power of a culture to bear in transforming an organization within its established philosophical framework:

1. Relate the new vision to traditional values. Spotlight those elements of established organizational values that, when revived, will reinforce the new vision.

2. Precisely articulate the values, purposes, and strategies that are congruent with both the (stated or latent) existing philosophy *and* the intended model. This new statement becomes the organizational vision for cultural modification. As in any other intentional effort, leaders must plan, develop a design, and visualize a clear

destination. If one calculates a profound normative change, one must develop a profound, written normative objective. Then one must "communicate these value-laden messages in a memorable and believable fashion, which will not be instantly forgotten or easily dismissed as corporate propaganda" (Tichy, p. 10).

3. Target the gap. Identify those behavioral changes that bridge the status quo and the new vision.

4. Precisely spell out the expected cascading derivative and complementary personnel strategies, the vision for personal behavioral change. Clearly spell out the results expected from everyone. These strategies should be specified in procedures, personnel manuals, and all formal and informal communications. When I talked with Marine Corps commandant General Gray about the culture of pride in the corps (personal communication, June 13, 1989), he said the corps taught every marine that he had to be "special" to be a marine and that to lead a marine he had to be "special special." Gray also mentioned aspects of the "way of life" that contribute to the esprit de corps and commitment of marines. These aspects are respect for discipline, self-discipline, a desire to excel, and a tight accountability. "When two marines are together," said Gray, "one is in charge." He also spoke of each marine's responsibility for the credibility of the corps, likening it to bank account deposits and withdrawals: "Every time a young marine goes out and demonstrates his commitment to excellence, that marine puts money in the bank. When they do not, then that money, plus interest, comes out." The U.S. Marine Corps obviously knows exactly what its culture expects in an individual's behavior.

5. Sincerely model the expected behavior. With a few notable exceptions, we do not expect actors to be our leaders. Or perhaps I should say we do not expect people to be acting as they lead us. Consistency, sincerity, and integrity are some of the qualities that an expressive normative leader must have in order to endure over the time span required for normative evolution. Leaders must continually symbolize the values of the culture. Even a perception of deviation can cause an organization to crater.

6. Communicate the vision. Through charismatic leaders and organizational heros, teach the needed strategies and train the participants with appropriate models and emotional motivations. Leadership through normative means is more than the application

of a few techniques; nevertheless, communicating the vision might include several effective techniques. General Gray noted his role in constantly speaking, reminding marines what the organization is all about. "The reason I am hoarse," he said, "is because I have made nineteen major speeches and many small ones in the past fourteen days. You have to do that!" Leaders at all levels who are communicating the vision in face-to-face gatherings and other communication channels should use the following techniques:

- Provide an orientation; include myths and legends from the past and describe current heros who exemplify the desired behavior.
- Demonstrate care and support for individual participants. The young Alexander the Great visited individual wounded soldiers after every battle, asking how they were wounded and listening to their accounts of the battle. This caring concern for his followers contributed to the legend of his love for his troops.
- Demonstrate confidence in others. When people are confident that others will meet their expectations, those others are more likely to do so.
- Appeal to people's hearts and minds. Mix substantive rational arguments with inspirational appeals to lead people in a new direction. Again, use symbols, stories, rituals, and ceremonies.
- Communicate through informal expressive leaders as well as the formal command networks. Pull the grapevines into the communication orbit.
- Ensure that all communications media, physical surroundings, technology, and hygiene factors are congruent with the new vision.
- Use face-to-face meetings profusely.
- After an initial success, reinforce desired change with ongoing education, including new myths, legends, and examples of benefits. The Marine Corps conducts an annual birthday ceremony at every one of its installations. The celebration reviews Marine history and traditions and, says General Gray, "is one part of a very broad training and educational program to build pride in our traditions."

7.   Consistently recognize and reward desired behavior that conforms to the new vision. Let small groups and all participants know how they are progressing toward the organization's goal. Remember that the voluntary sector is a realm in which intrinsic rewards are more potent than extrinsic ones.

Nonprofit organizations shape their cultures, not so much by the hierarchy of command or by rules and procedures as through coordinating groups. The most profound role of the effective leader in a voluntary organization is developing and maintaining group cultures with norms that are functional and compatible with both the expressive and instrumental ends sought by the organization. Groups are highly motivating for their members, and the time and attention of leaders is efficiently utilized when it is devoted to coordinating the groups that make up the organization (Handy, 1988, pp. 110–112).

Conclusion

Most voluntary and nonprofit organizations achieve cooperation from their participants because those participants comply with the norms of their individual organization's culture. The small task and affinity groups in the organization are the carriers of culture. The most successful leaders with the most profound impact will likely be those who work within the culture, or who modify the culture by modifying the norms of its constituent groups, thus leading by normative means. Normative leadership is still more art than science. The most potent practitioners of this mode lead intuitively or through emulating a mentor or through trial and error.

Needs for Further Research

More research is needed on the question the American Cancer Society asked of its CEO candidates: "What is the difference between the culture of nonprofit and for-profit organizations?" We need more research that identifies the effective functions of normative leadership. Scholars might study the practices of some of today's transformational leaders who have succeeded in more than one organizational environment. They might also study nonprofit organizations that intentionally tried to change their cultures. We need to know: How do we better define and measure cultural intensity? How does culture influence goal selection? What are the relationships among organizational, group, and individual goals? How do various group memberships influence an individual's behavior when he or she is a manager, a subordinate, and a peer? What are the key and the conflicting group loyalties? To what degree does communication follow status and authority lines? In exactly what kinds of organizations are people free to participate, challenge authority, and express opinions? Do leadership and group maintenance roles shift with topic and group needs? How are normative violations treated? (see also Rubin and Beckhard, 1972, p. 317).

Researchers working with a specific organization or in a discrete field might apply the hierarchy of values concept to their specific interest. Researchers might also study an organization or class of organizations to determine if organizations can host more than one culture. An interesting specific study might examine cases in which constituents struggled to choose between competing positive values. A study of cultural change in an organization since its founding should be productive, especially if the changes correlated with expressive and instrumental activity. The subject of organizational values alone beckons for specific studies within the segments of a single organization or within the organizations in a single industry.

Actions for Practitioners

Leaders should benefit from identifying their organization's culture, department by department, chapter by chapter, level by level, group by group, to discover how cultural differences relate to any internal tensions. They should identify the organization's expressive groups and elevate these groups' participation in decision-making processes. Effective normative leaders might identify the factors contributing to their own success and share their findings. Leaders who are not being followed to the degree they feel they should might sensitize themselves to their organization's culture and modify their perspectives. They can begin by identifying organizational values and any normative variations among the constituent groups. They might examine the role of small groups and then steer their organizational culture in a more desirable direction. If I could recommend but one thing to practitioners at this point, it would be that they accurately describe the mores of their own organizations and determine if the organizational culture is optimum for their purposes.

If the organization is not broken, do not try to fix it; but if something is askew, determine if the problem is due to incongruent group norms. Dilute or eliminate discordant elements. Staff members and volunteers alike can experiment by implementing what they learn about the potency of small groups. Fundraisers who are not yet utilizing small-group motivation may boost their results in their next campaign by attending to subgroups. Service provision that effectively utilizes groups will find both expressive and instrumental outputs growing.

Culture changes, if at all, in a succession of tides—each one encroaching a little further on the shore, in minuscule segments. An organization can experience the miracle of normative leadership—but not overnight.

This chapter discussed organizational culture, normative compliance, the role of values, the important functions of the small groups in which the culture resides, and what leaders can do to nudge a culture in a desired direction. If leaders can produce the right culture, the culture will produce the right mix of outputs. On those icy winter days, it is most effective to heat the house and let the house keep everyone warm.

Chapter Six

Building a Cohesive Organization

As leaders build organizations, many tend to concentrate on the bricks and neglect the mortar. They stack the instrumental elements on top of each other but ignore the expressive elements that bond those instrumental elements together, leaving cohesiveness to evolve on its own. Either the organization integrates into a cohesive unity or it does not. Without special attention to the factors that contribute to cohesiveness, organizational mortar may crumble, and the loyalty of individuals to each other, to their groups, and the encompassing organization will be insufficient on its own to hold the bricks firmly together.

The cohesion nonprofit organizations require comes from a positive expressive relationship among two or more participants. Nonprofit entities rely heavily on such social cohesiveness because they have neither the pervasive coercive power of government nor the strong financial incentives of business. Cohesion and expression are closely linked because the need for affiliation is a major expressive motivation.

This chapter will help leaders better understand the factors that build cohesion and the factors that contribute to disintegration. It will help them diagnose their organizations and better predict the potential an organizational action has for attracting and recruiting participants. When leaders want an organization to act, especially to act rapidly at a crucial time, they need cohesive unanimity. Members of an expressive unit can pull together, no longer single strands of wire but a woven cable with much greater power.

Cohesiveness, like a mason's mortar, is usually a mix of a variety of ingredients. No single factor produces group or organizational cohesiveness, but ideally, a mix of factors produces optimum bonding. Some of these contributing factors are endemic to organizations and evolve naturally. Others are produced by the long-range organizational purpose, structure, or strategy. Leaders may find tactical ways to stimulate participants in the organization in order to maximize cohesion to suit a specific situation or to compensate for some lack of another factor.

Participation in a purposeful cohesive community prevents alienation. The cohesive community provides support in time of trouble. From a management perspective, effective cohesion should increase participant satisfaction, productivity, and personal development and increase the organization's attractiveness to potential volunteers and contributors. It should provide social satisfactions in the form of excellent opportunities to relate to other individuals. The role of a church congregation as a mutually supportive extended family is an example. But as mentioned in Chapter Five, membership in a large organization does not guarantee immunity from alienation. The larger society may not meet individuals' personal need for recognition or for a sense of accomplishment or for fulfillment. Individuals may not be getting the kind of support they need. It is formal or informal association with a *cohesive* organization that provides people with a sense of legitimacy, with all the benefits described in the previous chapter, and with a group system of values and behavioral norms.

Cohesion is *both an end and a means*. It is an end because it enhances the expressive aspects of the organizations to their constituencies and to the society. Cohesion is a means because it is essential to the organization's instrumental achievement. Voluntary nonprofit organizations contribute to their constituencies by giving them a vehicle for expressive experience. Participants expect cohesion of them. Individuals will be attracted to and remain in the organization and the organization will remain viable as long as the cohesive forces are stronger than any disruptive forces. Human beings are naturally gregarious and a little forethought and encouragement by management will facilitate cohesive factors.

Cohesion is important for the well-being of individuals and society. When the mortar weakens and crumbles, the entire structure shakes. We once found our cohesive groups in family and village settings. Then, as W. H. Whyte, Jr., wrote, "the Industrial Revolution destroyed the solid moorings of an older way of life and cast the helpless workers adrift in a strange and difficult world. The peasant who had been reared in the intimacy of a small village . . . now found himself isolated and bewildered in a city crowded with strangers and indifferent to a common rule. The symbolic universe that had patterned the ways of man across the ages in village, manor, or guild had disappeared. This is the great moral tragedy of the Industrial system" (1956, p. 45). Industrialization in the Third World is causing the same social trauma. Migration to the cities and the breakdown of the tribal system with its strong cohesiveness may be "progress" to us, but it has many destructive results. People must find ways to replace the cohesiveness that has been lost, and leaders can make their organizations more attractive by providing it.

Cohesiveness is the very essence of the expressive aspect of nonprofit organizations. We enjoy voluntary activity and may immerse ourselves in it for its own sake. Cohesive forces usually operate spontaneously and informally; they may sometimes get in the way of formal instrumental ends, yet at other times they may contribute to those ends. Occasions often arise when keeping the system together takes precedence over objectives. Goals are forfeit. Trade-offs between human relations values and task values must be resolved. Occasionally efforts toward goal achievement can pull counter to those toward building cohesion. Cohesion not only contributes to expressive ends, it is also a means for achieving instrumental purposes. Think again of the mortar. It does not exist only for its own sake but for its function of holding together bricks. Elton Mayo's Hawthorne studies demonstrated many years ago the positive effect of cohesiveness on productivity in an industrial setting. "For all of us," said Mayo, "the feeling of security and certainty derives always from assured membership of a group." Mayo also observed that "man's desire to be continuously associated in work with his fellows is a strong, if not the strongest, human characteristic" (Whyte, 1956, p. 39).

An organization must elicit, store, and effectively channel energy to reach objectives. It is cohesiveness that can attract, hold, and apply the energy of a constituency toward the completion of tasks. This energy may be any resource elicited to fulfill organizational purposes. It may be money, equipment, surplus funds, talent, influence, skills, or work. It may be found within the bounds of the enterprise or in the outside environment. The more effectively this energy is applied and the more efficiently it is used, the greater the benefits the organization can provide the recipients. All of the individuals involved in contributing to these energy exchanges, utilizing them, and benefiting from them cohere together by their involvement and are potential sources of additional energy to recharge the system.

Cohesion further contributes to organizational productivity by facilitating the management of conflict and reducing the energy, time, and funds spent in internal disputes.

In addition, volunteers in cohesive organizations attend more regularly, have less turnover, participate more readily, and are better able to tolerate hostility and conflict than members of less cohesive groups. Volunteers in cohesive organizations tend to influence others to work toward organizational goals. Cohesiveness has a positive influence on self-esteem, which, in turn, tends to make a worker more productive.

It is possible for cohesiveness itself to cause some internal conflict, however. Organizational members' small-group cohesion may interfere with their cohesion with the encompassing organization. Suffice it to say that depending on the mix of cohesive factors, small-group cohesion may work for or against cohesion with the encompassing organization. While leaders of entities composed of smaller groups will prefer individuals to bond with the encompassing organization, leaders of the smaller units themselves may prefer individuals to give their primary allegiance to the smaller group. A leader of the local chapter of a national organization may be much more concerned about the loyalty of members to the chapter than about their loyalty to the central office. However, the leader of a fundraising team that will disintegrate when the drive is over may have a temporary limited cohesion goal for the team and an overriding concern for cohesion with the encompassing entity.

Interpersonal bonding generally produces greater small-group cohesion than loyalty to the encompassing organization. Typically, members give their small group credit for the positive affect of close personal bonds but lay any blame for negative affects at the doorstep of the encompassing organization. Therefore, one can easily predict that a given mix of cohesive attachments may work to fragment the encompassing organization because of members' loyalty to their competing subgroups (Yoon, 1994, p. 331).

Factors Affecting Peer Cohesion

I have not ranked the cohesiveness factors that follow; neither do I claim that the list is comprehensive. Moreover, these factors are not all mutually exclusive. Some are derived from others, some are components of others, and they are not equally important. But all of them strongly influence the cohesiveness of individuals within their particular affinity or task groups and within the encompassing organization.

Ceremonies and Symbols

Participation in a ceremony gives people a shared experience that reinforces their consciousness of shared history, values, associations, goals, and activities. Ceremonies build ethnocentrism and give participants a tie with the past. Induction or initiation rites are important, as are the rituals marking the movement of an individual from one level to another. A pledge to be loyal can obligate a person to be loyal. Otherwise, organizational expectations of loyalty or members' "duties" to be loyal demand a moral basis in the individual. The strongest influence on loyalty is the normative one.

Symbols help participants to feel an organizational identity. Symbols include such items as insignia, uniforms, flags, rings, pins, arm bands, certificates, or distinctive dress. Such symbols provide psychological separation between the organization and the broader society, which identifies the participant with the organization. The development of an organizational folklore, "in" jokes, and distinctive behaviors and speech patterns is also evidence of cohesion or can be utilized to develop cohesion.

Though groups tend to develop their rituals automatically, leaders occasionally develop rituals intentionally for the sake of cohesion. For example, when the U.S. Air Force Academy was established, it mandated many "traditions" copied from the pattern of West Point and Annapolis. The past can be honored in organizational literature, in speeches, and in annual ceremonies. An awareness of an organization's past tends to build loyalty above and beyond the daily routine, ensures continuity of purpose, and provides built-in momentum. Even past failures, if they were heroic enough, can become the focus of ceremonies. Look what Texans have done with the Alamo—a battle they lost.

Symbols and ceremonies are an important bridge between subgroups in large organizations with many autonomous subgroups. Handy has noted that "we need to be reminded to feel proud of the cause we serve. The rituals of armies and cathedrals may not be appropriate devices for a voluntary organization, but all the rituals, ceremonials, uniforms and banners have a purpose: to put the cause and the organization above self when it is life itself that may be at stake. Organizations often starve themselves of ceremony and ritual. Perhaps they are missing something, something which needs to be recreated in an appropriate form" (1988, p. 150).

Radcliffe-Brown tells us that

> The purpose of the rite is to affirm the existence of a social bond between two or more persons. . . . [It] compels the participants to act as though they felt certain emotions, and thereby does, to some extent, produce those emotions in them. . . . [A] strong feeling of personal attachment is produced when two persons join together in sharing and simultaneously expressing one and the same emotion. . . . [The] song first came into general use in human society because it provides a means by which a number of persons can utter the same series of sounds together and as with one voice. . . . When a group engages in a fight with another it is to revenge some injury that has been done to the whole group. The group is to act as a group and not merely as a collection of individuals, and it is therefore necessary that the group should be conscious of its unity and solidarity [1948, pp. 238–257].

Finally, Smith notes that "ritual can provide the satisfactions of a sense of belonging, of fellowship, of community, of acceptance and of self worth from the generation and/or affirmation of commitment to ideologies, to symbolic values, or to important social roles, statuses, categories or goals" (1972, p. 50).

Communication

The frequency and quality of communication among participants effects cohesion. Communication in voluntary enterprises must include more than factual data. It must also inspire, motivate, and build cohesion. Personnel constantly need reminding of their organization's traditions, purposes, and objectives. Praise for the good work of both individuals and task groups is part of the reward system of the enterprise. Organizationwide media stimulate interpersonal communications and play a direct part in bonding individuals to their groups and groups to the total enterprise. The organization's communication network is the nerve system linking the many parts into a cohesive whole.

While frequent and good communication tends to bond individuals together, the ostracism resulting from withdrawing all communication can be devastating. In World War II, for example, naval leaders discovered that serious problems arose during sea battles when ships' below-decks crews developed a sense of estrangement and loss of morale. The problem was solved by simply narrating the topside events, accompanied by the sounds of battle, over the public address system.

Communication in organizations must signal acceptance of others, convey personal feelings about things that are important to the speaker, and support the self-concepts of others. Individuals must perceive some degree of similarity among themselves as a prelude to cohesion. Therefore, communication must invest sufficient time in interaction and extend to an appropriate level of intimacy if it is to be effective (Gudykunst, 1991, p. 141).

Community Attitude

The idea of community is quite old. It was formalized, for example, in the ancient Greek concept of *koinonia*. Five prerequisites for *koinonia* were (1) free uncoerced participation; (2) a common purpose; (3) common ownership of jointly held resources, a collection of precious objects, or a repertory of shared actions; (4) *philia*, or a sense of mutuality, often inadequately translated as "friendship"; and (5) relations characterized by fairness

(Lohmann, 1992, pp. 58–59). The Latin concept of *communitas* had two related meanings: (1) common interest or the quality of fellowship and (2) a group having in common an external bond (Rosenthal, 1984, p. 219). Yankelovich says our modern word *community* evokes the feeling that "here is where I belong, these are my people, I care for them, they care for me, I am part of them. . . [I]ts absence is experienced as an aching loss, a void . . . feelings of isolation, falseness, instability and impoverishment of spirit" (1981, p. 227). The sense of collective consciousness implied here is almost synonymous with the concept of culture discussed earlier. It is a particular kind of culture, a culture of closeness, of sharing, of concern for others, and of needing others. It links one organizational generation to another.

Gudykunst (1991, pp. 147–148) recommends seven principles or attitudes for building community.

1. Commitment. We must be committed to the principle of building community.
2. Mindfulness. We must think about what we do and say. We must focus on the process.
3. Unconditional acceptance. We must value diversity and not judge diversity.
4. Concern for both oneself and others. We must engage in dialogue and consultation.
5. Understanding. We must determine how others' interpretations of events and/or behaviors are different from and similar to our own. We must search for commonalities.
6. Ethical stance. We must engage in behavior that is morally right in and of itself.
7. Peacefulness. We must strive for internal harmony and harmony in relations with others.

Conflict

Conflict? Isn't this chapter on cohesion? How did conflict get in here? That was my first reaction to the realization that I ought to discuss conflict, but respected scholars have long made a good case that in conflict a group finds itself—identifies itself—and that conflict ultimately contributes to a more cohesive body. Conflict serves a positive function in solidifying social groups and in shaping the complex symbolic and institutional apparatus needed to sustain them (Gager, 1975, pp. 79–80). Lewis Coser, distilling and applying some of the work of the pioneer German sociologist Georg Simmel to conflict in social settings, says that "conflict is a form of socialization" and that "groups require disharmony as well as harmony. . . . [F]ar from being necessarily dysfunctional, a certain degree of conflict is an essential element in group formation and the persistence of group life" (1956, p. 31).

In arguing that conflict is a group-binding function, Gager notes that this proposition is analogous to the finding in developmental psychology that an individual's process of rebellion against his or her parents helps that individual to define his or her identity. Gager finds that external conflict helps young, minority communities establish their own identity in the larger world. In addition, he cites Simmel's belief that internal "conflict also serves to strengthen group cohesion by reinforcing the inevitable divisions within increasingly complex organizations and by ventilating feelings of hostility associated with these divisions" (1975, p. 80).

Dreams

Every organization has some sort of dream. It may or may not be embodied in a formal mission statement or as a guiding purpose in the preamble to a constitution. It may be as idealistic and lofty as "To feed the world's hungry masses," "To teach the world to read," or "To unite all mankind in love." The dream may be as practical and finite as "To save the trees in Polk Park" or "To get our young people off the streets and provide wholesome recreation." The dream includes the group aspirations that members hold collectively. When groups believe something is going to happen, they behave as though it is going to happen, then it often does happen.

Whether the dream be idealistic or practical, the cohesiveness of the group depends in part on moderate expectations. When expectations are unrealistically high, frustration at not reaching the goal will result. Such frustration may be generalized to frustration with the group itself. When goals are set too low, there will be no challenge to members to pull together as a team. Though the idealism of the dream should not be forgotten, it can merge with practical action so that expectations will not be unrealistic.

The attraction of its organizational purpose, the relevancy of its goals, the ambitions of its leaders, the intensity of its activities, and the expectations of its constituency are some of the facets of any group's dream. The promise of its dream attracts human and financial assets. As long as the flame of a compelling purpose burns bright, participants will tend to bond together with a sense of common purpose. When the flame flickers, questions arise, and members' cohesive grip on each other relaxes.

External Threat

Nothing has the immediate bonding power of a common threat, a common enemy. Real or perceived, the common enemy increases cohesion (Blake and Mouton, 1964, pp. 420–425; Athos and Coffey, 1968, p. 131). Generally, the more ominous the threat, the tighter the bond. When we are confronted with an external threat, the fight or flight response embedded in our genes assumes control. Internal bickering grows silent. Centripetal forces reign. All the forces and energies are mustered for the sake of the common good.

When a film shows the Indians racing across the plain toward the settlers' wagon train, we know the trail boss will immediately circle the wagons and the settlers will abandon all internal struggles until the cavalry comes. Americans rallied together immediately after the bombing of Pearl Harbor. Political rivalries were no longer important. Where there had been fragmentation on December 6th, there was unity on December 7th. The cohesiveness resulting from external threats seems to be extremely widespread. It has also been observed among animals. For instance, musk oxen, when they perceive an external threat, form a circle with their horned heads down and facing outward.

The threat need not necessarily be deadly or the enemy necessarily hated. A threat may be no more ominous than the football team of a rival high school or a boot-camp drill instructor. Threats need not be real so much as perceived to rally people. Concocted external threats have always been a tool of the demagogue.

Among the many mistakes of the Bureau of Alcohol, Tobacco and Firearms at the Branch Davidian compound outside Waco, Texas, was their failure to anticipate how their attack would enhance the power David Koresh had over his followers. The outcome would have been different had they arrested him earlier when he went on an errand into town, rather than forcing a confrontation and a threatening situation that coalesced his followers.

Future Prospect

Cohesion is affected by whether the future prospect of the organization is one of hope or one of despair. The brighter the outlook, the more attractive the organization. When the future prospects darken, participants often seek scapegoats for the failure, and many will seek alternatives for their allegiance. The analogy of rats deserting a sinking ship is appropriate.

However, when the organizational prospect is bright, the constituents stake a claim on the promising future of the group. I like the image of a stake driven deep into the ground of the future. Tied to that stake is a sturdy cable on which everyone will pull together, drawing themselves into a new era. The effect of hope is not limited to the total organization. Hope is also a cohesive force when applied to subunits of the enterprise and to small task groups and individuals. Each needs that stake in the future. While people must be fed today, they must also have hope for more and better results in the future. Hope is an incentive. Staff and volunteers alike see a career ladder they can climb to that even better time.

Expectation of eventual success may be all that is necessary for an organization to make it through the rough times. However, one study indicates that "groups with moderate expectations gained significantly more than either groups with high or low expectations across the group experience. This suggests that the more cohesive groups are those whose members have more moderate and realistic expectations of what a group can offer" (Pereroy, 1980, p. 247). Thus, leaders should *not* intentionally exaggerate the prospects. Moreover, commitment to values that are developed throughout the history of an organization can encourage individuals to remain committed and dedicated even when the prospects are dim.

Harmonizing Differences

Disagreements arise whenever two or more people get together. Disagreements may be as minor as who steps into the bus first or as major as whether or not to drop an atomic bomb. However, the magnitude of the subject of the disagreement may not affect cohesion as much as the manner in which it is resolved. One of our greatest accomplishments in the United States is the manner in which we resolve differences of opinion as to who will be our chief of state. It is not that the magnitude of importance is less here than in Haiti or that citizens' views are less intense here than in Rwanda but that our culture mandates a peaceful transfer of power with the life, limb, and liberty of the loser still intact.

The ease and frequency with which differences among participants are settled in a manner satisfactory to group members, the greater the cohesion will be (Deutsch, 1968). Conversely, the potentially disintegrating influence of polarizing conflict can negate the benefits of expressive interaction. The goal of groups of all sizes should be an attitude of open, mutually respectful expression of all competing points of view before a group decides its course and the harmonious cooperation of all after making that choice.

Homogeneity

The more nearly homogeneous a group, the more likely it is to develop peer cohesion; and the more peer-cohesive the group, the more likely it is to become homogeneous (Etzioni, 1975, p. 293). Homogeneity may exist either because of a static similar cultural background or because of dynamic common values and goals precipitated by people's organizational membership. On the one hand, if participants come to a group with similar attitudes and a common orientation to life and the world, cohesiveness will likely develop quickly (Homans, 1951, p. 32). On the other hand, a group's common values and goals may attract persons without a common ethnic background. Once together, their homogenous common concerns are revealed and mobilized, and they begin to bond.

Individuals support each other by their perceived similarity of backgrounds or values. Homogeneity makes them compatible. Their similar backgrounds cause them to hold similar values and to develop similar objectives within the organization's structure. A study by Yalom and Rand demonstrated that compatibility of members correlated with group cohesiveness. Other studies show that homogeneous task groups are more cohesive, more efficient, and more productive than heterogeneous groups (Yalom, 1975, pp. 265, 270).

The vast literature of the church growth movement is built around the concept of homogeneous cells (McGavran, 1970). It contends that individuals are more likely to join a group if they do not have to cross boundaries of difference. However, my own experience has demonstrated that compelling homogeneity of values and goals can bridge ethnic, social, and cultural boundaries. Individuals like to be with people who share their values, but they want to stay away from people with different values, lest they be drawn into unpleasant confrontations.

Homogenous ethnic and social background correlates with cohesion in both small and large groups, but Etzioni suggests that the reasons for the correlation differ in the two: "In small groups, background homogeneity increases the chances that the members will reach consensus and hence exert social power to generate conformity; in large social units, it increases the probability that participants will share external loyalties which can be extended to the organizational unit" (1975, p. 297).

Interaction Frequency

The more people work together, the more likely they are to form cohesive ties. The more a task or proximity causes individuals to interact, the more likely social relationships and activities are to develop concurrently with the task relationships and activities (Homans, 1951, p. 4). Hence, task groups can also become affinity groups, and instrumental organizations can also develop into expressive organizations. The more exclusive and intense the interaction, the more cohesive the group is likely to become.

Conversely, the more interactions group members have with persons outside the group, the less strong their allegiance is likely to be to the group. Some tasks require group members to work as a unit all of the time, while others require members, perhaps as group representatives, to deal with external elements. In business, purchasing agents and salespersons constantly deal with outsiders. In government, members of Congress tend to have more and more relations in the District of Columbia and fewer and fewer in their home districts. Nonprofit organizations have their counterparts to these examples in fundraisers who bond with contributors, direct service personnel who bond with clients, and professionals who bond with professionals in other organizations.

Image

How attractive does the organization appear to individuals? Myriad components mix to form an organization's social character. Along with the organization's public relations effort, these components give an organization a distinctive personality that conjures up an image in people's minds. Some of the components of an organizational image are organizational significance, values, policies, property, personnel, and prestige. When a person visualizes the organization, he or she pictures its image as a whole, much as he or she would picture an individual. When an organization is very well known, just its name can call up its image. What images comes to mind when you hear such names as Tiffany, Wal-Mart, the U.S. Marines, the Ku Klux Klan, IBM, and Rolls-Royce?

Image incorporates an organization's level of prestige, the congruence of its values with an individual's own, and the quality of its personnel and services. Image affects whether potential constituents or customers are attracted or repelled. The image reflecting the character of an organization affects the cohesiveness of its members to the degree that they perceive the image as good and as worth their time and energy. Image grows out of the entire history of the organization and represents a capital asset that can pay high interest. Participants like to feel that they are part of a rich tradition and that the baton they carry has been passed on from one distinguished hand to another. Therefore, a high-status image of a group in relation to other groups tends to increase cohesion.

One of the most important positive components of a group's

image is the group's success in achieving its goals. Success encourages members to appreciate and like each other more. The more successful the group in accomplishing its task, the greater the cohesion. When the participants' image of the organization stirs up pride and raises their self-esteem, cohesiveness increases. The more attractive the group is to the participant, the more he or she respects its judgment and commits to its purposes. For example, many groups adopt their own vocabulary of "in" terms and phrases, whether the members be lawyers, college students, or Hell's Angels.

Integrity

The greater the integrity of the organization, the greater the cohesiveness. The soundness of the organization's values encourages trust in the leadership by the constituency. Group integrity results in members who trust each other. The ties that bind the organization do not depend only on laws, contracts, or formal agreements. There are also ties of trust based on integrity.

People must be able to perceive the organization's integrity. If members feel a lack of sincerity in either purpose or methodology, cohesiveness will crumble. Because of the voluntary nature of nonprofit organizations, the violation of trust or the appearance of exploitation will often cause participants to voluntarily disappear. Organizations need community involvement, but rank-and-file members are frustrated when they find influential members who do not mean what they say, do not do what they plan to do, and do not keep their promises and pledges to the organization that selected them for leadership positions.

The integrity of any group is also defined in part by the general attitude of appreciation among group members for one another's talents, time, and various other contributions. When each person feels valued by self and others for his or her unique combination of abilities and point of view, then members may have a greater desire to use their variety of gifts in the service of the group.

Leadership

The magnetism of a leader contributes to cohesion. This is one reason why the charismatic style of leadership often works well in a voluntary enterprise. Charismatic leaders can epitomize the value systems of their organizations and serve as role models. They set a pattern and a pace for the members and provide a magnetic core that holds them together. The leaders of a group, whether formal or informal, are often a powerful factor in determining the direction of the group's involvement. Commitment to the leaders often means commitment to their norms or the norms they represent, that is, those of the organization (Etzioni, 1975, p. 292).

Charismatic personalities are more effective in positions where cohesion is essential than in those where cohesion is unimportant. Strong leaders at various levels can utilize organizational purpose in recruiting volunteers, building their conviction, eliciting their energy, and inspiring them to their best effort. These strong leaders tend to be more effective than their pedestrian counterparts in motivating members around the organizational purpose.

Freud suggested that cohesiveness derives from a universal wish to be the favorite of the leader. He indicated that this wish grows from the child's wish to be the favorite of his parents even though each child realizes that his siblings are equally loved by the parents. In groups, this wish results in the solution in which all are granted equality in relation to the leader—producing a spirit of cohesiveness. Individuals in each group hold their group leader in common, and the groups hold the organizational leader in common.

While initial cohesion may be elicited by a single leader, a group intending to survive the long haul needs its principles stressed more than specific personalities. Leaders effective in facilitating cohesiveness should make themselves personally available to as many members as possible. Members need to be encouraged to approach the leader with ideas, feedback, problems, and counsel. Without such an open line of connection, volunteer members will likely come to feel that their contributions are unimportant, and their level of commitment will drop.

Shils and Janowitz (1948) found an interesting difference in military units between peer cohesion and hierarchical cohesion (between unit members and leaders). Where there was hierarchical cohesion with leaders who were committed to combat goals, there was a high commitment among the men to combat goals. When the leaders were excluded from the men's groups, high peer cohesion was not associated with high commitment to combat goals. Hierarchical rather than peer cohesion appears to affect goal attainment. Similarly, the often-cited studies by Lewin, Lippitt, and White (1939) and by Coch and French (1952) deal with the effect of hierarchical cohesion on morale and goal attainment.

Orientation

Some organizations induct members in groups and provide an orientation into the organizational culture for the group as a whole. If the inducted members come from diverse backgrounds and share an extended orientation period, they often form a cohesive bond that persists throughout the remainder of their experience in the organization. It seems that the more difficult the entrance requirements, and the more unpleasant or strenuous the orientation, the more cohesive the group. Examples of groups facing difficult entrance or orientation requirements are freshman classes in some colleges and universities, plebes at West Point, fraternity pledges, and circumcision groups in East African tribes.

Orientations that are intentionally designed to build cohesion apply factors such as a common enemy, sharing experiences, and symbols and ceremonies. Nevertheless, the bond that develops among participants who are socialized into a new society together is a factor in itself. As I mentioned earlier, when I spoke with General Gray about the legendary cohesiveness of the U.S. Marine Corps, he reminded me that from the moment of their induction into boot camp, recruits are taught that Marines are special and that each recruit must prove himself worthy of acceptance.

Ownership Roles

Organizations become more cohesive when participants have a sense of ownership and are given opportunities to formulate, implement, and achieve goals. Organizational membership should provide an individual with an opportunity to participate in organizational planning and problem solving and to influence decisions that affect a part of his or her life. Having an ownership role in achieving goals helps a person confirm his or her identity and purpose. Thus, cohesion increases with individuals' participation and when the organization provides resources and places value on the accomplishment of the task with which individuals are involved.

The ownership concept works in two directions: members of voluntary enterprises typically feel not only that they "belong" to the organization but also that in a very real sense the organization "belongs" to them. Cohesiveness has been credited with some of the success of Japanese industry for similar reasons. A Mitsubishi worker would describe his relationship to the company by saying, "I belong to Mitsubishi." In the United States we would say, "I work for Exxon," or, "I am with American Cyanamide." We reserve "belong to" for our voluntary enterprises: "I belong to the Museum of Modern Art." "I belong to the Lutheran Church." "I belong to the Rotary Club." Or, indicating possession even more, we identify ourselves with the voluntary entity: "I am a Mason." "I am a Teamster." "I am a Campfire Girl." "I am a Republican."

Proximity

As noted in the discussion of frequency of interaction, people tend to bond most intensively with those they are closest to. Group members are usually more cohesive within a small task group than within the larger encompassing organization. Members of local communities are closer to each other than to other citizens of their state, and to their states than to their nation, and so forth (Lawler, 1992, p. 334). The more individuals see each other, the closer their ties are likely to be. A study of 444 employees of a small industrial plant found that clique membership consisted of workers of the same sex who were near each other functionally and spatially (James, 1951).

Shared Experiences

Newly formed organizations tend to be less cohesive than established ones. The more individuals have the opportunity to interact and to work together and the more experiences they share, the more cohesive they will tend to become. The sharing of successes, opportunities for comradeship, and even shared failures will bond members together.

When Andrew Young told me about his experiences with Martin Luther King in the 1960s (personal communication, June 7, 1984), he said that their personal commitment to the civil rights movement, the intensity of the day-by-day struggle, their common faith, and the cloud of danger that constantly hovered over them bound them closer and closer together.

Any gathering of "old war buddies" demonstrates how shared experiences of an intense nature can weld individuals together for a lifetime in spite of their having different life-styles, values, and ethnic backgrounds. Police trained in dealing with hostage incidents learn of the "Stockholm effect," in which captors and hostages often bond when given sufficient time under stress. In such a case, the captors become reluctant to harm the hostages, and the hostages begin to sympathize with the predicament of their captors.

Size

All else being equal, a smaller group holds together better than a large one. Members of smaller groups interact with each other more and have stronger bonds. Chapter Five provides ample evidence of the small group's influence on cohesion.

Socializing

Meeting, eating, drinking, working, and having fun together builds cohesion. Church suppers, state dinners, formal toasts, the Indian peace pipe, all of these tend to facilitate friendship and establish cohesion and trust. Once again, proximity and frequent interaction develop cohesiveness. If cohesion is going to result from people's shared concepts about the group, it will come about as people interact, verbally and nonverbally, in social settings of all kinds.

Time

Cohesiveness can develop quickly through intensive relationships in isolated environments. My own experiences in hunting camps with previously unrelated persons have consistently shown the development of cohesiveness in a few hours. Individuals establish their individual identities and bond functionally to endure hardships that will arise during the course of the week with humor, ritual, common experiences of difficulty, and elation. However, all else being equal, the more enduring the interaction in a group, the more cohesive the group becomes (Etzioni, 1975, p. 290). If nothing else, time provides opportunities for the operation of a number of factors, such as common experiences, the influence of leaders, and more communication. High cohesion also requires a certain amount of stability in group membership since high turnover prevents the growth over time of mutual emotional investment (Etzioni, 1975, p. 286). In an analysis of primary groups, Fischer (1952, p. 276) found the best predictors of group intimacy among college students were frequency of contact and time spent in contact. The study also found that frequency of contact decreases as the size of the group increases.

Volunteerism

The fact that participants in a not-for-profit voluntary enterprise enter into it willing and of their own choice contributes to organizational cohesion. When people see themselves as volunteers, they are likely to act in a manner in accordance with the norms of good volunteers. Athos and Coffey illustrate that idea with this example: "Assume that a person is required to join a group even though he neither has much enthusiasm about its objectives and activities nor enjoys being with its members. We would expect him to behave quite differently from someone who joined the group because he advocated its objectives or enjoyed being with its members or both" (1968, p. 131).

Strong interpersonal cohesiveness usually improves member commitment to the larger organization. Cohesion across dissimilar positions usually has a more profound effect than bonding that occurs between similar positions (Yoon, 1994, p. 329).

Intergroup Congruence

All of the factors described above should not only influence the relation of an individual to the group and larger entity but also tie groups to each other and to the organization. Five additional factors that build cohesion are essential for holding groups together within an organization. They are functional interdependence, legal and contractual ties, solidary orientation, subunit congruence with the total organization, and a superordinate goal.

Functional Interdependence

The demands of the tasks required differ from organization to organization in the degree to which they depend on each other for success. While some require interlocking teamwork, others are best performed by an assemblage of individuals working independently. Members of a football team need each other in order to reach the goal, while members of an association of lighthouse keepers can function more autonomously. It follows that when individuals are dependent on each other for accomplishment, cohesiveness will result.

When there is functional interdependence, the work of individuals is woven together through teams for comprehensive and general functions. It is, however, possible to have too much as well as too little cohesion. Groups with a high degree of peer cohesion can become ineffective because members suppress instrumental communication in order not to endanger intensive expressive bonds. Conversely, Blau has shown that employees developed limited primary relationships in order not to block their instrumental relationships (Blau, 1955, p. 143). Medium peer cohesion, limited in scope, may be the optimum level from the viewpoint of organizational needs.

Integrating Subunits

Coordinating and maintaining solidarity is a challenge for organizations with little authority, control, or capital. Because organizations are groups of groups, and because organizations in the voluntary sector hold their groups together by normative means, the encompassing organization must maintain cohesiveness among its subunits. If they are not interdependent or properly integrated, the encompassing organization may disintegrate. Nonprofits have a special problem because of their relative lack of power over such disintegration. Religious entities are an extreme example. There have been more than fifty schisms in major denominations resulting in the founding of new denominations just in this century (Wuthnow, 1991, p. 7). Churches with weak central denominational offices are notorious for subdividing like amoebas. One may look at the yellow pages for names like Historic Mt. Zion, New Mt.

Zion, Little Mt. Zion, Greater Historic Mt. Zion, and Progressive Mt. Zion, and draw a family tree of subunits whose needs were not integrated at some past time.

The more an organization is moving forward, growing, raising more money, meeting its instrumental and expressive goals, and maintaining high ethics and morale, the more integrated the subunits will be. When there is a scandal, a fight over goals, a faltering economy—that is, when an organization really needs everyone pulling together—then subunit grievances will tend to emerge. Such times call for central charismatic leaders lest peripheral charismatic leaders pluck off part of the mother hen that once nurtured the whole nest.

While administrative safeguards, like central control of buildings, bank accounts, mailing lists, technology, and other property, may hold subunits together, the best defenses are normative. Commitment, trust, loyalty, and community may take years to nurture, but they also require years to undo.

Legal and Contractual Ties

One reason the state of Oregon can not secede from the union is because South Carolina and some other southern states once tried to and failed. Seceding is now against the law. The Popeye's Fried Chicken franchise on Weber Road cannot buy its potatoes from anyone that its headquarters does not approve. It is against church law for St. Stephen's Church to begin operating independently of its bishop. Various legal and contractual constraints can be used to bind units together within an organization.

Solidary Orientation

The more that individuals are drawn together by and oriented to the larger entity, initially joining a group because of that transcending entity, the more likely it is that subgroups will align with the larger unit. Let me illustrate with a negative example from an experience I had in 1969 on Long Island. A program under my direction to integrate an industrial plant recruited a group of eighteen "hardcore unemployed" youths from the surrounding neighborhood to work in the plant. Each member of the group had a prior relationship that superseded his relation with his employer. The youths were completely unresponsive to training efforts until we identified their leaders and began to motivate the group through these leaders. Never again did we attempt to recruit individuals whose cohesiveness depended more on preexisting relations than on their relationship with the employer.

Subunit Congruency

Just as individuals tend to be more cohesive when their goals coincide with the goals of their task group, overall organizational cohesiveness is increased when individual and group goals coincide with those of the total organization. Such congruency of subunits with the larger organization cannot be taken for granted. It is interesting, for instance, that humorous television series based on life in the armed forces center on cohesive subunits that work counter to the purpose of the larger organization. For example, consider the iconoclastic tone of *M*A*S*H* and the conniving of Sergeant Bilko and the characters in *Hogan's Heroes*.

The more cohesive a group of participants, the less the variation in the direction of their involvement. If workers are highly alienated and express this alienation by restricting output, the more cohesive the group, the more likely members will be to adhere to the restricting norm (Etzioni, 1975, p. 279).

Such attitudes lead to organizational fragmentation, declines in productivity, and failure to achieve organizational goals. Group norms are powerful regulators of behavior, and the individual is closer to his or her subgroup than he or she is to the total entity. Group leaders should develop cohesiveness within their groups but also link the group to the larger organization. To facilitate these functions, many organizations establish a group leader as a linchpin between two units. He or she is the leader of one subunit while being a member of a higher unit.

Superordinate Goal

A powerful superordinate common goal has the cohesive effect and power of the external threat, without the foreboding fear caused by the latter. Cohesion increases when group members subscribe to and work toward a common overriding superordinate goal (Sherif, 1958, p. 1). Superordinate goals are such sure-fire means of tying an organization together, so positive, potent, and instrumentally effective, that leaders often virtually institutionalize the method. For example, petty infighting among church members tends to subside during a capital building campaign when all must work together.

I believe superordinate goals have a lot to do with purely expressive organizations' evolution into expressive-instrumental organizations. Purely expressive organizations are highly cohesive since cohesiveness is virtually their reason for being. In time, some member or an external event focuses the homogeneous, purely expressive group's attention on some need, and fulfilling that need becomes a superordinate goal. The power of this common goal is so exhilarating and satisfying that it can drive the evolution of a complacent expressive organization into an organization with significant instrumental outputs.

Erosion of Cohesion

Each of the positive cohesive factors defined above has a negative aspect. For example, groups can be functionally independent rather than interdependent. Organizations can lack integrity. A leader can repel members. Communication can be dull, inaccurate, and confusing. Turn the coin over, and the same factors that draw people to organizations could be listed as alienating.

In addition to the negative aspects already listed, several other factors can undermine the mortar that holds the organizational bricks together. These factors are competition for resources, evolution of diverging goals, personality conflicts, and value conflicts.

Competition for Resources

Good management often requires that the various divisions of an organization compete for resources. A deliberate evolutionary plan is at work when those that succeed receive the resources required for expansion while those that are mediocre or tending to fail receive less. However, this plan puts the elements of an organization into conflict, and in some cases, the conflict can get out of hand. While competition may increase the cohesion within each competing unit, it can erode the cohesion of the larger organization.

Resources such as money, workers, supplies, accomplishments, prestige, recognition, and ample rewards feed cohesiveness. Conversely, cohesion starves when resources dry up. Personal differences multiply. Faith in the dream wavers. The image tarnishes. Success becomes more difficult. When environmental factors limit the encompassing organization's supply of resources—which in turn constricts its constituent subgroups, which in turn negatively affects all participants—there is little the leadership can do that it is not already doing on behalf of the total effort. However, leaders can do something about a destructive disproportioning of resources among its component groups, either when some are fat in times of famine or when some are starving in the midst of plenty. The values of most non-profit organizations plus the benefits of increasing cohesion should move managers toward a beneficial distribution of resources.

Evolution of Goals and Goal Displacement

Units within an organization and individuals within those units often are interested in the organization because of their allegiance to specific goals. As activities and organizational structure evolve to adapt to changes in the environment, internal conflict may develop because of conflicting purposes.

No enterprise sets out to plan destructive competing purposes. Yet time and expansion can cause conflicting purposes to evolve. For example, a new trade association searches for worthy purposes to justify its existence, to attract support from its constituent organizations, and to give itself a sense of magnitude. Within a few years, only twelve of its original programs survive. As the organization grows and demand for various services grows, each program changes shape slightly. With the passage of time and continued demand, there is more growth and modification. It is at this point that conflicts become evident, and conflict resolution becomes more difficult.

In large complex enterprises, the conflict between purposes can move outside organizational borders. The federal government provides many examples of the demands of one agency conflicting with the demands of another. For example, a rancher in Wyoming was involved in one federal program to eradicate a certain type of plant and in another federal program that insisted he must replant the same noxious weed on that portion of his land disrupted by mining. Another example is the organization that has both a senior adult program and a youth project. The senior adult program opposes a city ordinance to open a recreation center while the youth project supports the ordinance.

Personality Conflicts

Personality conflicts occur every day. Healthy creative organizations often seek to avoid members' blind compliance in order to stimulate individuality and innovation. But when unresolved personality conflicts become serious enough to disrupt harmony and productivity, the results can be devastating. The higher up in the organizational hierarchy the actors in the conflict are, the more serious its ramifications. Followers will tend to side with their leaders in these conflicts.

Value Conflicts

A leader or an entire tier of leadership may develop values or goals that are out of harmony with those of the organization. Leaders of unions and prisoners have been known to develop ties with outsiders that led to decisions disadvantageous to the rank and file. Organizations have both formal and informal social systems, communication networks, and lines of authority. The greater the deviation of the formal system from the reality of the informal system, the greater the possibility of eroding mortar.

Rifts between major segments of an organization can occur because of the value conflicts between the leaders of each. Such rifts can lead to the splitting of the organization and the creation of new entities.

Subunits such as task groups and chapters might come into

conflict not only with each other but also with the larger organization. As Athos and Coffey state, "A group might derive its satisfaction from thwarting the objectives of the required system and yielding a minimum of productivity. Another group might continue to perform well but still look on its tasks or fellow members with distaste" (1968, pp. 132–133).

Value conflicts also develop when individual participants respond to the call of values external to the organization. Voluntary nonprofit organizations almost always play a secondary role in the lives of their constituents; their demands are seen to be less urgent than familial or vocational demands. For instance, an individual cannot be expected to have a greater allegiance to his or her trade association than to his or her employer. When the external demands on the individual do not coincide with the purposes of the organization, the organization will usually suffer.

Conclusion

Organizations need a sense of community and cohesiveness. A major motivation for expressive satisfaction is the need for affiliation. Cohesiveness encourages expressive behavior. Some of the factors that build cohesion are ceremonies and symbols, communication, a community attitude, dreams, external threats, functional interdependence, future prospects, actions to harmonize differences, homogeneity, frequent interaction, positive image, integrity, leadership, legal and contractual ties, feelings of ownership, proximity, shared experiences, small size, socializing, a solidary orientation, subunit congruency, and superordinate goals. Some of the factors that undermine cohesion are competition among groups for scarce resources, conflicts among individuals, conflicts over values, and goal evolution.

Cohesive groups increase the satisfaction of their participants and stimulate warm supportive interaction. This member satisfaction, in turn, attracts outsiders who want to participate and holds those persons already participating. Cohesion enforces organizational compliance with productivity norms as long as groups support the goals of their encompassing organization. As long as an organization does not place a suffocating insistence on norms of uniformity, cohesiveness encourages personal development in an encouraging, supportive environment. Organizational cohesiveness is such an essential ingredient of success (and even survival) that its development and maintenance should not be left to chance. Leaders need to identify their organizations' optimum cohesion resources and apply them intentionally. Leaders need to build a healthy social system that encourages cohesion if they hope to develop an effective organization. The mortar is as important as the bricks.

Needs for Further Research

Voluntary sector scholarship needs a solid theory that integrates and coordinates cohesion factors such as those listed here. We need to know more about factors that build subgroup cohesion but distance the subgroup from the enveloping organization. When opportunities or problems concerning a cohesive social system develop, does the wise leader simply apply his or her diagnostic skills and seek to deal with each matter in isolation, or are there universal principles? Empirical studies might consolidate or amplify my list of cohesion factors and determine which factors are most prevalent and/or effective in various classes of organizations. We might investigate several organizations with notable cohesiveness and determine whether it evolved naturally or was produced by a calculated technique. Researchers interested in a specific nonprofit field might study the roots of schisms in a disintegrating organization.

Actions for Practitioners

Managers should identify the factors that specifically contribute to cohesion or disintegration in their own organizations. Organizational and mid- and lower-level leaders could intentionally incorporate one or more cohesion factors into units needing more cohesiveness and/or minimize the presence of disintegrating factors. A leader might benefit by investigating a single factor in depth and incorporating his or her findings into the management of the unit.

This chapter described an array of factors that build the cohesion essential to expressive outputs and also discussed the factors that contribute to organizational disintegration and the starvation of expression. The next chapter describes a sequence of management functions and activities that can increase expressive outputs and integrate some of the cohesion factors into an organization's systems.

Chapter Seven

Enhancing Expressive Outputs Throughout the Management Sequence

When I read *Theory Z: How American Business Can Meet the Japanese Challenge* (1981), in which Ouchi commends the Japanese management model, I thought, "That is the way good nonprofit managers operate." When *In Search of Excellence* (Peters and Waterman, 1982) described exemplary corporations, I thought, "That is how we manage our better nonprofit enterprises." When J. M. Burns "discovered" transformational leadership in organizations, I thought, "Nonprofits have always been that way!" As management experts come to understand the realities of nonprofits, they are also beginning to appreciate effective nonprofit management more (Young, 1986; Drucker, 1989b; Mason 1990c; Billis, 1993; Morgan, 1994).

Management is the process of answering the questions: What do we want? What shall we do? How shall we do it? Typically, management answers are a series of steps, a process, rather than a bag of simultaneous acts. These processes apply to such functions as planning, organizing, and supervising. Some may be completed as a weekend project, some over the four years of a presidential term.

This chapter will scan the discrete functions and activities of a typical instrumental management sequence adapted to enhance an organization's expressive outputs. The sequence begins by assessing the results of previous management activity, followed by planning, organizing, and staffing for the next cycle. Managers guide all participants through the sequence, and feedback on participant progress controls the movement toward optimum expressive outputs until a new sequence starts.

Unbridled expressive behavior in an organizational context could lead to anarchy. At best, an entity would remain small and chaotic. Herding cats in a desired direction, even when the destination is a more innovative expressive environment, requires an instrumental process. The sequence of management functions that follows is typical of thousands of organizations, though some activities in the sequence are rarely acknowledged as overtly as I will describe them. I did not base this sequence on any one source or, for that matter, on any body of literature. It evolved through the fifty or sixty successful annual management cycles (some concurrent) in which I have participated. The process will work.

Management as we know it today began a century ago. Imaginative entrepreneurs created the new railroads, steel mills, and auto companies, enterprises that demanded ways to coordinate masses of employees engaged in a myriad of complex tasks. Leaders scrambled for methods that worked, and they abandoned methods that did not. Through trial and error, modern management evolved, bringing a degree of order to the tremendous new endeavors. Managers, consultants, and educators have subsequently developed and refined the processes that are the core of modern management (Kotter, 1990, pp. 3–4).

Without these processes could the United States have even dreamed of a Hubble Telescope circling the globe? Would Denver ever have broken ground on the first new massive airport to be built in two decades? Could England's venerable Baring Bank hope to span the globe and serve even the modern markets of Southeast Asia? Well, as the problems that have beset these particular enterprises demonstrate, management is not a precise science like chemistry or physics. Nevertheless, its processes are the best tools we have developed so far to engineer an idea into tangible realities in people's lives. And my personal experiences with the following processes have been overwhelmingly positive.

The steps in a typical management cycle might follow the following sequence:

Assessing
> Reviewing organizational purposes
> Evaluating present posture
> Identifying core values

Planning
> Clarifying organizational purposes
> Forecasting probable destination
> Setting organizational goals and component objectives
> Developing long-term strategies
> Detailing a program of activities
> Budgeting organizational resources
> Predicting stakeholder responses
> Setting detailed procedures
> Developing policies

Organizing
> Establishing a relationship structure
> Informing stakeholders of intentions
> Reviewing and adapting to stakeholder response
> Designing tasks
> Preparing position guides

Staffing
> Assigning staff
> Recruiting governance and advisory volunteers
> Recruiting direct service and administrative volunteers
> Orienting all personnel
> Instilling conviction
> Training participants
> Developing and upgrading

Guiding
> Prioritizing tasks
> Motivating personnel

Monitoring personnel

Increasing efficiency

Reviewing and evaluating performance

Feedback evaluation

Establishing a reporting system

Developing criteria

Measuring specific results

Reviewing overall progress

Recognizing and rewarding effort and accomplishment

While the following discussion scans all the management functions listed here, it focuses on those that leadership can adapt to increase expressive outputs and thereby benefit the organization and its participants. One could write volumes about each step, so my comments will be suggestive and provocative rather than exhaustive. The process is primarily for organizations with a paid staff, though all-volunteer groups may implement the broad brush strokes by choosing those activities appropriate for enhancing their expressive outcomes.

Assessing

An organization's leaders end one management cycle when a project is over, a major goal is reached, or new leadership takes over, or simply when year's end arrives. Next, they may immediately set goals for a subsequent round of activity. A more judicious approach, which will advance the entity more aggressively, incorporates a Janus-like pause for looking toward both the past and the future, "listening," and assessing the organization's posture. Reflection after evaluating a concluded sequence and before planning a subsequent one is especially important when leaders intend to enhance the organization's expressive aspects. I suggest the assessing function should include the following activities: reviewing organizational purposes, evaluating the organization's present posture, and identifying its core values.

Reviewing Organizational Purposes

An unambiguous, clearly understood statement of purposes is the starting point of an effective organization. If providing expressive outputs is realistically part of its reason for being, as is often the case, its purpose statement should clearly say so. I will use the terms *purposes, goals,* and *objectives* as three cascading levels of the concept of destination. Purposes are the most profound, general, and long-range destinations; goals are midrange destinations; and objectives are the most immediately attainable and specific destinations. The terms *vision* and *mission statement* form a similar hierarchy. A vision connotes a hope, and a mission statement connotes movement, the pursuit more than the end itself. The planning function in the management sequence must be based on a clear statement that defines an organization's purposes and considers cultural and emotional factors.

Once the statement becomes the officially pronounced North Star of the organization, it has rational-legal authority, like a crowned king or queen. The formal abstract conception exists and has significance apart from the interests of individuals. A purpose statement represents traditional authority, to which participants owe obedience and the allegiance attached to offices, not to the persons occupying them (Blau and Meyer, 1987, pp. 64–71). Therefore, the management sequence should begin with a review of the present statement of purposes.

Evaluating Present Posture

Malls often help bewildered customers find their way through colorful floor plans with an arrow that declares, "You are here." One's present position is the only starting point of a good plan, even though some may consider this point too self-evident to address systematically. Complacent U.S. automakers let the nation's highways clog with imports before they awoke to the smell of sushi and bratwurst and discovered they had been slow in facing reality. A preliminary evaluation of where the organization stands with its purposes audits its strengths and weaknesses. Such an evaluation reviews the interests of all stakeholders: founders, past investors, volunteers, clients, members, staff, patrons, and regulators. It establishes whether or not the organization is presently accomplishing the goals it started out to achieve. It diagnoses where the organization is and why. The evaluation should consider clients' needs and the service-providing system, contributors' and regulators' needs, the fundraising system, and the volunteers' expressive system.

A close look may show that an organization's present posture is quite different from the purpose statement. Perhaps the organization needs a radical shift back to its roots. Or perhaps it may need a more realistic version of an outdated purpose statement. While a business can maximize its profits by enlarging its product line or expanding its services, its desire to make money remains its chief purpose. Nonprofits have a more dramatic option: they can change their entire purpose. The classic example is the March of Dimes, which was originally set up to fight polio, with the strong support of Franklin Roosevelt. After Jonas Salk discovered a polio vaccine, the March of Dimes changed its purpose and focused on eradicating birth defects.

Identifying Core Values

Organizations hold values that define the organizational culture, just as values define an individual's character. Values are at a higher level of generality than goals, representing general directions rather than specific destinations. They define the ways participants deal with each other and with others outside the organization.

Parsons states that a participant must be "grounded" in three main directions: "First in his existential beliefs about the world, second in his own motivational needs as a personality and third in his relations to others in the society" (1968, p. 172). As a first step toward greater effectiveness, every few years an organization should conduct a survey, form a focus group, or hold a leadership retreat to rank its paramount values. *As an entity embarks on a sequence of activities to enhance its expressive outputs, it must make certain that the intended journey is congruent with its core values.*

Planning

If an organization does not know where it is going, any course will take it there. When we have a destination in mind and want to get there quickly, we should study a chart, plot a course, and equip the best vessel at our disposal before we pull away from the dock. An intentional reformulation of an organization to enhance its expressive outputs requires planning—something one does with a pencil. Through planning, management applies available resources to the tasks of the organization to produce optimal benefits at minimal costs.

A cognitive vision of a desired future is the first step in an iterative process for achieving organizational ends. A written plan with numbers, dates, and dollars turns wishes and dreams into a road map to a better tomorrow. A thorough process begins with the results of an assessment, then moves to clarifying purposes, forecasting the organization's future, setting its goals and objectives, developing its strategies, predicting the response of its participants, budgeting its resources, programming its activities, setting its procedures, and establishing its policies.

Managers need not slide from one week to the next, from one meeting to another, from today's shortfall to tomorrow's crisis. They need not be creatures of the winds of circumstance. Good managers are architects of circumstance. Plans build tomorrow's great organizations out of the circumstances of today. As Thomas Carlyle wrote, "From the same materials one man builds palaces, another hovels, one warehouses, another villas, bricks and mortar are mortar and bricks until the architect can make them something else" (*Correct Quotes*, 1991).

Managers who plan on building optimal expressive outputs into their organizational systems must recognize a paradox: opportunities for activities that are expressive for the individual participants should be explicit and instrumental for management. Management is a conscious, intentional instrumental function, even when building a framework for relatively spontaneous expression.

Who should start the planning process? Ordinarily the CEO takes the initiative. The top professional should be the most motivated and best-equipped person to do so. Occasionally, the board, a funding source, or a regulating body might demand a written plan. Expressive concerns tend to run informally and parallel to the instrumental system. Planners rarely include expressive outputs in formal statements, even though they are intuitively aware of expressive demands at each step. But why omit written plans for optimum expressive outputs? Why not take advantage of management processes and skills that make all organizational aspects more effective? Should the Scouts plan to meet needs of boys and girls and neglect the needs of den mothers and scoutmasters? Should a literacy council plan for the needs of its students and ignore the intrinsic needs of tutors? I think not.

Many people are short-run oriented, driven by the "crisis du jour." Effective managers know that over the long run, planning saves time. The surgeon who has three minutes to save a boy's life should not cut without a plan; nor should the helmsman of a ship watch the waves rather than his compass; nor should the carpenter cut without sharpening his saw. A good plan usually saves time because it avoids false starts, detours, dead ends, and backtracking. Interestingly, organizations that plan well tend to do well—even though they later deviate from their initial plans. Action-oriented leaders should act like thinkers if they want their thinkers to act.

I believe that a planning retreat for the board of directors is the single most effective method for initiating organizational planning and usually the most pleasant. Retreats are marvelous mechanisms for top leadership expressiveness. The retreat site should be located close enough for all members to attend but too far away for them to run back to their offices for phone calls, correspondence, and minor emergencies. Retreats are so effective in building participants into a team that those who miss a retreat may begin to think of themselves as outsiders. Of course, in addition to unifying the group, the retreat provides a large block of uninterrupted time for substantive progress.

Consider several techniques for increasing expressive outputs at the retreat. Members might break into pairs in which each partner tells the other about himself or herself and then each partner introduces the other to the group. Introductions should allow enough time to include information about hobbies, dreams, and other interesting information attesting the uniqueness of each person. Warren Avis, who founded the car rental company that advertised itself as "number two," suggests that retreat planners assign relative strangers and not friends as roommates. Encourage socializing with appropriate settings. An opening informal reception, dinner, or get-acquainted party can be an effective catalyst.

Clarifying Organizational Purposes

The first step in planning is clarifying an organization's purpose. This will be followed by delineating component goals and selecting appropriate objectives within those goals. By whatever name one calls it, a clear purpose holds two precious gifts: one is a direction to a destination, and the other is a mysterious propelling power toward that destination. Statements of purpose should be lofty without being ludicrous. They should be at the horizon, not underfoot. They should require some dreaming and a degree of stretching and should be worthy of the organization's wisest and most vigorous efforts. They must be greater than any one person and worthy of all people. Handy recommends that organizations should have "a cause, a vision or an overriding purpose, one which is long on rhetoric and short on numbers. . . . [I]ts purpose is to inspire rather than to direct activity" (Handy, 1988, p. 127).

Writing about the purpose-driven organization, Pascarella and Frohman suggest six benefits of a purpose statement: it provides direction, focus, policy, meaning, challenge, and passion (1989, pp. 33–36).

Direction establishes what the organization wants to succeed in doing, what it does, and what it does not do. It presents the parameters for resource allocation, strategic and annual planning, and acceptable opportunities for new or expanded expressive experience and instrumental service.

Focus emphasizes activities that distinguish the organization from others, specifying how and where to channel efforts to sustain the organization's strengths and competitive advantages. When participants clearly understand the breadth of the organization's focus, they know what to work at and, as pressures increase, what to work at harder or smarter.

Policy defines constraints or boundaries for participants, specifying how the organization wants to appear both internally and externally, expressively and/or instrumentally, and how it wants to attain its goals.

Meaning is the definition of something to relate to that is greater than the job itself. Meaning offers a broad expressive context into which people can fit their daily work. People want their work to enhance their self-respect and satisfy their desire to achieve.

Challenge comes from establishing goals and measures of achievement, describing what success looks like, and prescribing how to achieve or maintain success.

Passion increases participants' enthusiasm, commitment, and pride in the organization. People in organizations respond to a statement of purpose that gives them everything they need in order to play the game and keep score, stimulating their desire to win.

Any organization that does not clearly understand where it wants to go will drift with every changing fad. Nonprofits are responsive to their participants' desires and thus tend to accumulate multiple purposes. Nevertheless, management should periodically define, examine, and clarify even complex sets of purposes into coherent and integrated wholes, an enlightening and challenging exercise.

Once an organization clearly defines its purposes, the destination takes on a magnetic life of its own. It pulls, motivates, and excites participants in its direction. Perhaps its power is in the passion it elicits. Perhaps its power is in the challenge that lifts members' sights, ennobles members themselves, and lifts them to their highest selves (Covey, 1991, pp. 173–180).

Voluntary organizations also need to rank their purposes in a hierarchy. For example, an expressive-instrumental organization would list its expressive purpose before its instrumental one. Ranking purposes may present many political problems, but this prioritizing builds a framework for complex aspects of the organization and establishes a concrete way of thinking and talking about them. The exercise of ranking purposes often uncovers additional purposes and clarifies relations among objectives, postures, and directions.

Forecasting Probable Destination

After clarifying its purposes, an organization should forecast where its movement will lead if its present course continues. Forecasts provide premises for planning; they stimulate looking to the future and providing for it. The process of forecasting may disclose areas where feedback mechanisms or other functions are inadequate. When organizational members widely participate, forecasting may also help them unify and coordinate plans.

External factors to consider include the general environment; the political, economic, social, technological, and ethical climates; similar organizations; and public policy. Forecasts should look at the specific agendas of key stakeholders and the need for the organization's services. They should consider location, labor, materials, and money. Internal factors include equipment, buildings, personnel, morale, policies, and major programs. The production of resources and the provision of services are two distinct systems in a voluntary organization. Forecasts, like all other activities, must deal with each of the two systems. Forecasts should consider recent experiences in the organization's expressive status, funds growth, and services record. They should consider interest group expectations. Among the key stakeholders are the larger society, board members, founders, collaborators, contributors and prospective contributors, regulators, suppliers, paid staff, unpaid staff, clients, and volunteers.

Setting Organizational Goals and Component Objectives

Goals, the midrange destinations, should be subdivisions of organizational purposes, the long-range destinations. At a minimum, these midrange destinations should consider the organization's expressive nature and the growth in its fundraising, expenditures, and services as well as such adaptive needs as property acquisition or geographical expansion.

Even broad goals should be specific enough to help participants choose between alternative courses of action. Good goals have a built-in time dimension and are consistent with one another. Participants should be able to state goals in terms of organizationwide missions. Goals are hierarchical. Goals may represent hopes or wishes but must also be reasonably attainable and practical. Setting challenging goals in situations calling for personal responsibility for results can be especially stimulating to individuals with high achievement needs.

Planners should align objectives, short-term destinations, under each goal, getting down to the specific aims of the current management cycle. Objectives should also stretch an organization and make participants reach. Objectives should include departmental or divisional programs, be set for each level and each unit, and ultimately involve every participant. If every participant reaches every objective, goals will move closer, and the organization will move toward fulfilling its purpose. Objectives should specify who is responsible for what and, like goals, should include a time frame. They may specify where to perform the tasks, any constraints, and a budget. Objectives answer the questions of a good journalist: Who? What? When? Where? How? and sometimes, Why?

Traditional management aimed toward instrumental purposes pictures the father, king, general, or CEO on top of a pyramid—thinking. The children, subjects, soldiers, employees, and volunteers are below—doing. The person at the top gathers information, sets goals, decides what subordinates should do, and commands them to produce. This approach places an emphasis on intention and effort rather than results and is more suited for Theory X than Theory Y personality types.

Peter Drucker popularized management by objectives (MBO), a cascading systems approach in which those accountable for operating each component of an organization choose measurable objectives within the broader goals set at higher levels. I have found the MBO process an excellent vehicle for expressive involvement throughout an organizational system. Each task group undertakes to accomplish an objective at a certain cost in a specified unit of time. This approach integrates thinking with acting. It relies heavily on clearly stated discrete objectives through which the results of an organization's assessing step present givens to those responsible for planning. The objectives specify what to do, when to do it, and who does it. The schedule follows a sequence in which top leaders decide where the organization should be by a certain time. After establishing the overall broad outline, the next tiers contribute their efforts to the overall objectives. The process establishes mechanisms that monitor progress toward objectives, then it feeds back results to accountable parties.

Planners tend to ignore expressive purposes when the time comes to plan and formalize goal and objective statements. True goals almost certainly include a major hidden agenda—the satisfaction of the participants who contribute time and money. Defining only instrumental goals and objectives results in an incongruence of stated purposes and true purposes, but this is a correctable error. Management can specify, with numerical measurements if possible, the expressive goals along with the instrumental ones.

From a management perspective, inclusion of expressive goals and objectives is probably the key activity for enhancing expressive outputs. It sends concentric persistent waves throughout the system. Besides devising a lofty statement of overriding purposes, leaders must support that statement with goals for areas of specific activity and measures indicating what success in each task looks like (Handy, 1988, p. 127).

Goals and objectives should be as specific as possible. For example, "teaching people" is too vague to be an objective. It leaves many unanswered questions: Teaching what? To whom? To how many people? By what means? To what level? When objectives are specific, the manager knows the probabilities of success, the risks involved, what to do, and the resources and "stretch" required.

Quantified verifiable destinations are much easier to achieve than vague ones, so goals and objectives should quantify everything that can be quantified. Organizations with multiple goals should rank them through a bargaining process. To overcome conflict, organizations often attempt to satisfice rather than maximize their objectives. When the cost of time is considered, satisficing can be an optimum choice. Organizations also need to cope with different time frames for different objectives. For example, the end of the calendar year may be an excellent season for fundraising but poor for volunteer recruiting.

The Points of Light Foundation found that high effectiveness in utilizing volunteers included building understanding and collaboration in certain areas. Paid staff should fully participate in planning, decision making, and management related to volunteer involvement. And a conscious active effort should be made to reduce the boundaries and increase the teamwork between paid and volunteer staff.

Member participation in defining goals and objectives helps organizations in several ways. Involvement taps more and perhaps better ideas from those who deal with day-to-day operations. Broad participation in the process can lessen the potential for future conflict by developing goals that consider participants' objectives. People like to understand what they are doing and to feel they have a part in choosing their tasks. Moreover, members' understanding of goals and participation in forming them is the best assurance of member loyalty to the goals. And people who set specific goals for themselves not only are more likely to commit to their goals but also are more likely to achieve them.

People who reach their current goals set higher goals for the next cycle, while those who fail set lower subsequent goals. Success not only builds momentum, it also increases the desirability of the goal (Handy, 1988, p. 31). People's search for psychological success and self-esteem enhancement includes setting challenging goals for themselves. When organizations allow people to participate in goal setting, determine their own ways of reaching their goals, and "own" their tasks, the organizations tap this desire for success and make it more likely that people will reach their goals.

Developing Long-Term Strategies

While purposes, goals, and objectives move from the *why* through the *what*, strategies are the *how*. The most effective organizations over time will be those where why, what, and how are consistently integrated. In these organizations, the purposes reflect values, and goals and objectives conform to the purposes. There is an integrity of organizational strategy and culture.

Like values, purposes, goals, and objectives, organizational strategies should be written down and disseminated so they are as clear in the minds of their readers as they are in the minds of their authors. In values-expressive voluntary nonprofit organizations, this body of written definitions may incorporate the organization's *vision*. In spelling out *how* the organization will achieve its purposes, the strategy answers several questions. Knowing where the organization wants to go, the strategy asks: What is the best way to get there from here? How fast shall we try to go? How much are we willing to risk?

As always, the more participation in formulating the strategy, the more the expressive output. However, some people are better and more experienced in strategy than others, and unqualified individuals should not be allowed to produce a strategy that would bankrupt the organization. Often the chief leader, especially if he or she is a strong charismatic personality, will formulate a personal vision. The leader than tests this road map of how to reach the goals with an astute inner circle. The effective leader sincerely seeks assistance and modifications in crafting the strategy statement. The statement then moves to the board of directors and thence throughout the organization.

A concise statement of strategy must not only reflect organizational values and purposes and implant goals and objectives, it must shape all subsystems. It is not a ceremony or an academic exercise resulting in superficial window dressing. Strategy should modify behavior and structure. It should influence organizational design, staffing, allocation of resources, guidance of paid and unpaid personnel, and organizational feedback systems.

The Ford Motor Company's current motto, "Quality is Job One," is an ultra-simple strategy that should be easily understood by anyone wanting to know where the company wants to go and how it intends to get there. "IBM means service" is a similar basic strategy statement.

Detailing a Program of Activities

Programming orders and schedules the activities necessary to translate the strategies and details for implementing objectives into action within a time frame. It involves a complex of the policies, procedures, rules, assignments, and other elements necessary to carry out a given course of action. Programming is finite in that it deals with a specific set of objectives for a specific period of time. It should establish the priority, order, balance, and timing of steps necessary to apply plans to programmatic interactions and organizational activities. Few programs stand alone. One primary program may call for many derivative programs, and all these subordinate programs will require coordination and timing also.

Budgeting Organizational Resources

Whereas programming orders and schedules activity, budgeting apportions and schedules resources within a strategic context. This activity represents the organization's financial goals, reflects its priorities, and plays a gatekeeper role as it opens or bars the door to almost every activity. Budgeting assigns funds to plans, balances anticipated receipts and disbursements for effective use of capital, and compares actual to planned cash flow.

Usually, the process begins with lower-tier estimates and requests that move upward for incorporation into upper-tier budgets. Departments define major objectives and then analyze their financial needs and plan spending to achieve the objectives. The budgeting process is full of political considerations. Certain units may tend to receive the biggest budgets irrespective of objectives and performance. Participative budgeting, wherein the operator of a unit contributes to the budgeting process, may give individuals some control over their own turf and a feeling of ownership. Moreover, wide participation in the budgeting process, especially at the lower levels, makes more people aware of how their contributions coordinate with the total program. Increasing participation here usually increases expressive outputs.

Except in purely expressive organizations, instrumental activities require more money than expressive ones, since most expressive behaviors occur in the pursuit of activities budgeted to reach instrumental goals. Therefore, allocations that produce expressive outputs are rarely seen to be earmarked as expressive funds. This is good news and bad news. The good news is that expressive outputs may appear to cost little. The bad news is that the uninitiated may think expenditures reflect importance and thus assume that expressive outputs are unimportant.

Many organizations fail to appreciate the crucial influence of the budgeting decisions that allocate resources between providing the outputs (the services for which the organization exists) and generating further resources for continuing operations (recruiting volunteers and raising funds). As mentioned earlier, unlike businesses, which have their resources and services linked into a single system, many nonprofits have two relatively independent subsystems, in somewhat the same way as a hook-and-ladder fire truck has dual steering mechanisms, one for the front end and another for the wheels far in the back. One subsystem provides the services for which the organization exists; the other generates the resources to fuel both systems. Ideally, they work harmoniously, in tandem, but the linkage between them is not as direct as the pattern we see in business, where the sale of a product or service provides the resources for more goods or services (Mason, 1984a, pp. 63–73).

To take the analogy of the fire truck further, consider the gasoline that fuels the fire truck and the water that quenches the fire. Both the gasoline and the water are essential in fulfilling the fire-fighting mission. Both must be available in sufficient quantity. The water must be ample to put out the flames and kill any embers that might reignite. The gasoline must fuel the rush to the fire, keep the water pumps working, and return the truck to the fire station so it can respond to the next alarm. Never can the water do the gasoline's job, or the gasoline the water's. Fortunately, fires are short, and fire chiefs have solved this allocation problem. The fires that nonprofit organizations fight burn continually. Supplying an effective balance of water and gasoline demands a mix of crucial choices more serious than most managers realize. Perhaps the decision that influences the financial health of an organization most is the way the organization answers the question, How much should we spend on water, and how much on gas?

When a leader is confronted with an array of variables in budgeting, his or her best choice is an intentional process to reduce subjectivity and provide a narrow decision window in which outputs of service can be equated with potential inputs of funds. Decision makers may then examine the trade-offs between the two systems and choose an optimum balance for achieving organizational objectives in both systems during the next cycle of operations (Mason, 1990b, p. 3).

Predicting Stakeholder Responses

If leaders expect followers to follow, they should test the followers' emotional reactions to the proposed plan. As the curtain rises, people who have helped develop the plan will tend to applaud rather than jeer. It is at this point that leaders begin to recover time and effort they may have thought lost through the time-consuming involvement process. As time passes, planners may gain even more because a preview of the program will help people to correct problems while they are small enough to fix quickly.

Predicting the response of the constituency need not require a mass membership meeting or a special issue of the newsletter.

Leaders can test the plan by moving down the chain of command, offering each level an opportunity to express its reactions. Representative focus groups are another avenue.

Setting Detailed Procedures

Procedures are standardized customary methods for implementing plans. Much more specific and numerous than policies, they are very specific guides to action, especially at the direct service levels. It is procedures, bound into manuals, that are appropriate for training new or temporary personnel.

Procedures are followed throughout an organization, becoming more exacting and numerous at lower levels. They have a hierarchy of importance and often cut across departmental lines. They often sum up what organizational veterans think of as second nature. Procedures may take time to prepare, but they are long-term time-savers, answering many questions and explaining the best way of performing tasks.

Developing Policies

Policies are standing decisions on important, recurring matters, general statements that channel thinking for the decision making of subordinates. They delimit an area within which a decision is to be made and assure that the decision will be consistent with, and contribute to, organizational ethics, norms, and purposes. Policies define the character and personality of the organization and generally cascade to as many levels as there are in the organization. They set the organization's attitudes toward clients, employees, volunteers, services, property, and money, and thus, are determinants of its culture.

Organizing

Organizing arranges the relationships of an entity's elements, situating personnel and property to facilitate the accomplishment of goals through the allocation of functions and responsibilities. Organizing designates the persons to work together, the things to do, the place of work, and the work process. Organizing creates a structure of roles. It groups individuals to accomplish goals that they cannot achieve alone. In an organized system of parts, each part makes a contribution and each is dependent on the other parts of the system for its own needs.

The activities in organizing include establishing the relationship structure for both paid and unpaid participants, informing the constituency, reviewing and analyzing constituent response, defining relations in detail, and finally preparing position descriptions.

Establishing a Relationship Structure

Even our basic social unit, the family, functions with some division of labor. Similarly in every organization, everyone must know who is accountable to whom and for what. Handy suggests looking at relationship structure as a skeleton, since skeletons come alive when people and groups and tasks get the blood surging and the nerves and sinews working. The structure of voluntary organizations needs to be as informal as possible and as participative as practical (Handy, 1988, p. 103).

The structure, symbolized by the organization chart, should clearly picture the lines of authority and responsibility. Organizers should consider that voluntary organizations have a special kind of constituency, often composed of multiple stakeholders, and that the organization's chief tool may be volunteerism elicited by persuasion. Therefore, the structure must use the energy imbedded within its constituency. Organizers must shape the organization in order to achieve the various purposes established in the hierarchy of purposes during the planning phase. Three structural models that encourage expressive outputs are the flattened structure, federalism, and the *Chlorophytum comosum* model.

A *flattened* as opposed to a tall, elongated structure usually improves expressive outputs. Tall organization structures are like skyscrapers, with many levels of authority between top management and the entry-level bottom tier. Flattened structures are like malls, with few intervening levels from top to bottom. While many people associate tall structures with very large organizations, the massive Roman Catholic Church has but three tiers: the papacy, the diocese, and the parish. The fewer the intervening levels of authority, the more participatory expressive behavior. Flatter structures increase discretionary power at the middle and lower levels, encourage diversity, and disperse power and control.

Federalism is a profound adaptation of an organization's distribution of power, a balance of centralization and decentralization. A strong centralized base provides a high level of knowledge and technological expertise for an organization. Centralized power can promote a unity of outlook and purpose across the organization, stimulate growth in areas remote from established units, speak loudly on national issues, and do so with a firm, positive grip on the controls. As the role of government relentlessly encroaches on every crevice of our society, and the massive centralized communications media expands to Orwellian proportions, national organizations require strong centralized voices in dealing with big government and influential communications media.

However, decentralization characterizes the U.S. nonprofit sector. Local autonomy frees units effectively to match local preferences for services, providing revenues for their provision and autonomy in allocation decisions. Typically, decentralized organizations give highest priority to local preferences. From 85 to 90 percent of nonprofit revenues are raised and spent in the local community. Decentralized nonprofits typically satisfy their local donor bases and rarely transfer resources between communities. Greater centralization would reduce such support and reduce expressive motivation. Donors would realize fewer direct benefits from their contributions and would subsequently reduce their giving (Wolpert, 1993).

Federalism means holding onto the expressive benefits of decentralization while retaining some of the advantages of a potent center. It is a means for two or more autonomous entities to share power over the same constituency. It divides the powers and functions between central and regional powers, giving each its own rights and responsibilities regarding the composite whole, and it takes advantage of the economics of coordination.

Morton Grodzins suggests the vivid metaphor that compares federalism to a marble cake, in contrast to a hierarchical layer cake: "Wherever you slice through it you reveal an inseparable mixture of differently colored ingredients. There is no neat horizontal stratification like a layer cake. Vertical and diagonal lines almost obliterate the horizontal ones, and in some places there are unexpected whirls and an imperceptible merging of colors, so that it is difficult to tell where one ends and the other begins" (1966, pp. 3–4). In the marble cake model, initiatives come from the disbursed components that generate the energy. Ideally, the central power does only what the parts cannot or will not do—facilitating, enabling, coordinating, and maintaining unity. "The parts delegate authority and responsibility to the center, not the other way around" (Handy, 1988, p. 115). Federalism views diversity as strength and builds on diverse means to common ends. "It operates on the theory that vision and not rules bind people together" (Handy, 1988, p. 18).

The federal shared-powers model can be applied not only to large national organizations with local geographical components but also to multicomponent organizations in a single location. In a local entity, the center may be the executive offices, and the dispersed entities may be the various departments with discrete functions. For example, the central power of a church may reside in its pastor, board, and business manager, while the dispersed components may be its church school, youth department, senior adult department, nursery school, community outreach program, and evangelical visitation ministry. Everything I cite concerning shared power and responsibility may also be applied to the center and components of a single site.

In citing *Chlorophytum comosum,* or the spider plant, as a metaphor for an organizational structure, Morgan visualized a commonly used structure with highly desirable aspects that maximizes expressive opportunity. A single spider plant will generate numerous small new plants on long stems. Morgan suggests that this is a model for growing large while staying small, for re-creating an organization through decentralized replication. He stresses the importance of the stems, or umbilical cords, that connect the plant and its offspring. In the organization, these may be information systems or means of transferring resources, accountabilities, vision, values, and rewards (1993, pp. 63–89).

The *Chlorophytum comosum* model suggests not only national nonprofits with their geographical chapters but also the cell growth method detailed in Chapter Ten. It is an ideal model for an organization that uses expressive motivation for starting new programs or iterative geographical units.

Informing Stakeholders of Intentions

Organizations that elicit energy from participants must inform and educate those participants regarding any structural changes that affect them as a constituency. Besides rational explanations of the changes and their anticipated benefits, leadership should also include cultural and emotional appeals in the presentation. Again, people who participated in the process that produced the changes are those most likely to welcome them. Those who did not participate are most likely to object. Changes in any social structure will surely change social relationships, and not everyone will have reason to rejoice. It is better to give everyone (or at least those directly affected) an opportunity to preview the changes than to give them news of an fait accompli. The leadership should throw the organizational changes in front of the lion and see if it purrs.

This preliminary field test should dispel the inevitable rumors and provide leadership with a sample of the degree to which they may be able to tap organizational energy. The message about the change should communicate the form of the new structure, whom it will effect, and why the organization will benefit from it.

Reviewing and Adapting to Stakeholder Response

After constituency members learn how structural changes will affect their lives and have a chance to react to those changes, leaders must determine whether modifications are required in response to the reaction. Putting pride of authorship aside, the decision makers should consider what the reaction suggests about the future availability of key individuals. Will anyone stop participating? They must integrate the resources of their constituency with the goals and programs of the organization. They must ask, Who purred? Who stood on his or her hind legs and roared? How might the reaction affect the implementation of the new structure of relationships? Are modifications of the structure necessary? At this point, the leadership may also undertake modifications.

Designing Tasks

There is a lot of difference between sanding the arms of one hundred rocking chairs and building one whole rocking chair. While in the short run specialization may put out more chairs, a design to enlarge and enrich builders' tasks may produce better chairs and more expressive outputs. If one expects the builders to work for free, a more satisfying task design may make the difference in whether or not there are any builders at all. An organization working toward optimizing expressive outputs must consider redesigning some of its tasks to enlarge and/or enrich them and assigning some of them to autonomous task groups.

Most volunteers have the capacity for more responsibility than they currently carry. Expanding their assignments may benefit them and produce more for the organization. Horizontal task *enlargement* gives a task more variety, challenge, interest, and responsibility by incorporating more tasks requiring the same general abilities. Vertical task *enrichment* increases expressive outputs by giving the worker a complete module of work and increasing his or her responsibility to include planning the task, doing it, and then evaluating it and feeding back progress.

Leaders may also assign clusters of tasks to autonomous task groups. Many nonprofits are constantly undertaking projects that lend themselves easily to this work design. Autonomous groups are highly motivating and require little supervision time (Handy, 1988, pp. 110, 112). Members of each independent group (see Chapter Six) participate in specifying its objectives and deciding who will do what and when, spinning off expressive outputs galore.

Preparing Position Guides

After top leadership outlines the organizational structure with broad brush strokes, subsequent echelons must put flesh, nerves, and sinew on the skeleton by filling in the blanks down to the lowest level. Position or job descriptions are work assignments or position guides, concisely written statements delineating the objectives, contents, and essential requirements for each job. The considerations and processes are much the same as for determining the structure of the entire organization. Management arranges relations to facilitate sharing, cooperation, and goal achievement.

As was just discussed, to increase expressive outputs and improve concrete results, managers must redesign jobs to be more challenging, to require greater resourcefulness and creativity. Managers should design every job so that each worker can do enough components of a task to produce and see some end product. The resulting position description is the step that finally applies all the planning and organizing to the individual worker, describing the scope, relationships, responsibilities, and authority of a specific position.

Implementing the Process

In the late 1980s, a retired airline pilot and his wife bought a deluxe Winnebago motor home and set out to explore the American West. Just three miles past the city limits, a state trooper found the Winnebago smashed into an oak tree, steam hissing from the radiator. Extracting the dazed, lacerated, and bruised couple from the cab, the trooper overheard the wife berating her husband: "I don't want to catch you ever again putting it on 'cruise control' and going back to the kitchen for coffee!"

There is much more to reaching one's destination than merely plotting the course, stocking and servicing the vehicle, and setting the cruise control. An organization's leaders must select appropriate personnel, direct and guide both employees and volunteers, and continue to control the direction by giving accurate feedback on the progress of its many components.

Staffing

Individual hard yellow kernels of popcorn do not pop simultaneously into their full fluffy white glory. That is because each kernel is different from the others. Each pops in its own time and its own way. So it is with people. People are the most important things about organizations. Organizations are different or similar, strong or weak, positive or negative, attractive or repulsive to a large degree because of their people. Drucker asserted that the function of managing an organization is to "make the strengths of people productive and their weaknesses irrelevant" (1974, p. 307). Staffing is the process of recruiting, selecting, and matching the right people to the right jobs.

The ease and success with which an organization shifts into a more expressive mode depends more on the CEO than any other individual. The CEO can either accelerate the process or block, sabotage, or discredit it. The board usually selects this person and must be certain that she or he commits to the expressive concept and is competent to implement any shift toward it.

The CEO usually plays a major role in filling senior management positions and must be equally firm in ensuring that persons in these key slots commit to facilitating the process. Essential people who are unlikely to acquire the skills for adapting to more involvement may need to shift from line to staff positions or to line positions requiring less skill in working through others. An outside consultant can help orient managers to the new mode of doing less and facilitating and empowering others to do more.

The hiring process must include the development of an initial psychological contract. Handy describes this unstated contract as a set of expectations between an organization and its participants. The individual assumes that the organization will satisfy his or her needs in exchange for the individual's work to satisfy the organization's needs and vice versa. Most people participate in several organizations and have several such psychological contracts; therefore, no one contract has to satisfy all of a participant's or organization's needs. This psychological contract comes into being when the participant accepts and identifies with the organization's purposes and goals and commits to work with a group in the pursuit of those goals. In return, the group gives the participant a voice in the selection of the goals and discretion in the choice of means to achieve them. "The management relinquishes a large amount of day-to-day control but retains ultimate control partly through the right of selection of people, partly through the allocation of financial resources that gives it a power of veto on certain of the goals" (Handy, 1985, p. 44).

Staffing continues beyond the beginning of a new cycle. It

reoccurs as new employees replace those who leave, as people change jobs, or as expansion opens new positions. In addition to selecting staff and recruiting volunteers, activities in the staffing function include orienting, instilling conviction, training, and developing and upgrading.

Assigning Staff

The CEO or another manager often reassigns staff members at the beginning of a new cycle. When the assignment deals with expressive outputs, management should consider the staff members' interests, aptitudes, skills, and commitment to involving volunteers. Many professional specialists are so intrinsically motivated that they may not want to work through others, preferring the direct contact with clients themselves.

Recruiting Governance and Advisory Volunteers

Management or a nominating committee must recruit qualified and available unpaid personnel for appropriate positions. The beautiful thing about recruiting high-level volunteer personnel is their quality. The organization can recruit a volunteer with experience and qualifications it could not afford to employ.

Recruiting key people at this level requires more than a routine letter or telephone call. Instead, the process may be ceremonial. An appropriate high-level manager and/or board member might make an appointment for lunch with the prospect. Several people will then attend this recruiting meeting, at least one of whom will probably be a close friend of the prospect. One of the group describes the opportunity (need). Another appeals to the prospect to serve the cause in a certain position for the ensuing year. (The committee may want to have a less time consuming backup job ready to offer, in case the prospect turns down the first request.) My personal experience in hundreds of such meetings has taught me never to oversell a position nor to minimize its liabilities. Better to have to repeat the appeal to another candidate than to have the first choice begin and then quit at the shock of negative surprises.

Recruiting Direct Service and Administrative Volunteers

People work best and accomplish most when they accept a definite job for which they are mentally, emotionally, socially, and physically suited. Written position descriptions are being used more and more as a recruiting tool precisely because they let the prospect know that the organization knows where it is going and what it expects. When coupled with an explanation of how the task fits into an overall plan and where it is on an organization chart, the written description gives the prospect a clear picture of what is being offered.

Selecting volunteers requires the participation of the person who will be the volunteers' supervisor. The supervisor generally has full veto power. Management should consider the composition of the constituency so that what it considers progressive elements are in appropriate positions. Expressive organizations sometimes have the opportunity and duty to create a job for a person. One of their purposes, after all, is to serve as a means through which people attain their own ends.

In addition, effective organizations recognize the value of involving people as volunteers from all segments of the community, including those segments the organization seeks to serve.

Orienting All Personnel

A good orientation not only familiarizes new personnel with their role in the total program but also enhances morale, increases cohesion, reduces turnover, and begins the process of socializing people into the organization's culture. Even a brief orientation is important because a new work situation is intimidating for most people. Since many people view any change as negative, existing personnel may greet newcomers with hostility, thinking they represent the forces of unpleasant change.

Because the organization must begin integrating the new person into its culture and social matrix, the orientation might begin by showing how the organization fits into the society. It might tell when, where, why, and how the organization started, what it has accomplished, and what its dreams are. The orientation might describe organizational structure, introduce key people, and take the newcomer on a tour of the facilities. It should introduce new people to their job site and their co-workers and show them how their tasks fit into the tasks of others. It should tell them how they can get answers to the questions they will have in the future.

Instilling Conviction

During the orientation period and the first few weeks newcomers are on the job, supervisors and co-workers should intentionally begin to transfer to those newcomers their own enthusiasm for their cause, their organization, and their task group. Instilling conviction should be an iterative function going on in every unit in every division. Its purpose is to convince all the personnel of the high purpose and worthiness of their efforts.

This should not be too difficult a task if properly developed goals and objectives are clear. A widely accepted definition of organizational commitment sees commitment as the strength of an individual's identification with and involvement in a particular organization. Conviction has three characteristics: a desire to remain in the organization, a willingness to exert considerable effort, and a belief in and acceptance of organizational goals and values (Porter, Steers, Mowday, and Boulian, 1974, p. 607).

Training Participants

Training makes people proficient when it is a combination of instruction and practice. It can take several forms or mix these forms. *Vestibule training* duplicates working conditions in a simulated work environment. *On-the-job training* is work performed under the supervision of an instructor. An *apprenticeship* puts trainees under the long-term guidance of an experienced supervisor. An *internship* is an apprenticeship for professional and managerial personnel. *Job rotation* familiarizes members of a group with a variety of skills. *Temporary promotions* while supervisors are otherwise occupied familiarize workers with the requirements of a higher position. *Off-the-job training* can include lectures, group discussions, seminars and university programs, computer programs, and tapes.

Nancy MacDuff points out that training performs two functions in nonprofit organizations: it establishes a minimum level of competency and it is a benefit of belonging. She cited a survey showing that 87 percent of board members listed learning as a membership benefit and suggested that "nonprofit organizations should publicize how their training can help people on the job or in their personal relationships" (1994, pp. 591–592).

Developing and Upgrading

Management is responsible for establishing a climate for personnel development. If development is unorganized, the results could be negative for the organization. Thus, the organization should try to increase individual effectiveness through programs of education and training that develop people's inherent capabilities. Management should give attention to the motivators that attract volunteers initially and cause them to try to excel, and carefully consider the status of volunteers who need upgrading within the structure.

Organizations concerned about their human as well as their instrumental aspects view the development of people's understanding and skills as a significant output, and it stands to reason that an organization should upgrade its competency to enhance expressive outputs. The Points of Light Foundation found that high effectiveness in utilizing volunteers included helping them learn, grow, and change; being open to the possibility for change; being eager to improve performance; and consciously organizing efforts to learn from and about volunteers' experience in the organization.

Guiding

Guiding includes all activities and functions designed to help subordinates work effectively and efficiently. Guiding involves motivating and activating the efforts of all workers to accomplish organizational goals. Supervisory styles used in guiding can range from autocratic to laissez-faire, with the democratic style falling in between these two extremes. Each style has its appropriate time and place. The autocratic style works in times of crisis, when there is no time for discussion or debate, as in war or an America's Cup race. The laissez-faire style may be appropriate for Miles Silverberg in the *Murphy Brown* television series, who supervises famous journalists who make higher salaries than he does. The democratic, participative style is usually the most effective one for most organizations made up of volunteers and professionals. This team and coach approach allows workers to contribute to decision making. Supervisors think of employees as whole persons and collaborators, not simply as means of getting the work done. Consistently, the data show that this approach relates highly to positive attitudes, strong motivation, and subordinate success. Studies by White and Lippitt (1960), for example, reported that participants in experimental task groups performed more effectively under democratic than either laissez-faire or authoritarian leaders.

Prioritizing Tasks

Nonprofit organizations usually have more work to do than they have resources with which to do it. Since it is not likely the organization will ever catch up with society's demands, it must not waste time on the least important jobs. This reality requires everyone be involved in constant selection of the most effective tasks and in discarding or delaying the less important ones.

Motivating Personnel

Motivation is very complex; its character depends on the nature of the tasks, the organization, the management, and on the types and needs of workers. Motivation concerns the *why* rather than the *how* of behavior. Usually, multiple factors motivate or demotivate behavior, and everyone in the organization will react to at least some motivational factors. Good supervisors learn the art of selecting the best motivators for certain persons at particular times.

If an organization is to optimize its expressive outputs, it must structure tasks and the work environment to motivate workers by means of the work itself, thus providing intrinsic or task-mediated outcomes. While good hygiene factors (see Chapter Four) can reward volunteers with job satisfaction, discipline is not an option as a motivator except in the most rigid cultures. Cordial interpersonal relationships between workers and their supervisors and the provision of appreciation, recognition, and contribution toward goal attainment can motivate. Co-workers are typically a source of socially oriented motivation.

Monitoring Personnel

Monitoring includes observation of personnel to see that duties are being performed, that incomplete work is reassigned, and that everyone gets essential resources or support. Regular contact with workers demonstrates a supervisor's interest and can ensure that workers understand their objectives as well as the supervisor does. What is clear in the mind of one must be clear in the mind of the other. Training or replacement may be required if monitoring reveals serious problems. Monitoring can help upgrade individuals and results or identify superior work methods to share throughout the organization. Since values and high ethical standards are especially important in the culture of most nonprofits, they too must be monitored.

However, leaders must recognize that the internal politics of most voluntary organizations affect the ability of paid personnel to supervise volunteers. People may hold voluntary positions because they represent a politically potent force, such as a major source of resources.

Increasing Efficiency

Increasing efficiency has to do with improving productivity per unit of time and resources expended. Efficiency is essential in the machine model of organizations, especially in manufacturing. In voluntary and nonprofit organizations, efficiency is a matter of good stewardship, especially when it comes to the productivity of salaried employees. Responsible managers are agents of the contributors, who give money they could spend otherwise. As the agents of donors, managers should work smart and fast to get the most out of each dollar toward producing the optimum instrumental outputs.

Expressive outputs may present an efficiency paradox. The more expressive the outcome sought, the more concern exists in regard to effectiveness versus efficiency. Managers tend to concern themselves more with employee efficiency than with volunteer effectiveness. For instance, contrast a proprietary nursing home and a nonprofit nursing home introducing a new safety program. The business can require all employees to attend a training seminar and will want to spend as little as possible to produce a given level of competency. Since most of the training cost is employees' wages while in training, management wants the session to be as short as possible. The nonprofit can also require all employees to attend and also wants to spend as little as possible to produce the same level of competency; however, the nonprofit realizes the seminar will also be a benefit for volunteers and might be a catalyst for recruiting persons considering a volunteer job. The nonprofit might benefit, then, by transforming the seminar into an attractive social occasion, utilizing volunteers to arrange refreshments and attractive decorations and to recruit potential attendees. Board members and patients' families might join the group for lunch to hear about the institution's concern for safety. When one considers the benefits of this approach, efficiency might give way to effectiveness.

Reviewing and Evaluating Performance

The business sector has benefited by the introduction of periodic reviews of employee performance. Workers want to know where they stand with work and their boss. Bosses find it easier on their own emotions and more productive to their work if they update subordinates' understanding of their personal status quarterly rather than waiting for a crisis to precipitate an evaluation of performance. We can assume the workers are likely to stay on their toes with an upcoming review on the horizon and likely to sleep better if they are not apprehensive about their superior's views of their effectiveness.

Though periodic reviews of unpaid workers might take time to implement, I see no reason why a review policy cannot become part of any organization's norms. Informal or team reviews are more acceptable than a formal approach. If an organization has an MBO process, reviews of progress toward objectives will provide an automatic review of instrumental progress. If a unit has defined its expressive goals as part of its system, then members can discuss interpersonal relations and other touchy matters objectively.

Feedback Evaluation

Feedback of results is a means of controlling work. "Control consists in verifying whether everything occurs in conformity with the plan adopted, the instructions issued and principles established," wrote Fayol (1949, p. 57). This pioneering manager argued that control points out weaknesses and errors "in order to rectify them and prevent recurrence. It operates on everything, things, people, actions" (p. 59). The whole concept of control has been losing favor in our society. However, control in management refers to control of work outcomes rather than control of people, and it remains important.

Feedback about, or evaluation or control of, organizational outputs is the final function of any given management cycle and a database for the next cycle. Feedback completes the circuit between goals and results. It enhances the accuracy and predictability of an organization's systems, increasing the confidence of all participants in what they have accomplished and the prospect for future accomplishment. Feedback costs time, but the investment pays dividends in future effectiveness and satisfaction.

Feedback requires an evaluation of the reasons operating results are different from those planned. The process I have described here reduces aspirations to written goals, objectives, and specific procedures. Participants should know their group's intended destination. Periodically, then, they should check to see if they have arrived. If they have fallen short, what should they do to get to the goal? If they exceeded their goal, how did they do it, and how can others learn to do the same? If they are not where they had planned to be, is it a better or worse place, and what can their journey teach others? Feedback should report any deviations, and leaders must initiate action when operations deviate too much from previously established objectives. The more one keeps a record of progress toward achieving the goals to which he or she committed, the more the new commitment is likely to influence his or her future thoughts and actions.

Organizations in the voluntary sector tend to neglect or even ignore the feedback function. If things seem to be going well, if goals are being met or exceeded, leaders hate to hesitate in order to take stock of themselves. Momentum may stall. If the organization is failing or fumbling, who wants to rub his or her own nose in it? Yet leaders need to analyze the cause of success so there will be more successes. How can one avoid another failure if the cause of a past failure remains a mystery? Intrinsic expressive motivation may actually get in the way here. If the gratification is in the work itself, then the result of the work may not appear as important as the impatience to get on with more work. Perhaps there is little overt gratification in the often numerical activity related to evaluation, review, and feedback.

When supplying feedback, managers must decide which is more important: the value of a particular mechanism or the morale and esteem of a volunteer (or the good will of the group that volunteer represents)? Management should exercise diplomacy in enforcing controls or establishing some predetermined and generally acceptable agreement as to authority in enforcing controls. Positive feedback, of course, can enhance intrinsic motivation and expressive outputs (Yoon, 1991, p. 191).

Koontz and O'Donnell (1961) suggest ten specific requirements for those who wish to produce effective feedback, some of which I have already described: reflect the nature and needs of the activity, report deviations promptly, be forward looking, point up exceptions at critical points, be objective, be flexible, reflect the typical organizational pattern of doing things, be economical, be understandable, and indicate corrective action (p. 35). In addition to these requirements, I suggest there are five specific steps in the feedback process. Feedback begins with establishing a reporting system. Then the process develops performance standards, reviews progress toward objectives, takes corrective action, and finally, recognizes and rewards.

Establishing a Reporting System

To establish a good information system, managers must consider the information needed, the types of reports that will provide this information, who will write or compile the reports, and when the reports will be completed.

Developing Criteria

The most important aspect of the whole feedback function is determining how to measure progress toward objectives. Ideally, this activity will have taken place as the final step in the goal-setting part of the planning function. If the nature of the measurements is decided too late in the process, the results of a program may influence the selection of criteria, in a subconscious duplication of the little boy who shoots an arrow into a wall and then draws a bull's-eye around the spot where the arrow hits.

The performance standards should say what conditions will exist when people have completed the key duties well. The standards should describe the destination so that the organization will recognize the appropriate goalposts. At this point, I am tempted to describe Roy Reigel's spectacular Rose Bowl run in 1928, which brought him to within one foot of the goal line—his own goal line—but I will resist the temptation.

The interests of various participants will affect an organization's definitions of effectiveness, and the variety of stakeholders and points of view in a typical nonprofit is another argument for written goals and objectives. Each organizational subsystem and each task group should have its own objectives and its own criteria. It is unlikely that a single indicator will suffice. The criteria should reflect not only whether the objectives were reached but also to what degree of quality and quantity and at what costs. Some examples of performance measures are physical criteria, such as the materials consumed, labor employed, and services rendered; monetary criteria, such as costs; capital criteria, such as financial worth, level of investment, and returns on investment; fundraising criteria, such as amounts and methods; program criteria, such as performance, timing, quality, and quantity; and personnel criteria.

Measuring Specific Results

With results and criteria in hand, the next step is to ascertain the extent of deviation of actual results from quantitative objectives and qualitative standards. As much as possible, measurement should be projected into the future, to detect the potential for deviations before their actual occurrence. If one develops appropriate standards, both measurement and appraisal of results are fairly easy. Overall organizational objectives should be the major consideration when comparing results to standards. Measurements are often stated in terms of ratios because the process of calculating ratios is fairly straightforward, and both managers and potential founders find them useful (Fisher and Cole, 1993, pp. 154–156).

Businesses that manufacture or sell products enjoy precise output measures. They can use profit-and-loss measures to evaluate the contribution made by virtually every unit in the company. Their organizational purpose is clear and unambiguous as compared to nonprofits' purposes. However, nonprofit managers may move their organizations toward precise, measurable objectives and, thus, reduce uncertainty. As people identify and utilize valid and meaningful units of service, the fog will dissipate. The quantifiable unit of service integrated into objectives and purpose is often an adequate stand-in for the profit measure of business. Managers should develop quantifiable units and objectives that are truly congruent with expressive purposes. However, if purposes defy measurement, managers should not abandon purposes for the lack of a tool. The best things are, indeed, often unmeasurable.

Reviewing Overall Progress

Nonprofit enterprises drift off course easily. An organization needs to evaluate its posture against its purpose intentionally and systematically. Often, the officially stated purpose of the organization is not the true ad hoc purpose. Often, its valid expressive purposes are unwritten and even unspoken. This allows for much hypocrisy and game-playing in which the organization's pronouncements and practices do not mesh. Written statements should be tools; like a ship's compass, they should be watched by the helmsman and periodically checked by the captain. If the owners, passengers, captain, and crew want to change course, they may do so. Until they do, they must periodically measure their direction against their destination.

Of course, it is all right for a ship to have more than one destination and for voluntary enterprises to have more than one purpose. One passenger may undertake a voyage to go to Rio *and* to get a suntan by the ship's pool. Another may wish to go to Rio *and* read *War and Peace* on the way. Another may want to get off at Trinidad.

Recognizing and Rewarding Effort and Accomplishment

The threshold of planning another tier of goals is an appropriate time to recognize and reward the success and effort that brought the organization to its goals thus far. However, there is never a bad time to recognize and reward, and the nearer the recognition is to the action that earned it, the more positive reinforcement the reward bestows. B. F. Skinner's carrot hypothesis is that good results come more from rewarding good acts than from punishing bad acts.

Pet owners recognize and praise the successes of their dogs and discipline their failures. To a degree, the same pattern holds all the way up to, say, the relationship of a U.S. president to his secretary of state. Good reward systems should acknowledge growth in recognition, responsibility, and stature; they should encourage creativity and initiative.

Leaders must take care that recipients will positively value rewards. If a person receives something that she or he does not want, it is not a reward. Rewards can be either intrinsic to the person's own behavior, such as a feeling of accomplishment, or extrinsic, provided by others. For predicting future performance, the most important thing to remember about rewards is "their perceived size and their perceived degree of connection to past performance" (Porter and Lawler, 1968, p. 29).

Nonprofit organizations enjoy a range of reward possibilities. Purely expressive orders and lodges establish complex hierarchies of positions with grandiose titles, honors, and privileges. To a lesser degree, such hierarchies are ubiquitous in all but the most informal organizations. They provide a latticework of nonmaterial incentives for advancement. Prospects of climbing this latticework may induce even the most sophisticated and able individuals to serve or to serve harder and better. Such hierarchies also facilitate pride of accomplishment and other important general incentives. Of course, when work is expressive, then it may be a reward in itself. Jonas Salk once said, "I feel that the greatest reward for doing is the opportunity to do more."

Conclusion

Organizations can drift into serious trouble if they simply extend one year's activities into the next without intentionally directing their efforts toward where they should be going. Planning and organizing include various activities that affect an organization's effectiveness and the number and degree of its expressive outputs. Expressive outputs will increase if more individuals participate in setting an organization's direction and in selecting its strategy for reaching its goals. Organizations should acknowledge and include expressive as well as instrumental objectives in the management process. Certain arrangements of relationships within the organization, such as flatter rather than taller structures, enhance expressive opportunities.

An old adage teaches us, "You can't plow a field by turning it over in your mind." One must keep one's eye on the goal—but to actually reach the goal, the plow must move forward, dealing with every inch of the surface along its route. Implementing an organization's strategy through staffing, guiding, and feedback functions ultimately affects everyone. The enthusiastic participation of everyone will achieve more objectives in more units. Progress need not be left to chance. Leaders at all levels can benefit by understanding and applying the various goal-achieving activities discussed in this chapter. Uncertainty and lack of predictability in the environment make such calculative management more, not less, important.

Nonprofits must have priorities. An organization should order and rank its priorities into a hierarchy of purposes. The two systems of every nonprofit, one for developing resources and the other for providing services, profoundly affect management. Neither can be neglected. An organization should coordinate them; they may require two organizations and two marketing plans. For true progress, an organization should not depend on the incidental interest generated by the service-providing system to limit the development of resources. It should set coordinated goals for each system and intentionally allocate appropriate amounts of seed money so that each may reach its objectives.

The needs and demands of constituencies give nonprofit organizations their politically charged character. This distinctive character is the nature of the nonprofit creature. It is in the genes. Selection of staff, design of the organization chart, method of decision making, guidance of workers, and control of the work must be appropriate for the kind of organization. Management should monitor the relationships between paid staff and volunteers at all levels, include volunteers and members of the constituency in the communication system and in the management sequence, and recognize that implementation of tasks may take more time than in a utilitarian or coercive organization. Because of their constituencies, their legal status, and the general position of regard voluntary enterprises enjoy in our society, vast resources exist for them to do their job. Organizations should not rely on chance to tap resources but develop a system for identifying need and potential sources of gratification.

Needs for Further Research

What are the best ways for organizations to measure expressive outputs? Of value would be an extensive study that compared organizations with clear written statements of purpose and regular intentional planning to organizations that segue from one year to the next with no such process.

Are expressive outputs simply parallel to the pursuit of instrumental outputs, or do good expressive outputs actually improve the instrumental ones? There are needs for additional study of each of the management functions discussed here. Researchers working with a specific organization or in a discrete field might investigate the degree to which an organization has identified its typical management sequence. What are the weakest functions in the sequence? Is the stated sequence actually for management's use rather than merely ceremonial widow dressing or a document to include in funding proposals?

Actions for Practitioners

The entire chapter consists of recommendations to practitioners. If they have not already done so, leaders should look into the congruency of their purposes, values, goals, objectives, and expressive outputs and also examine their feedback process for assessing this congruency. However, if an all-volunteer group or an organization with a small staff were to undertake only one step, I would recommend that they begin to include expressive goals and objectives statements in their plans.

This chapter scanned the discrete functions and activities of a typical management sequence adapted to enhance an organization's expressive outputs. The sequence begins with an assessment of the results of previous management activity, then progresses to the planning, organizing, and staffing for the next cycle. Managers will guide all participants through the sequence, and feedback on people's progress will control the work until a new sequence starts. Some management sequences are brief; others are long. A mother might go through many of the same steps outlined here in getting her children off to school; a nation might reiterate the sequence as it engages in a four-year war. And there are more management process functions, which we will examine in the next chapter.

Chapter Eight

The Expressive Dimension of Concurrent Managerial Functions

Sir Ranulph Fiennes planned an expedition to circumnavigate the earth vertically along the prime meridian (Fiennes, 1983). His team spent seven years conceiving this first-time adventure, shaping the vision and strategy. Team members charted their course; organized a board; and recruited, trained, and tested personnel. They secured contributions, including a ship, a plane, and a million dollars worth of fuel. They spent three more years on the journey itself. Hundreds of volunteers assisted, including sailors, pilots, camera crews, and radio operators. Yet the record-breaking adventure's success ultimately depended on Fiennes and the one or two others who actually trudged, one foot in front of the other, across the Antarctic and Arctic ice.

In addition to carrying out the sequential functions described in the previous chapter, all the members of the Transglobal team communicated with each other, made decisions, secured emergency funds, and boosted morale. The men solved routine daily problems while chopping a trail through ice across the Arctic Ocean, floating for three months on an ice floe, and moving through torturous winds across Antarctica. They had to interpret weather and terrain conditions, deal with interpersonal conflict, avoid marauding polar bears, and perform other day-to-day functions. These concurrent functions and activities were as essential to their success as the sequential functions.

Besides implementing the activities that are steps in a management sequence, all managers also function in a process to enhance both the expressive and instrumental aspects of their organizations all day, every day. Some of the concurrent functions in this process are universal, common to all organizations. Others are characteristic of the voluntary sector. Yet others are especially important in managing volunteers. In this chapter, we will examine some of the concurrent functions that contribute to the process of producing expressive outputs.

Adapting or Expanding Universal Functions

All managers perform concurrent functions like *communicating, decision making, delegating, innovating,* and *politicking.* Nonprofit managers who want to increase expressive outputs may need to adapt or expand on their application of these functions.

Communicating

Communicating with others is one of the expressive opportunities an organization offers to its participants. *Inclusive* communications enhance expressive involvement vertically and horizontally, formally and informally. Communications networks share and shape values, establish norms, influence priorities, reduce the need for formal decision making, and substitute interactive influence for the exercise of raw power.

The *vertical* flow consists of communications going from the top down and coming from the bottom up. Typically, 40 to 60 percent of all work involves communication. Leadership is exercised through *top-down* communication. Top leadership devotes 75 to 95 percent of its time to communicating. Participants in expressive organizations all appreciate being "in" on what goes on. They want access to their leaders. The more leaders project their personalities through communication, the more energy they elicit from rank-and-file participants. Leaders can encourage expressive outputs with an intensive flow of downward expressive communication (Etzioni, 1975, p. 244).

Organizational levels affect vertical communication. Taller organizations with their longer communication chains tend to distort the objective aspects of messages and dilute the subjective aspects. Generally a flatter organization structure facilitates effective communication. The nonprofit organization should possess an ample number of liaison individuals, participants infused with the organization's values, committed to its purposes, and enthusiastic about its progress, to inform both individuals and component groups.

Major free-flowing *bottom-up* communication channels are vital for expressive organizations. These channels include progress reports, counseling, grievance and suggestion systems, opinion surveys, and emotional and social intercourse. Upward communications should include any information for which superior tiers may be ultimately accountable, such as potentially controversial matters, factors influencing morale, ethical concerns, deviations from normal procedures, and ideas that might improve performance. Being able to contribute to the upward flow also satisfies lower participants' needs for influence and recognition.

Effective expressive organizations need ample *horizontal* communications for camaraderie, bonding, cohesiveness, the imbedding of organizational values, cultural enrichment, and cross-communication between different departments. Part of the function of such lateral exchanges is nonfunctional (not directly concerned with instrumental outputs). The exchanges are ends in themselves, serving social and emotional purposes, and are legitimate contributors to the expressive output. Lateral communication between co-workers should include the task and affinity groups and personnel operating on a specific level, and should provide information, evaluation, and instruction and carry out some persuasive and ceremonial functions.

Leaders should do their best to see that both horizontal and vertical communications are compatible with organizational and subgroup norms, values, and objectives.

Formal media economically transmit essential information. Instrumental managers rely heavily on memos, procedural manuals, and the chain of command, recognizing that time-consuming face-to-face meetings eat up money. However, memos rarely inspire. Effective expressive organizations value involvement, purpose, cohesion, motivation, and instilled values, so they encourage large gatherings, inspiring speeches, face-to-face meetings, and occasional skipped links in the chain of command, as when a direct-service volunteer talks directly to the board chairperson). Other formal media, such as magazines, newspapers, newsletters, faxes, electronic-mail networks, and special mailings, should intermix information for both volunteers and staff.

Informal interpersonal networks, or grapevines, occur in spite of formal structure and official functions. Moving horizontally, diagonally, and elliptically from one central figure to another, such networks are especially vital during change and crisis. An individual may be part of many communication vines: some will be social, others will be political, advisory, informational, racial, sexual, or recreational, and some will represent particular individuals' mutual trust. Some leaders see the grapevine as an evil growth that spreads rumors, destroys morale, ruins reputations, and threatens authority. However, a grapevine can be a good thing, a safety valve, and rapid transmitter of news (Davis, 1987, p. 84). An organization cannot afford to ignore grapevines. Leaders cannot control grapevines, but they can influence them by finding ways of integrating grapevine activities with the organization's objectives.

If the manager wants more communication, for example, she or he should increase the number or the effectiveness of the liaison individuals who transmit on the grapevine, keeping in mind three well-known communication principles that affect liaison individuals: tell people what will affect them, tell them what they want to know rather than simply what you want them to know, and tell them soon (Davis, 1987, p. 87).

Not all communication is verbal. An inclusive organizational culture relies heavily on nonverbal signals. Body language quickly communicates whether one party welcomes another or considers the other an intruder. Nonverbal communications include the answers people see to such questions as these: How much time does a key person have for specific others? Who plays golf with whom? Whose spouse is in what social circle? Whose secretary lunches with whose assistant? Who is part of which loop of prestige networks?

Decision Making

Participative management emphasizes employees' involvement in decisions that affect them. It relies on commitment, self-control, and self-management. "Making decisions which affect one's work life allows one to experience a sense of self-determination and are therefore intrinsically rewarding" (Deci, 1975, p. 223).

People are more likely to abide by decisions in which they have participated, even when the decisions did not go their way. Effective performance rewards itself. Leaders of departments, important committees, and representatives of constituencies should be included in decision making—especially for those decisions that affect them. Inclusion does not always mean each party has an equal vote. It does mean they have a voice to some degree. For instance, they can help with data gathering in preparation for decisions and with conducting informal "what if" probes. They can join in opportunities for sharing information, ideas, and opinions on alternative possibilities. Once a decision has been made, they should be briefed immediately, with a full interpretation of the decision and its implications. A quick way of ruffling the feathers of anyone at any level is to leave that person out of the loop.

Delegating

Farming out work to a subordinate and making sure the tasks are accomplished is the primordial organizational act. When there is little to do and all the time in the world to do it, managers do not need to delegate; but when there is much to do and little time, they must either learn to work faster or get someone else to do the work—delegate.

A systematic way of delegating is, first, to list all of the tasks that are your responsibility; second, list all of the employees and volunteers you might call on for help; third, go through the lists of tasks, designate those persons who might perform them, and then select the persons who might do those tasks best; fourth, describe the objectives of each task and ask the selected persons to assume responsibility (a real pro, not finding a match for each task, will prepare a profile of the desired person and recruit an outside person who fits the profile); and fifth, follow through. In particular, be aware that effective delegation demands that the quality and quantity of results expected be clear to both parties.

Because of job overlapping, difficulties often arise in the delegation of authority. One cannot fully delegate responsibility. Responsibility is an obligation to perform that which one owes to one's superior and cannot diminish by delegating to another. The process of delegating to volunteers may seem difficult to persons who have no experience of organizations where that practice is part of the cultural norms. How can a manager assign tasks and delegate authority and responsibility for accomplishing these tasks to someone who is not financially accountable? Successful and effective nonprofits do it every day. Several principles point the way toward this absolutely necessary activity—absolutely necessary for attracting and holding potent, responsible decision-making unpaid staff.

First, the organization must acknowledge nonpaid personnel as part of its formal structure—something it wants, not just something it needs.

Second, nonpaid personnel must have responsibility, authority, and sufficient staff support to attain assigned objectives.

Third, paid staff working with nonpaid staff must be evaluated, at least partially, according to the degree they can recruit, motivate, and support nonpaid staff to whom objectives are delegated. Success will come from a team effort with shared responsibility.

Fourth, organizational norms must evolve that include the following: formal public acceptance of responsibility by nonpaid personnel, the practice of reassigning (firing) those whose applied time and/or talent is insufficient for meeting objectives, the "promotion" of those who consistently fulfill their responsibility, and respect for paid staff whose careers depend on their success.

Delegation is a precarious venture for the novice, but it is the veteran's ultimate management skill. Effective delegation multiplies potency and productivity, especially delegation to volunteers whose time costs the organization nothing—multiplying the final outputs once again. Delegation can reduce costs if managers assign work to appropriate levels. Higher-level participants then have more time for higher-level decision making, results are better because tasks are executed by those closest to them, and delegators get the best out of participants who have a say about how they work.

Innovating

Organizational innovations result from the ideas and efforts of creative people. While all organizations can benefit from new approaches to solving problems, voluntary nonprofits, especially expressive ones, are unique in that they do not have to make money from innovations. Part of the purpose of innovations may be to provide expressive opportunities for creative persons.

Schumpeterian theory begins with the idea of the innovative nonprofit entrepreneur, driven by intrinsic expressive motivation, who creates for the sake of the resulting innovation itself (Schumpeter, 1934). Creativity is primarily intrinsic and expressive. Extrinsic rewards may even distract the creative personality. Many of the same conditions that stimulate expression also stimulate creativity and subsequent innovations.

Nonprofits have virtually unlimited resources available to alert leaders who are innovative enough to tap them. An excellent example is the series of Boy Scout commercials that utilizes U.S. presidents as on-camera talent. Attired in their uniforms, these former Scouts promote this nonprofit to which they once belonged. The air time was free for these public-service announcements, and the ad agency contributed its services. The Boy Scouts' only costs were some negligible production expenses. The presidents would not have been available to a business.

Organizations can stimulate innovations through good communication and a friendly atmosphere of cooperation. Everyone associated with the organization should be busy identifying resources and foraging for fresh ideas.

Understanding Political Activity

Vic Murray stated, "There is more destructive political game-playing and badly handled conflict in our sector than in either business or government. I would suggest this is because there are usually so much more expressive kinds of commitment in these organizations. People invest their egos in the ideologies of their voluntary organizations. They also feel that, because they truly believe in the mission, one should not ignore or contradict their ideas. Because goal attainment is so difficult to measure, there is always much room for debate as to what we should do or who should do what. So conflict is rife and much more difficult to manage effectively" (personal communication, December 15, 1992).

Nonprofit organizations are political systems with defined

boundaries, goals, values, administrative mechanisms, and hierarchies of power. Politics is the activity of influencing, changing, or controlling the hierarchy (Handy, 1985, p. 20). Nelson Rockefeller once said, "I learned my politics at the museum," referring to the Museum of Modern Art in New York, the nonprofit in which his mother played a major role (Mason, 1984a, p. 116). George McGovern once told me, "There is no way anyone can function effectively in a voluntary organization without some knowledge of diplomatic or political skills. That is really what it is all about" (personal communication, September 4, 1984).

Why is political skill especially important in nonprofits? The more voluntary the participation, the more the exercise of power is relative rather than absolute. The currency of many nonprofits is recognition and influence more than it is dollars and cents; political aspects are prominent. Power is diffused, and in a real sense the organizations are more governed than managed. The artful marshaling of support for special interests through internal politics and the external positioning of the organization in its environment of resources are critical for control and success. However, the more lofty the organization's perceptions of its values, the less participants can openly acknowledge its politics, and the more artful ones must practice their politics with subtlety. Politics lubricates the inevitable competition for influence among interests.

When individuals choose organizations as vehicles for applying their energy, when they identify with organizations' values and commit themselves to the causes, they develop a vested interest in the organizations' processes. All organizational activity reflects these interests. Though cultural etiquette dictates that most discussion will be couched in terms of what may be best for the cause, personal and clique interests and power concerns are an inevitable reality. Participants rarely discuss private interests or organizational politics in formal deliberations, but informal discussions among cohorts are rarely about anything else.

With knowledge of the reality of the role and exercise of political power, effective leaders acknowledge there are dimensions other than rational efficiency. Expressive goals and normative and emotional factors are legitimate and bear on overall organizational effectiveness. All participants are motivated, to a degree, by their desire for power and control. Morgan has noted that "even the most altruistic persons may find their action following a political script in the sense that their orientation to organizational life is influenced by the conflicting sets of interests that they bring to issues of immediate concern" (1986, p. 196). Successful managers need to be successful politicians in the sense that they understand and are sensitive to the causes of conflict and to political tactics and strategies. As Handy reminds us, "The belief that organizations can and should be entirely rational is both erroneous and harmful in that it has inhibited much study of the organization as a political process" (1985, pp. 255–256).

Characteristic Marketing Functions

Two concurrent management functions in particular are characteristic of the voluntary nonprofit sector. Both are marketing functions: *fundraising* and *volunteer recruiting*. We might say that, by definition, these two functions are unique to the sector; however, governments and businesses sometimes have volunteers, and both of these sectors occasionally solicit contributions. For example, some mayors are volunteers. Government volunteers work in public hospitals, fire departments, schools, and prisons, and provide clerical help in public offices. Businesses often sponsor nonprofits—for example, softball teams and committees for social events. Whatever the umbrella entity, each of these subunits is a voluntary organization.

An organization to which people donate money and then volunteer to work for it for nothing is doing something right. David Rockefeller observed that people often ask how nonprofits can benefit from adoption of business methods. He acknowledged that nonprofit and for-profit organizations are basically different when he said, "That is something to me like the song from *My Fair Lady* which asks, 'Why Can't a Woman Be More Like a Man?'" (Mason, 1985b).

Persuading

Nonprofit marketing is primarily based on persuasion, appealing to people's values or offering expressive opportunities rather than a quid pro quo exchange. We will touch briefly on persuasion's role in both fundraising and recruiting volunteers. Both were activities in the sector long before someone coined the term *marketing*. The two relate closely because volunteers who give their time are more likely than other people to give their money.

Persuasion is endemic to a healthy voluntary sector. Involuntary organizations exercise coercion, or more often implied threats of coercion, to get their way. Market-based businesses get their way by quid pro quo exchange. Children are not born into membership in voluntary associations. One does not come under the authority of a voluntary association by virtue of her or his residence, as in the case with people under a government. Voluntary and nonprofit organizations depend on participation by means of voluntarily contributed time and money. Hence, their very existence depends on marketing themselves through persuasion.

Persuasion is one of the most obvious and least objectionable methods an individual uses to get others to do something. It relies on clear logic, effective argument, and mobilization of facts. Persuasion also depends to a degree on the recipient's evaluation of the source of the persuasion.

Moreover, persuasive influence is compatible with the current emphasis on the rights of the individual and a contractual system in which the subordinate has the right to say no. Persuasion implies a flexible, participative style (Handy, 1985, p. 132).

Fundraising

Unlike business sales in which an organization provides a service or a product for a payment, giving is not a quid pro quo exchange. Typically, the elicited contribution pays for a service to society or to third parties. A government entity or foundation may see the nonprofit organization as a contractor, a grantee, or an agent, but to most individuals, the recipient nonprofit organization is a *channel of expressive acts*. Those seeking funds can enhance the whole donor experience by emphasizing that a contribution is shared expressive participation. And many people do donate primarily for an expressive rather than an exchange transaction. They see their donation as instrumental for an expressive purpose. Many good solicitors understand donors' expressive motivations, and their appeal for funds reflects this understanding. These solicitors, usually volunteers, approach prospects as intrinsically motivated persons who may want to share an expressive opportunity to help a cause that espouses the prospects' priorities. Such an approach also empowers the solicitor. The solicitor is in no way a beggar or supplicant, but is expressing her or his own values and interests in partnership with the donor.

Organizations enhancing their expressive dimension will include board members, salaried employees, and all volunteers in their appeals for contributions. They should go after the larger givers first, then ask the large donors to solicit others. Donating, like water, flows downhill. A major contributor's solicitation carries the weight of sincerity. The campaign should also approach companies and individuals for in-kind gifts of what they have—space from building owners, food from grocers, printing from printers, medicine from pharmaceutical companies, and office supplies from office suppliers. Development directors and campaign chairpersons may take advantage of small expressive groups, as described in Chapter Ten, for raising funds as well as for enlarging membership.

Volunteer Recruiting

Though all unpaid workers volunteer, there is some ambiguity about the use of the term *volunteer*. Some organizational cultures relegate the term to lower-level direct service providers. Board members then are simply described as board members; committee members are simply members of committees. Volunteer scoutmasters, choir members, tutors, docents, church school teachers, and little league coaches rarely attach the adjective "volunteer" to their titles. While I recognize that in many organizations, a director of volunteers usually works with unpaid direct service people, while other managers recruit and work with the higher-level specialists, committee personnel, and board members who work voluntarily, I approach the subject of recruiting volunteers by looking at *all unpaid workers* as *volunteers*.

All functions related to volunteers (recruiting them and organizing, guiding, and motivating them) are virtually confined to the voluntary sector. Recruiting activities will be particularly distinctive in any organization offering an expressive experience, for its philosophy must pervade its entire recruiting strategy and process. The volunteer is not only an input resource but also a recipient of outputs. The organization offers not only work but also values to be shared. Philip R. Warner, once vice president of the National Executive Service Corps, an organization that provides top-level business executives to nonprofit organizations, described one aspect of the special situation this way:

> One of the things we worry about when we recruit retired execu-
> tives is whether they have the sensitivity to be able to transfer from
> the kind of operation you have in business to the nonprofit field.
> In business, you have total control of the situation. In the nonprofit
> area, many workers are volunteers. Therefore, you may want some-
> thing done instantly, but no one does it instantly. It is much harder
> to control. One has to be sensitive to that. It is the executive who
> can make the transition and who has the sensitivity to work well
> with other people that work best for us [Mason, 1988, p. 34].

Clary, Snyder, and Ridge (1992, pp. 341–342) suggest three steps for successful volunteer recruiting:

1. Consider the target audience. Organizations should identify the population from which they intend to recruit, and assess the prospects' motivational concerns before promoting an organization's means of satisfying these motivations.
2. Assess each prospect's motivation, gaining valuable insights into the prospect's interests. (Clary, Snyder, and Ridge recommend their Volunteer Functions Inventory as a tool for such assessment.)
3. Tailor persuasive messages to the prospect's relevant motivations, matching the organization's activities to the target audience's interests.

Applying Specialized Functions

Concurrent functions relating to ethics, inspiration, managing professionals, decision-making levels, and the identification of resources also have an essential importance in voluntary and nonprofit organizations.

Emphasizing Ethics

Leaders must not only conform to a complex code of mores but are also responsible for creating moral codes for others. They subordinate their individual interests to the good of the community (Barnard, 1938, p. 279). Most voluntary and nonprofit organizations accept a concept of binding duty that mandates that the moral status of behavior should depend not only on its consequences but also on its intention (Etzioni, 1988, p. 12).

Institutions that enunciate, transmit, and defend ethical values fall within the boundaries of the voluntary sector. Educational, religious, and advocacy organizations constitute a majority of nonprofit organizations and have shaped the form of the sector itself. This society expects a high ethical standard of its nonprofit organizations and, as Elizabeth Boris of the Council on Foundations points out, expects nonprofit professionals and volunteers "to be role models of moral responsibility" (Van Til and Associates, 1990, p. 190). Nonprofits mediate many of the values in our society from one generation to the next. Organizations that preach and teach ethics are part of the voluntary sector. The link between nonprofits and ethical standards is so strong that it makes all nonprofits seem part of the same extended family. Moreover, when one member of the family slips and falls in the mud and the press waves the dirty laundry in the public's face, typically someone will suggest that the whole family needs to wash.

The fact that founders establish nonprofit organizations for (usually idealistic) reasons other than profit and that the nonprofit social character is distinctively moral and idealistic, draws employees, volunteers, and contributors. They care about right and wrong and about what happens to their society. But that does not necessarily simplify their decision making in comparison to other organizations. They will still struggle with value-based decisions between competing positive values. Before they make such decisions in any intentional way, they must identify their own value system, their own hierarchy of values. Robert L. Payton summed it up when he said, "It is the transformation of moral sentiment and imagination into collective action that has shaped the core of the philanthropic tradition. . . . [I]t is within the philanthropic tradition that the moral agenda of society is put forward" (1988, p. 119).

The most potent weapon in the donative nonprofit marketing arsenal is the public's trust and its perception that the "purity and nobility" of nonprofits' goals have a "halo effect," producing "superior quality and services" ("The Forbes Nonprofit 500," 1990, p. 100). Similarly, Weisbrod suggests that the public perceives "nonprofit status, particularly tax-deductible status, as a mark of quality—as indication that the organization is trustworthy" (1988, p. 11). The opportunity for expressive participation in an ethically positive sphere is an essential benefit that nonprofits offer, and thus, many nonprofits can seek and receive public support. And public trust is essential if they are to continue generating this participation. It is ethical behavior itself that builds trust. Without trust, participation will weaken. Cynicism will further erode trust and confidence. Contributors will cut off funds. The solidarity of constituencies will dissolve. People who give their time and allegiance will lose their incentive. Governments may withdraw a nonprofit's special legal privileges.

Nonprofit organizations tend to have complex multiple motives and purposes as they serve multiple constituencies. The effective interfacing of these facets is so complex as to defy legal enforcement and requires instead all members' acceptance of undergirding principles. Self-interest mandates consistently ethical behavior, and managers have learned that they cannot govern behavior in such a milieu as easily "by the book" as by the cultivation of a cohesive culture bound by culturally approved patterns of conduct. A nonprofit organization that wants to succeed yet condones sloppy ethics is like Humpty Dumpty trying to balance atop a slippery parapet—picture it.

Inspiring

Inspiration, a subclass of communication, is so important in expressive organizations that it merits special attention. Leaders should apply the motivational power of the organizational purpose to all task levels. They should build resolve and confidence. Organizational participants do not work for material rewards, and inspiration feeds many of the hungers that motivate them. It is a major advocacy tool. It elicits energy in the form of contributed time and money and builds an intrinsically motivating culture. Productivity tends to increase when inspirational appeals augment rational persuasion (Falbe and Yukl, 1992, p. 638). A nonprofit organization can easily focus all its energy on its process and inputs. Therefore, the leadership must persistently inspire participants and draw attention to the high-priority outputs desired.

Inspiring practices, according to a leadership skills training program conducted by the Boston-based Forum Company, include developing people's talents, recognizing the contributions of others, enabling others to feel and act like leaders, and building enthusiasm about projects and assignments (Conger, 1992, p. 97).

A 1992 study by Falbe and Yukl of business managers' use of various influence tactics found that the most effective tactics were "soft" inspirational appeals and consultation. The least effective were "hard" tactics like pressure, legitimating, and coalition tactics. Intermediate in effectiveness were rational persuasion, ingratiating, personal appeals, and exchange tactics. Inspirational tactics were used mostly in a downward and lateral direction and usually in combination with another tactic (p. 650). "Pure" inspirational appeals are often not as effective in generating task commitment as inspirational appeals combined with rational persuasion (p. 640).

Managing Professionals and Dedicated Persons

Both professionals and "dedicated" people require ample space for expressive opportunity. Professionals, such as educators, social workers, and clergy, predominate in nonprofit organizations. They are often the most important people in an organization, and they constitute almost 40 percent of the philanthropic labor force. Though philanthropic organizations employ only 5.7 percent of the total labor force, they employ 14.1 percent of all professionals and technical workers (Powell, 1987, p. 57). Among many professionals, the title of "manager" or, more often, "administrator" is used in a condescending way—as a reference to a sort of unavoidable but lowly function. Professionals' primary loyalty usually lies outside the organization that pays their salary. They might march to one drummer while the organization has a different beat. They are most strongly attuned to the expectations, values, and mores of their profession. They often get their rewards from the satisfaction of their professional goals and think of themselves as individual practitioners rather than as organizational people. Professionals' memberships in transcending communities whose norms state that professionals should be mutually protective can present nonprofit organizations with special constraints.

Dedicated persons also have a transcending loyalty and motivation that may supersede their allegiance to their employer and supervisor. Dedicated individuals do not necessarily have the special knowledge of professionals, but they perceive themselves to have a special anointing that immunizes them from needing to follow the mandates of anyone whom they do not see as also anointed. Managers must follow much the same approach with dedicated individuals as they do with professionals. They must recruit a person with the proper potential, then let go of the details of the process, allowing the professional or dedicated person to be self-managing. When analyzing an organization, management should be sure to recognize the existence of highly dedicated individuals in both the volunteer corps and the staff. The more cause-oriented an enterprise, the more likely it is to have many of these individuals. Managers need to be aware of dedicated persons because they are a mixed blessing. The fires in their boiler rooms were lighted by the cause, and these individuals generate much energy that can be available to the organization. They produce much heat and sometimes light. They have much energy and sometimes ability. But to these individuals, the cause is everything. The organization is just so much machinery. Should the organization shift its course, their course will not shift. Inside or outside the organization, under this banner or another, nothing really matters but their personal commitment and relation to the cause.

We will often see three subcultures in an encompassing organization—an organizational culture, a professional culture, and a true believers' culture—and they may compete. On the one hand, the professionals and dedicated true believers see themselves as part of transorganizational cultures. On the other hand, organizational people see their values and goals residing within the agency. The management of professionals and dedicated people includes providing an enriching environment, subsidiarity, decentralization, autonomy, participation, and tolerance of risk taking. It means providing opportunities for achievement, interesting work, personal growth, and responsibility for contributing to a worthy goal. It requires understanding and the application of intrinsic motivation in an expressive environment.

Satisficing

Simon (1976) defines *satisficing* as a rational decision-making procedure that terminates the process of considering all possible alternatives by selecting the first alternative that fully meets the criteria. Most voluntary nonprofit organizations do not have in-house capability for conducting thorough research as input for management decisions. In addition, activities are not expected to have a quid pro quo return to the degree that for-profit activities are. Quantifiable measurement of nonprofit outputs in general and expressive outputs in particular is often too difficult to be worth its cost. The difficulty of quantifying expressive aspects contributes to the scarcity of scholarly attention and has much to do with the organizations' being in this sector (Mason, 1984b). Therefore, it is often functional for nonprofits to act on the first alternative that meets their criteria, rather than exhaustively identifying all options and then selecting the best.

Applying Subsidiarity

Subsidiarity is the principle that no higher-level authority should make decisions that could just as well be made at a lower level. Decisions should be made and actions should be taken as close to the bottom of the organization as possible. This principle is fundamental for stimulating expressive outputs.

This same principle was promulgated by Pope Pius XI in his encyclical letter of 1931, *Quadragesimo Anno*. He held it to be a fundamental policy of social philosophy "that one should not withdraw from the individual and commit to the community what they can accomplish by their own enterprise and industry. So, too, it is an injustice and at the same time a grave evil and a disturbance of right order to transfer to the larger and higher collectivity functions which can be performed and provided for by lesser and subordinate bodies." Subsidiarity is not only moral; it also increases expressive outputs. People should have as much responsibility as they can handle. "To do anything else is in a sense to steal people's choices from them; and since most people in a voluntary organization are there because they believe in the work, they will want as much of that work as they can reasonably handle" (Handy, 1988, p. 105). Lawler evaluated quality circles, gain-sharing plans, job enrichment, self-managed work teams, and other subsidiarity practices for their impact on productivity and found that "overwhelmingly, the evidence that I reviewed supported the idea of giving individuals at the lowest levels in organizations more information, knowledge, power and rewards" (1992, p. xi).

Subsidiarity makes some managers fear losing control. An intrinsically motivated superior fears lost opportunities for his or her own hands-on involvement in the work itself. Some supervisors are not receptive to others' ideas, cannot tolerate subordinates' mistakes, and are psychologically unable to resist meddling. Some fear their subordinates will work so well that they will compete for the supervisor's job. Some feel they are shirking their work when those below them carry much of the load. Nonprofit managers must learn to overcome these fears, because subsidiarity is an important factor in expressive outputs.

The most costly and extreme failure to exercise subsidiarity that I know of is the World War I battle of Passchendaele. It was a sunny day when the British strategists planned the battle, far behind the lines. Not one senior officer from headquarters set foot on the battlefield during the four-month battle during which British troops advanced four and a half miles while 250,000 fell! The attack plans might have worked except that steady drenching rain turned the battlefield into a mud field. Rifles clogged, heavy equipment bogged, and soldiers could hardly slog through the deep thick mud. But the strategic thinkers remained ignorant of the conditions under which their orders were executed (Mintzberg, 1994, p. 187).

Identifying Resources and Exploiting Opportunities

I couple the concurrent functions of identifying potential resources and exploiting opportunities. I see the former as a developmental activity having to do with inputs, and the latter as a program activity having to do with outputs. Both functions utilize expressive activity and require alertness, creativity, flexibility, and initiative. A person can build a successful career on the foundation of being alert enough to see resources and opportunities, creative enough to imagine how to use them, flexible enough to adapt them to the organization's purposes, and innovative enough to seize the right moment.

In an organization worth one's commitment, anyone should be able to exercise these functions. Everyone in an organization can recognize potential inputs and opportunities for outputs for its services. The alertness and creativity of participants are the only constraints because any participant may be in the right place at the right time. For example, the editor of a nonprofit publication in Colombia, South America, was on a speaking tour in Minnesota when an executive with a large paper manufacturing company approached him following a speech. After exchanging a few pleasantries, the executive told the editor his company could donate a large amount of paper if the editor could to get it to South America. While the executive was verifying the contribution with his company, the editor told his executive director in New York about the offer and the expensive transportation problem. The executive director called friends in other agencies and located an ocean freighter willing to carry the paper free on a space-available basis. When the paper arrived in Colombia months later, the editor found the paper unsuitable for his press because it was in large rolls instead of flat stacks, but the donation was still valuable because the publisher sold the paper to another printer for $70,000.

Program personnel are usually those who are in the right place at the right time to exploit opportunities for maximizing outputs. Others in the organization may be better placed to recognize inputs. Petr Spurney, who managed the 1984 Louisiana World's Fair in New Orleans, managed this input function as well as anyone I know. He developed an extensive wish list of resources the fair would need, then approached corporate and other sponsors to contribute everything from airline transportation, buildings, and fine art to coffee mugs and ballpoint pens.

Managing Unpaid Personnel

By definition, volunteers have more options than a typical employee. At will, volunteers may enter an organization or depart it, vary the intensity and quality of their efforts, and vary the amount of resources they contribute. Their presence and intrinsic motivation mandates *cohesion maximization, management of conflict, dual personnel systems, empowerment, growth by cell division, hygiene factor maintenance, morale enhancement, redundancy,* and *support systems.*

Maximizing Cohesion

As discussed in Chapter Six, cohesion is the (expressive) mortar that holds the (instrumental) bricks in place. Organizations should intentionally integrate newcomers into task groups and into the organization as a whole and confirm and further commit existing members. Chapter Nine also identifies ways and means of building cohesiveness into the organization, as well as factors that produce disintegration.

Managing Conflict

The public perceives voluntary and nonprofit organizations, especially religious organizations, as contentious and perpetually involved in petty squabbles. This may be due to the weak authority structures of many nonprofits; participants feel free to criticize and complain without fear of reprimand. Perhaps it is simply due to nonprofits' expressive nature. Participants feel strongly about their organizations, and many work in them to satisfy values-driven intrinsic motivations. They tend to express themselves freely and to object to constraints of that expression. Coercive and utilitarian organizations restrain overt conflict to a degree because of their more direct means of enforcing compliance.

Whatever the reasons for disagreement, voluntary organizations have much at stake in these dissensions. Aggrieved parties can withhold their effort and/or financial contributions as a result of unresolved conflict, and a conflict may distract and inhibit the activities of uninvolved but proximate participants.

Some of the traditional strategies for regulating conflict are arbitration, when an organizational superior or outsider judges the issue and decides the outcome; rules and procedures that allow issues to be decided through predetermined policies; coordinating devices in which a specified individual or group mediates; confrontation, in which the concerned parties fight it out between themselves; separation, in which a higher ranked individual isolates the conflicting parties; and neglect, in the hope that the conflict will simmer down or go away (Handy, 1985, pp. 252–254).

Conflicts grow out of several seedbeds. Some lie more in the perception than the reality of differences. Skilled managers can recognize such perception problems and gently help the parties resolve difficulties by clarifying reality. Some conflict is structural, growing out of the way the organization has established roles and goals. Leaders on a higher rung of the organizational ladder than the disputants should deal with structural conflicts because they can precipitate other conflicts. Some conflicts have nothing to do with the organization, but when they flare on organizational turf, the supervisor of the conflicting individuals or groups must mediate. Many conflicts—often major ones—occur along the boundaries of organizational subcultures. For example, they may occur between paid and volunteer personnel, overlapping specialty areas, staff and line management, people focused on ideology and those focused on organizational necessity, departments and groups, program and development people, expressive and instrumental interests, and organization-oriented and profession-oriented personnel. Value conflicts and conflicts over the multiple organizational purposes are among the most serious.

It is also useful to consider the four types of organizational conflict identified by M. Afzalur Rahim (1985, 1992)—intrapersonal, interpersonal, intragroup, and intergroup—and his five styles for dealing with conflict—integrating, obliging, dominating, avoiding, and compromising.

The *integrating* style is useful for dealing with complex strategic conflicts when there is sufficient time and the persons involved are concerned about the outcome. This process involves an open exchange of information and an examination of differences in order to integrate the interests of both parties into the solution. The *obliging* style is useful when the interests of the two parties are unequal and one party is willing to give up something in exchange for some future reciprocating benefit. This approach helps participants play down differences in favor of interests in common goals. The *dominating* style is used for implementing higher-level interests and unpopular courses of action. It is often necessary in cases where speedy decisions are needed. This style does not work when the parties are of equal rank, when the outcome is not important to the superior party, or when the issue is complex and there is ample time to use another method. The *avoiding* mode allows participants time to cool off, and it works with trivial and tactical issues in instances where the potential negative results of getting involved in the conflict outweigh the benefits of positively resolving it. Avoidance is not appropriate when the outcome is important to a party, when one is responsible for a decision, or when waiting is dysfunctional. Finally, the *compromising* style, involving a give-and-take exchange of benefits, is appropriate when the parties have relatively equal power, their goals are mutually exclusive, and the issues are complex but do not involve value differences.

Rahim suggests that in *intrapersonal* conflict, managers should optimize individual and organizational goals by matching individual goals and expectations with task and role demands. For managing *interpersonal* conflict, he suggests teaching participants the aforementioned styles of handling conflict so they can select the appropriate style for attaining individual and organizational goals. *Intragroup* conflict is best handled with the integrating style in order to help the group attain group goals. *Intergroup* problems are also best handled by the integrating technique since that has the best chance of optimizing the benefits of group cooperation to the encompassing organization.

In short, conflict does not always have to be bad. Recognizing that a certain amount of tension and even conflict may be good for an organization, some experts are moving away from the idea of *resolving* conflict and toward the idea of *managing* conflict, seeking more constructive and less destructive conflict. Organizational success may depend on well-managed conflict. We are not talking here about haranguing and pushing and shoving, but about innovation-spawning conflict over the best jobs to do and the best ways to do them. Open, fair, and forthright discussion of opposing views precipitates creative solutions.

Working with Dual Personnel Systems

The central altar in many managers' organizational faith is the organization chart. Its image burns into their minds and souls, and they make no decisions—indeed, they think no thoughts—without booting up an image of "The Chart" that defines the formal units and the lines of authority and accountability. Informal networks and unofficial positions are usually too complex and messy to include on the chart. Expressive concerns, such as unpaid positions over which managers exercise only "soft" authority, complicate a neat chart.

Somehow, managers must delete this mental image of "The Chart." Only then can they understand how expressive components fit into the organization. One solution is to draw up two charts. If the mind cannot easily adapt to a chart including both paid employees with "hard" lines of authority and accountability and volunteers with "soft" lines of influence and responsibility, why not have one chart for paid personnel and another for volunteers? Another choice is to have an opaque chart that includes all organizational units and their paid personnel, and an acetate overlay that shows where unpaid personnel fit. Either alternative gives the mind visual symbols for the relationships among *all* the people.

Recent decades have seen the emergence of professional directors of volunteers. These persons are skilled and often formally trained in recruiting, placing, training, supervising, and recognizing and rewarding volunteers. The relationship they have with the CEOs, department heads, and directors of human relations in their organizations will vary from group to group. Often, they work solely with direct service providers and seek to enhance expressive outputs with the volunteers at that level. Establishing such a position is a positive step in the right direction, but the profession of director of volunteers is still evolving and is not an established norm in all nonprofit industries.

A major characteristic of any voluntary organization large enough to employ staff is the difference between the paid and unpaid workers. The organization rewards paid personnel with extrinsic (and perhaps intrinsic) incentives and volunteers with only intrinsic incentives. Paid staff are kept on a relatively tight rein, and they may undertake the more boring and unpleasant tasks on relentless schedules. Conversely, one leads more than one manages volunteers. Volunteers undertake boring and unpleasant tasks only briefly, spurred on with the promise of significant rewards, and their work is normally intermittent. Managers may employ different styles with the two types. Leaders and managers at mid- and junior levels may work exclusively with either paid or unpaid personnel. At the highest levels, managers must be able to consider both types of volunteers. The manager who chooses to work only with the more controllable paid personnel chooses a less challenging lower road, one that leads toward reduced outputs.

Empowering

Empowerment is strengthening others' belief in their own sense of effectiveness and sharing leadership power with others, thus increasing subordinates' self-efficacy. The last thing leaders want to do in many for-profit organizations is to empower anyone except themselves. (This is not necessarily a bad approach, since power is what leaders use to do their job.) In voluntary organizations, however, power in the hands of one's subordinates usually enhances the power of the supervisor. In these organizations, effective leaders want participants to feel expressively potent. They want participants to share a sense of ownership in the organization and in their specific area of responsibilities. To a degree, leaders are judged by their skill in endowing their subordinates with as much power as they can optimally handle.

One way a leader may empower others is simply by providing more opportunities for self-determination. I have found that a surefire method of building a subordinate's sense of self-efficacy is to encourage the person to undertake successively difficult tasks that she or he can then master.

Vineyard and Lynch (1991, p. 36) list six ways to empower an organization in general.

1. Be clear about the purpose and vision so they infect others.
2. Identify and create total commitment.
3. Enjoin everyone to work toward making the organization the best possible vehicle for achieving its purposes.

4. Create a purposeful workplace in which all individuals know they are needed and how they fit into the whole.
5. Eliminate, without compromise, anyone not committed to the purpose.
6. Maximize human resources through raising workers' sights with access to information; investing energy in people who are potential future leaders; sharing responsibility with all participants; providing sufficient authority for every responsibility, mutual support and trust, and a learning climate with permission to make mistakes openly; encouraging and modeling creativity; and encouraging expressive behavior.

As a leader considers expressive philosophy, she or he will see the vital need for co-worker empowerment. Participants need a sense of community, a feeling that everyone is joined in a common effort toward shared goals. They need to feel that they are learning and growing as persons and as individuals with significant responsibilities. A good leader can build a sense of ownership into each newcomer by pointing to a clear worthy goal and showing each participant how his or her participation enhances the common mission.

Growing by Cell Division

Expressive organizations suffer when their size is static, and nonprofits have traditionally metered their success by their rate of growth rather than their bank balance. They also enjoy an organic means for expanding their size, their resources, and the services they provide. Building organic growth into their systems is a vital concurrent function for stimulating expressive outputs while enlarging the organization. The details of growth by cell division are presented in Chapter Nine. Here, we can begin to understand why nonprofits need to foster this kind of growth.

Growth is critical to nonprofits because a growing organization tends to hold its better workers and attract effective new workers—both paid and unpaid. If an organization is coasting and losing momentum, top participants may want to find greener pastures. Conversely, if people's responsibilities are growing with their present organization, they will tend to stay and grow with the group they know best. A growing organization with a reputation for vitality attracts the more talented people, and the larger an organization's pool of personnel, the more people there are from which to choose new leaders at all levels.

Growth improves the psychological climate that fuels the organization with energy. Some of the attitudes engendered by a growing concern are optimism, pride of membership, enthusiasm, excitement, and confidence. In summary, there is much to the adage "Nothing succeeds like success."

Maintaining Hygiene Factors

The primary revelation of Herzberg's 1966 study of engineers and accountants that defined motivating factors and hygiene factors (see Chapter Four) was that while business employees are happier with a better work environment, they are not more productive. The nonprofit venue differs. Volunteers in nonprofits can depart with less provocation or penalty than can employees of a business. Hygiene factors, therefore, are elevated to greater significance for retaining effective personnel.

Hygiene, or maintenance, factors such as working conditions, status, and interpersonal relationships prevent dissatisfaction, low morale, absenteeism, and turnover. They meet needs on the lower levels of Maslow's hierarchy. Businesses can focus primarily on factors that increase employee productivity; nonprofit organizations know their volunteer workers need satisfaction in order to participate. Some satisfiers are a friendly and complimentary supervisor, attractive surroundings, coffee breaks, air-conditioning, clear policies and guidelines, harmony, contact with top charismatic leaders, emotional support, appreciation for hard work and loyalty, status symbols, and fringe benefits.

Enhancing Morale

As a young CEO of a local voluntary organization, I was annoyed by some members' expectations. I thought I was doing a great job in accomplishing my instrumental tasks, and the organization was growing dramatically. I was frustrated by several board members' hints that Mrs. X or Mr. Y felt neglected. I felt that I had gone to school too long to learn to do my job to waste my time sipping tea with someone who simply needed reassurance. Every hour I spent in the office of an influential businessman, listening to his hare-brained ideas, seemed an hour lost in implementing my success-ful program. One day, I realized there was a word for the result of this seemingly wasteful activity—morale. The light went on. Morale building was a legitimate part of my executive function.

The more voluntary and expressive the organization, the more important its morale. To a degree, volunteers participate because of the "vibes" they get from high morale. Morale in the group is like temperature in the body—it indicates either well-being or an infection, perhaps a serious sickness. When the mechanical indus-trial model was at its zenith, companies conducted morale "inven-tories." Even then, management saw the importance of employee attitudes as a quantifiable measure of employer-employee relations. Morale indicates some organizational strengths and weaknesses, tests reaction to new policies and programs, and yields informa-tion about potential problems. However, one does not treat low morale directly, as one does a fever with an aspirin or injection, because morale levels indicating human relations health and go up or down as root causes fluctuate. It is these root causes that must be addressed.

If an organization does not directly assess its morale level peri-odically, it must check attendance, production, participation lev-els, and other indirect morale indicators. It should evaluate rumors of morale problems to determine their validity and react quickly to valid negative indicators. Managers can ascertain morale fluc-tuations through the grapevine, supervisors' reports, informal interviews with participants, and formal attitude surveys.

Applying Redundancy

In nonprofits, redundancy is a management tool that produces expressive effectiveness in the face of apparent instrumental inef-ficiency. Redundancy is seemingly superfluous duplication, exceed-ing what is necessary. However, what may at first glance appear unnecessarily repetitious may occasionally be an astute tactic. Observe a roof for example. A bottom layer of shingles keeps water off the roof deck. A second layer of shingles keeps water away from the bottom layer. A top layer of shingles sheds the rain as it falls, keeping it off the other layers. The relationship of rain to roof to wind to leaks is one of life's great mysteries—one of the last strongholds of nature over technology. As housing contractors struggle against the natural phenomena of wind and rain, they find redundancy works. When one works with volunteers whose energies and schedules are imprecise, the redundant approach is also often a winner.

An example of the functioning of redundant systems is the promotion of a banquet or seminar. If the organization depends on volunteers to publicize the event and sell tickets, one group might solicit mail orders. Another group might contact other organizations. Another might work through the mass media. Another might recruit teams of ticket salespersons. Each unit has a sales goal, and when these goals are added up they do not total 100 percent of the overall sales goal but 150 percent. If some groups fail to reach their goals, the others should have compensated. If all succeed, the organization declares a great victory.

Supporting Personnel

People work with nonprofits to fulfill their expressive hunger for relatedness, rootedness, affection, approval, admittance, security, esteem, affiliation, and other expressive activities. It is small groups of friends that primarily feed such needs. As a group enables and lifts up its members to accomplish more than they would accomplish alone, it also buoys them up and supports them expressively. Individuals' efforts and emotions are not constant. They are intermittent and fluctuating. A group can mediate with and support its members during low periods, making these periods shorter and shallower than they would otherwise be.

Outside of immediate families, the small groups within religious congregations are perhaps the best examples of supportive communities. As Robert Wuthnow has noted, "In an otherwise atomized and commercialized society, churches and synagogues remain one of the few places in which members of different families, age-groups, occupations, and neighborhoods can interact at a deeply personal level over extended periods of time. They also provide one of the few places (other than therapy groups) in which frank discussion of the problems and gratifications associated with caring relationships within the family, the congregation, and the wider community can occur" (1991, p. 3). Note that Wuthnow falls short of saying that congregations are the *only* locus of such supportive communities. I have experienced them as an expressive output of other voluntary communities.

Leaders in voluntary enterprises tend to need affiliation more than power or achievement. They play their roles by developing strong support systems. Supportive relationships are in the nonprofit organization's best interests. If the organization wants the individual to be there when it needs him or her, it should be there when the individual needs support. The better its support system, the more the organization offers potential participants; the more and better the participants may work, and the lower their turnover may be. Strong support is good for public relations, for a high-quality culture, and for the kind of cohesive spirit that holds the organization together in times of triumph and stress alike.

A supportive organization develops more through a genuine caring attitude than through following a checklist of actions to take. A support system is not something a computer creates. It is not something an employee manual creates. Support is something only individuals in a community can do well.

Conclusion

Management activities do not simply fall into place as the pages of a calendar turn. Specific management functions apply day by day and as opportunities open and problems arise. Some of these functions are common to all sorts of organizations, some are especially important in the voluntary sector, and some are unique to it. Managing and leading a nonprofit is a complex job, requiring a wide range of complex skills. The more a manager understands the functions that are effective, the more effective will that person become.

Needs for Further Research

Are there additional concurrent functions regularly employed in nonprofit organizations? Researchers might survey a sample of organizations to test the list presented in this chapter and to uncover additional practices. They might compare the frequency of use of selected concurrent functions in different fields and across sector boundaries. Researchers working with a specific organization might identify the concurrent functions emphasized in that organization.

Actions for Practitioners

Leaders and managers should see if they are acknowledging each concurrent function that is legitimate for their organization. They would benefit by paying out-of-pocket expenses for a graduate student to study the expressive outputs of one of their concurrent functions. They might want to chart the various political coalitions in their entity and determine which ones are the most powerful. If they are not taking advantage of the redundancy technique, they might use it in a forthcoming project. If managers of all-volunteer groups were to act on only one item at this point, I would suggest they determine to what degree they are practicing a concurrent function such as subsidiarity or delegating. Organizational personnel who have not yet employed some of these functions toward improving organizational outputs should apply them to appropriate opportunities and problems. An organization should build these functions into its systems. Staff and key unpaid participants should learn appropriate concurrent management skills.

This chapter listed some of those concurrent functions that contribute to the process of producing expressive outputs. Some are common to all organizations; others are characteristic of the voluntary sector. Some are especially important in managing volunteers. The next chapter focuses on leadership, the catalyst that draws everything together and precipitates action.

Chapter Nine

Strengthening Leadership Substance and Style

The thundering hoofs of the knight in shining armor, the bugle of the galloping cavalry, and the "Hi Ho, Silver," of the masked stranger foretell bigger-than-life leaders on white horses who save us in the stress of crisis. In contrast is the harried middle-aged scoutmaster who rolled down his car window as he pulled up to the Dairy Queen and implored, "Quick! Tell me where they went. I am their leader."

Dwight D. Eisenhower defined leadership as "the art of getting someone else to do something you want done because he wants to do it" (*Correct Quotes*, 1991). Leadership makes the difference in whether or not an organization stands still or goes somewhere. Good leaders move organizations forward and upward. Bad leaders move organizations backward and downward. Therefore, when organizational participants choose a leader to achieve optimum expressive outputs, they must choose wisely because they are setting the direction their organization will take—and by definition, they will not outpace their leadership. Once they have found a good leader, they should hold on to him or her and follow that leader as long as the he or she takes them where they need to go. When their leader fails to take them in the optimum direction, they should either help correct the course or find a new leader. Regardless of an organization's potential, regardless of the resources at its disposal, its direction depends on the efficacy of its leadership.

Leadership is more important today than ever before because of the range of potential participants', or followers', choices. A static organization without good leadership will not attract the best participants or the necessary money, and it will not operate the best programs. People will commit their time, money, and interest elsewhere because they have a choice. Even if there seems to be no choice today, tomorrow an effective leader will offer an alternative. Leaders make the difference, so choosing and developing the best leaders is the best thing an organization can do when transforming itself toward better expressive motivation.

This chapter spotlights the leaders who are the catalysts who will make things happen. An organization may know everything there is to know about the importance of expressive outputs in invigorating its people. It may communicate just the right images and appreciate the need to socialize people into an ideal culture to achieve the optimum structure and programs for fulfilling its purposes. It may understand how small groups can bond most cohesively, and it may set up a perfect management sequence. But it must *also* have leaders to point the way, stoke the fires, ring the bell, and push the buttons to precipitate action. I will suggest differences between managers and leaders, describe different types of leaders, suggest the charismatic leadership style as optimum for instrumental-expressive organizations, and prescribe the cultivation, selection, placement, and constraining of charismatic leaders.

The voluntary nonprofit sector is a special venue for leadership. Certainly, the world of politics and government is a marvelous platform for leaders, but that platform is also narrow and shaky. There are many more candidates than vacant offices, and once the successful candidate is in office, the opposition promptly strives to unseat him or her, and the press forever strains to find a place to plunge its barbs. In our adversarial system, government leaders have built-in enemies.

The military makes heros of its leaders, but sometimes it does so posthumously. One trouble with being a military leader is that one must kill people in order to win. Win or lose, the leader may himself be killed.

Business leaders gain financial rewards along with their power. Some businesses even change the world for the better. Nevertheless, most business concerns itself first with the quest for money. A business leader can make millions and control a giant corporation yet still be accomplishing nothing but making jeans, hauling gasoline, or selling soda pop.

The voluntary nonprofit arena, in contrast, is bite-sized, people oriented, and user-friendly. A leader here may espouse a truly profound cause, if only at a neighborhood level. Nonprofit leaders have opponents, for certain, but the adversaries' proportion of the constituency is relatively small. The extrinsic benefits are limited, but the intrinsic expressive rewards are vast. People adore their voluntary nonprofit sector leaders and engulf them with appreciation and love. These leaders operate in a venue of important values, "highs" of intense inspiration and warm supportiveness, and best of all, volunteers can be leaders in their spare time.

Leaders and Managers

To this point, I have usually written "manager" when the tasks are calculative and systematic and "leader" when the tasks are more emotional and relational. Apart from that, I have used the terms interchangeably, as we tend to do in everyday life.

However, in order to talk about leadership substance and style, it is important to draw a distinction between the two terms. The work of Bales and his colleagues is helpful here. Bales found that small groups naturally draw out two types of leaders as the groups work toward goals. A task leader specializes in directing and controlling goal attainment activities. In exclusively instrumental organizations, task leaders may suffice. A socioemotional leader specializes in motivating members and reducing tensions (Bales, 1953; Slater, 1955). For our purposes, we can designate the person taking charge of task attainment as an instrumental manager and the one responsible for socioemotional matters as an expressive leader.

Are there deeper differences between leaders and managers? Managers can be leaders, and leaders managers; but not every manager is a leader, and not every leader a manager. Managers appeal to authority and reason while leaders appeal to cultural norms and emotional persuasion. Blau pointed out that managerial authority is rooted in the formal powers and sanctions the organization bestows on managers (1964, p. 210). Managers use the physical resources of organizations, operating on organizational capital, human skills, raw materials, and technology (Bennis and Nanus, 1985, p. 92). Covey describes organizations that have excellent management systems but no heart, while others have heart but lack good systems. Potentially excellent managers may accomplish little because they exhibit "no feeling, no heart; everything is too mechanical, too formal, too tight, too protective" (1991, pp. 247–248).

Leaders envision an inspiring future and focus followers' energy toward a vision. Leaders use their personality to inspire— they stoke and ignite those fires in followers' boiler rooms. Managers use their legal authority to set the thermostat and keep the steam flowing to the right places at the right time. Leaders use the emotional and spiritual resources of an organization, operating on an entity's values, commitment, and aspirations (Bennis and Nanus, 1985, p. 92).

From times deep in the recesses of the past, humans have acknowledged the difference between head and heart as the source of two different approaches to action. Contemporary brain theory carries forward that concept. It pictures the manager dominated by the left half of his or her brain, working with logic, words, parts, and specifics. The brain's right side dominates the leader, who works with emotions, images, wholes, and relationships among the parts.

Kotter's significant recent work differentiates between managers and leaders and the ways both contribute to success. Management assists complex organizations to achieve consistent results. Managers decide what to do, create networks to accomplish an agenda, and then ensure that the job is done. Leadership mobilizes and directs people and/or ideas. Kotter sees leadership as establishing direction and strategy. Leaders project a vision of the future, often the distant future. Leaders' strategies show how to produce the changes needed to achieve that vision. Leaders align people and communicate the direction to all whose cooperation they may need, creating coalitions committed to the vision and its achievement. Leaders motivate and inspire, keeping the organization moving in the right direction in spite of major political, bureaucratic, and resource barriers. Leaders appeal "to very basic, but often untapped, human needs, values, and emotions" (Kotter, 1990, pp. 3–5).

Management may be adequate for achieving some instrumental organizational purposes, but leadership is vital for generating and directing expressive energy. The charismatic leadership style, so prevalent in the nonprofit sector, is functional for those organizations in the sector that understand how to work with "gifted" personalities. Leaders are always important. They are especially important for instrumental-expressive organizations.

The voluntary component in organizations with major expressive ends endows leadership positions with extra potency. Citizens are stuck with their political leaders until death or the end of a term. Employees have little choice of bosses and must often make a life change to get new ones. However, a volunteer can abandon a leader between coffee break and lunch. Therefore, appealing leaders are crucial for voluntary sector success.

But precisely which leaders are responsible for producing expressive outputs? Should the focus be on leaders at the first-line supervisors' level, middle-management's level, or the CEO's level? The answer is yes. All leaders are responsible, although the most responsible should be the top leader, the chief executive officer. Responsibility for expressive behavior is a lot like responsibility for public relations. A specialist might be named to be responsible for PR. An organization might even give him or her the title of vice president. But when public relations go down the tube, the public wants the CEO's head to roll because it is he or she who is supposed to set the tone. Similarly, while it might be good management to assign expressive outputs to another office, the top leader is still the one to determine whether that office is doing the required work.

Styles of Leadership

Before we look at specific leadership styles, we can note some of the situations that call forth different styles of leadership. Gamson's intensive analysis showed that expressive leadership is typical in normative organizations, whereas instrumental leadership is more likely to appear in utilitarian ones and that communication of values, as distinct from mere knowledge or skills, is associated with expressive leadership (1967, p. 282).

Strong leadership is crucial during change. A relatively inexperienced helmsman can hold even the largest ship on an unchanging course, but steering even a tiny craft around dangerous shoals in a raging storm requires much more ability. The greater the potential for change, the more the ability required of leaders and the more people may think of changing leaders. Political incumbents are often both praised and criticized for the status quo. Political hopefuls promise how much better things will become when they are at the helm. Succession in business leadership may be less public and more orderly than in governments, but "under new management" is always meant to imply good changes.

Leadership style also has to do with power. Organizations endow their leaders with differing amounts of power. Fear of abuse of power causes many entities to provide no more power to individuals than is necessary for them to execute the specific tasks assigned to them. Power can intoxicate the heart, so organizations fear that no leader is good enough to trust with unlimited power.

The attention Etzioni gave to appropriate leadership styles as they relate to the expressive aspects of normative organizations is particularly helpful. (One way to distinguish between the formal and informal leaders mentioned in the following passage is to recognize that people elect or appoint the first while they spontaneously follow the second.)

> Expressive activities usually require moral involvement of the actor, Hence, they are best supervised by elites having normative power over the performers, for normative power, we have seen, is most supportive to moral involvement. Although this power may be derived from a position, personal characteristic, or both, personal rather than official normative power tends to be more effective. Hence the elites that are most likely to control expressive activities effectively are informal or formal leaders; officers, who have the power of office but little of their own, are less effective. Informal leaders tend to be more effective than formal ones because . . . they can be more 'purely' expressive [1975, p. 208].

Etzioni hypothesized that people rely more on expressive leadership than instrumental leadership in the more normative organizations and that we associate the communication of values with expressive leadership.

Yet another way to look at the situations in which leadership occurs is to recognize that leaders face followers inside the organization and the general population outside the organization in the social environment. They are like the tiny center of an hour-glass, controlling what flows from one end to the other. They interpret the environment and control much of how it affects the organization, and they are the organization's agent in dealing with the world outside. Some leaders work well in both directions. Most are better at one job than the other.

Leaders come in many sizes, colors, and shapes, and exhibit a wide variety of styles. The basic styles of leadership are as follows:

Autocratic.   All authority and decision making is centered in the leader. A military leader or ship's captain is a good example. For a charismatic leader to function in an autocratic mode, he or she must have a compelling cause or crisis and a clear, undiffused goal.

Laissez-faire, or free rein.   The laissez-faire leader assumes the role of a group member. She or he assumes the followers are self-motivated. An example is the leader of a sports team.

Participative, or democratic.   The participative leader gains the cooperation of followers by allowing them to participate in decision making. An example is a congregational church.

During the 1930s, Kurt Lewin and his colleagues at the University of Iowa launched their empirical study of leadership. They found a greater amount of aggressiveness in autocratic groups, both in reacting to the leader and in interacting with others. Their research revealed greater attention to group-minded suggestions and work-minded conversations in both the laissez-faire and democratic groups. However, their study also showed that laissez-faire and democratic leadership differed significantly: the lower level of psychological involvement among employees in the laissez-faire groups resulted in less work and poorer work than in the democratic groups (Lewin, Lippitt, and White, 1939).

Tannenbaum and Schmidt (1973, p. 165) describe a continuum of possible leadership actions that are contingent on the leader, the situation, and the workers and that reflect the styles described above.

1. The boss makes a decision and announces it to the workers.
2. The boss makes a decision and "sells" it to the workers.
3. The boss presents an idea and initiates questions.
4. The boss makes a tentative decision, then listens to discussion with the possibility of modifying the decision.

5. The boss presents a problem and gets suggestions, then makes a decision.
6. The boss defines constraints, then asks workers to decide.
7. The boss permits workers to function.

Supervisors and managers who see employees as whole human beings rather than just workers consistently get the best results. Likert (1961) found that study after study showed that treating people as human beings rather than as cogs in a machine is a variable highly related to the attitudes and motivation of subordinates at every level. The superior whose attitude and behavior demonstrated that he or she saw the subordinate as a whole human being was perceived by subordinates to have the following qualities:

- Is supportive, friendly, and helpful rather than hostile
- Shows confidence in the integrity, ability, and motivations of subordinates
- Shows confidence in subordinates, which leads him or her to have high expectations for workers' level of performance
- Sees that each subordinate is well trained for the particular job
- Coaches and assists employees whose performance is below standard

Finally, Warren Bennis (1984) studied ninety effective leaders. He found four competencies in each of his effective subjects. They focused on commitment to a vision or an agenda. They communicated and interpreted the vision so others aligned themselves with the vision. They maintained a reliable, consistent posture. They knew their strengths and deployed them effectively. Ideally, a leader's style should match the needs of the organization and the demands of a given situation. However, individual leaders mature in their competency or wane in their energy. Organizations do the same. Situations constantly change, so organizations must usually be content with an optimum rather than an ideal match. The material presented here should assist participants in selecting an optimum match.

I now shift to a consideration of charismatic leadership because my research showed what a profound influence such leadership exerts on voluntary organizations (Mason, 1993). Charismatic leadership may overlie the autocratic and democratic, and occasionally even the laissez-faire styles. Charisma has more to do with a leader's source of power than with his or her style in exercising that power.

Charismatic Leadership

The Branch Davidian cult attributed extraordinary charismatic powers to David Koresh, as did John Kennedy's fans to the young president, as did members of the People's Temple to Jim Jones, as did allied troops to Dwight Eisenhower. The audiences for Michael Jackson, Selena Quintanilla-Perez, and Joe Montana and the followers of Boris Yeltsin and Martin Luther King, Jr., similarly found a charismatic quality in these performers and leaders. People seek the *collective effervescence* of charismatic experiences (Durkheim, 1934), and it is a special kind of leader who precipitates these experiences, which are essential for expressive outputs.

Voluntary and nonprofit organizations are an appropriate environment for the collective effervescence precipitated by charismatic personalities and provide many events and sites for them. Charismatic leaders are plentiful and effective in the sector. They elicit energy in the form of time, talent, and money, heighten motivation and aspiration, and infuse and mold values. The voluntary sector needs these powerful personalities. They are one of its chief assets whether, as Shakespeare said, they are born great, achieve greatness, or have greatness thrust upon them.

My data on charismatic leadership come from three sources. The first source is a survey I conducted with 142 successful voluntary and nonprofit organizations in eleven states. The organizations ranged from tiny volunteer groups to ten of the United Way's top seventeen. The fields they operate in include health, education, and welfare, among other areas. Some are trade associations. Some are foundations. I intentionally omitted churches and other spiritual religious organizations because I assumed that they would tend more than other types of organization to gravitate to the charismatic leader. Eighty-eight percent of the founders of these 142 organizations were perceived as charismatic leaders. Second, I systematically contrasted a list of fifty-four charismatic leaders and fifty-four noncharismatic leaders I have personally known or observed. Third, although this chapter does not look at all the literature that Conger reviewed so well (1989), it draws on published research in sociology, political science, business management, and the rare input dealing specifically with the voluntary sector. The recent interest in organizational culture has elicited a number of studies on charismatic leaders and their relation to their organizations' cultures (Avolio and Bass, 1987; Boal and Bryson, 1988; House, 1987; Pfeffer, 1981; Pondy, 1978). Several writers have specified negative aspects of charismatic leadership (Bennis, 1989b; Conger, 1990; Conger, Kanungo, and Associates, 1988; Kets de Vries, 1988; Roberts and Bradley, 1988; Zaleznik, 1989).

Innovative charismatics pouring out their lives for a cause founded most voluntary and nonprofit organizations. Gifted leaders are too valuable to be shunted away from the leadership track. Not only are they virtually essential in establishing a movement, but existing organizations also need leaders who can be heros when an organization requires transformation or revitalization or faces distress, change, or rapid growth (Bass, 1985; Conger, Kanungo, and Associates, 1988; Kuhnert and Lewis, 1987; Yukl, 1989). Charismatic leadership is and always has been an appropriate style for voluntary organizations because of their dependence on eliciting contributed time, money, and other resources (Mason, 1992). Writers have used the term *charismatic* for two millennia to designate qualities considered so mysterious that they must be gifts from God. I feel that recent researchers tend to neglect charismatic leaders in relation to their importance. Objective, patient, rational, meticulous researchers are often on the opposite end of the personality scale from charismatics who tend to be emotional, subjective, people oriented, impatient, and prone to rear their white horses on their hind legs as the riders brandish their glistening swords toward a distant enemy. Nevertheless, scholars should focus on the relationship of charismatics and their organizations if they are to better understand leadership in the sector and have a profound positive impact on our organizations (Mason, 1992, p. 14). Avoidance of charismatic leaders would alter the culture of the sector and limit the effectiveness of its component entities.

While charisma is still somewhat mysterious, Conger, Kanungo, and Associates have suggested that charismatic leaders' effectiveness consists of formulating a vision and instilling faith, articulating the vision, building and maintaining trust, and symbolizing (1988, p. 34).

A charismatic personality with a vision can seem to float in a solution with a group in distress, with no change taking place. *Faith* is the catalyst that links the leader and the group and precipitates action. The followers' faith sees a leader's strategic vision matching their own aspirations. Faith empowers the leader's ability to harness a tremendous amount of human energy and ensure a group's commitment. Such faith is primarily an emotional rather than a rational reaction and allows the leader to attract the loyalty, trust, commitment, and involvement of followers (see Avolio and Bass, 1987; Conger, Kanungo, and Associates, 1988). Followers with faith willingly obey and trust the leader. They become attached to him or her and have a sense of empowerment and group cohesion around their shared faith in the leader's vision. Zaleznik refers to the "strong feelings of identity and deference or of love and hate. Human relations in leader-dominated structures often appear turbulent, intense, and at times even disorganized. Such an atmosphere intensifies individual motivation and often produces unanticipated outcomes" (1989, p. 132).

Faith in a charismatic leader's vision of a desirable future generates tremendous energy that becomes available for change. That is why charismatic leaders are virtually essential at the beginning of an organization, when it needs revitalization, or when it faces distress, change, or rapid growth. Let us look at aspects of a charismatic leader's power in formulating a vision, articulating that vision, building and maintaining trust, and symbolizing.

Formulating a Vision

Vision has to do with seeing. A vision is more than talking about an idea, it is conceptualizing a picture of the future others can see in their mind's eye. Charismatics have the imagination to see beyond current realities, to imagine the desired future as if it already exists in the present. As the charismatic leader Napoleon noted, "Imagination rules the world" (Conger, 1989, p. 37).

Effective leaders possess a frame of reference that enables them to "put the whole of life in perspective, to envision goals which encompass the needs of the common person, to draw out the best and downplay the worst in followers, to elicit the courage for followers to be the best that they can become, to call forth hidden capacities, to work miracles and wonders in the names of goodness, wisdom, justice, and love" (Mitchell, 1990, p. 103). An ideal vision is a clear overall strategy that is involving, relevant, linked to needs, memorable, meaningful beyond work, and seen as a challenge to move toward something better than the present situation.

Articulating the Vision

How can a visionary help followers share in ownership of a vision? The Points of Light Foundation found that high effectiveness in utilizing volunteers in community service organizations included laying a foundation for service through mission and vision. The mission was framed in terms of the problem or issue the organization was addressing. A positive vision was clearly articulated, widely shared, and openly discussed throughout the organization. Volunteers were treated as valuable human resources that could directly contribute to achievement of the organization's mission.

Lenin is purported to have launched the Communist Revolution by vividly articulating his vision: "The Tsar is dead, the land is yours, go and take it!" Lenin had sensed an opportunity and formulated a vision perceived as an end desired by followers. In his formula, he stated the opportunity, shared the vision, and called for action. He could have phrased the vision like this: "Our beloved Russia is currently enjoying a leadership vacuum. Why should an oligarchy of royalty and hereditary landowners maintain control of the land and other national resources? The people who have worked the land, and who are now in such sore distress, have as much or more right to it as anyone. I therefore strongly suggest that the people, themselves, undertake a program of acquiring the land for their own use. Take advantage of this opportunity and begin the process."

Instead, his manner of articulating the vision was emotional and charismatic, designed to pluck the sympathetic cords of the aspirations of his audience, encapsulating their dreams better than they could have themselves. My apocryphal rational version lacked the charismatic touch. Charismatic leaders, says Conger, "may also sense that by creating perceptions of a freely chosen commitment they can tap deeper reservoirs of motivational energy within their subordinates . . . [creating a] powerful bond that is unique to charismatic leaders. It results in performance that is often far beyond expectations and certainly beyond that achieved by most organizations. It also results in a level of commitment and loyalty to the leader and his mission that is quite rare" (Conger, 1989, p. 125).

Building and Maintaining Trust

Trust precipitates confidence that the leader's vision is the solution to followers' distress and will bring about desired change. Causes usually require sustained effort long beyond an initial surge of energy. The vision, once unfurled, must elicit continued effort, commitment, energy, and encouragement. Charismatic leaders may restate the vision so many times that it loses its efficacy. The most ardent followers tire, stagger, and need support. Followers hunger for affirmation, reassurance, and the renewed energy of sustained trust in the leader for the difficult climb ahead, and charismatic leaders feed these hungers. They "show a sympathetic concern for the welfare of their followers, rather than concern for self-interest" (Conger, 1989 p. 104). "Developing other people's talents, caring for others, staying in touch, listening, understanding, feeling responsible, taking initiative, empowering, and including others in decision making are highly correlated with the perception of effective leadership" (Conger, 1992, p. 129).

Trust is characteristically established, enhanced, and maintained through the perception of the charismatic leader as a unique individual. McGregor described the phenomenon this way:

Since human beings respond most deeply to other human beings, there should be something in the leader which differentiates him from the crowd and marks him as unique. It is in the nature of style that it does not fit a standardized pattern in human personality but is a variable attribute peculiarly distinct and specific to its possessor. At the same time, whatever it is, it must touch a responsive chord in other people. It may involve a whole gamut of human qualities . . . clarity of mind and expression, sustained enthusiasm, sympathy, courage, wisdom, originality, humor, sensitivity, and cultural refinement. However style is expressed, it must be a visible manifestation of unique personality [McGregor, 1960, p. 29].

In field studies that compared charismatic to noncharismatic leaders, Conger consistently found the charismatics to be more effective and powerful speakers (1989, p. 69). Charismatic leaders are immensely persuasive. They derive deep satisfaction from persuasive processes. Warren Bennis (1989a, p. 13), too, writes of "leading from voice," in which trust is the underlying element. He says leading from voice can and should be present in all organizations but is a necessary condition in any situation in which the leader is dealing with volunteers. Bennis lists four characteristics of leaders who generate and sustain trust.

1. *Constancy.* Whatever surprises leaders themselves may face, they do not create any for the group. Leaders are all of one piece; they stay the course.
2. *Congruity.* True leaders walk their talk. There is no gap between the theories they espouse and the life they practice.
3. *Reliability.* Leaders are there when it counts; they are ready to support their co-workers in the moments that matter.
4. *Integrity.* Leaders honor their commitments and promises.

Symbolizing

Evangelist Jimmy Swaggart's fall had nothing to do with his singing, speaking, or managing skills. It had everything to do with his contradicting through his behavior the values he espoused. The effective ethical leader models the values of his or her organization. Pat Buchanan should not have owned a Mercedes at the time he spoke against foreign cars. Perhaps the charismatic leader's symbolizing and embodying the vision instills deep and abiding trust most effectively. "They embody and personify collective goals and aspirations so intensely that other needs—those of both the leaders and the led—may be swallowed in the purposes of the movement" (Burns, 1978, p. 248). As followers internalize the values of the leader, the leader becomes the ego-ideal, the model, of the potential followers; followers' commitment is the internalization of the values and beliefs that the leader symbolizes (Mitchell, 1990, p. 159).

Charismatic leadership occurs and is valuable at various organizational levels, not exclusively at the pinnacle. Departments, chapters, and smaller subunits can benefit from such leadership.

Since successful founders exercise a charismatic style more often than not, they are valuable in the formation of new units or the introduction of new services.

Born or Made?

Training may enhance charisma, but we have not reached a point where education can create a charismatic leader. There is no orchard where we can pluck one. Charismatic leaders are where you find them—wherever a body of people is following and acknowledging a person with charisma. Identifying leadership candidates inside the organization must be exercised with great caution. Importing one from outside the organization may or may not work. A leader may be more easily acknowledged as charismatic when coming from the outside, without negative baggage ("a prophet is not without honor except in his own country"). But charisma is often specific to a situation, and may not travel well from one organization or cause to another. Not every leader with the capacity to exercise a charismatic style does so in every position or at all times.

Moreover, different types of charismatic personalities can be contrasted on the basis of dyadic criteria, and one dyad of special importance for nonprofits has to do with the audience on which the leader concentrates. One leader may direct his or her message toward a general public, such as all the members and potential members of an organization at the base of the organizational pyramid. Another type may direct his or her message to an intervening tier of subordinates, intensively inspiring intermediaries and enabling them to influence the broad base of members and potential members.

Top leadership and rank-and-file members alike must take full advantage of the leader's massive contributions while developing an understanding and tolerance for her or his weaknesses and blind spots. Neutralize or compensate for negative qualities by proper management procedures, because the gifts of the leader are not likely to be easily found with a classified ad under "Savior Wanted."

However, one school of thought believes organizations can effectively develop synthetic charisma in their leaders. An experiment by Harvard University psychologist Ellen Langer and her associates showed that people can get their way by using the word "because" to preface even nonsensical reasons for compliance. She said it is a response of the human brain to obey after hearing this potent B-word (Langer, Blank, and Chanowitz, 1978, pp. 16–18). A group of experts in nonverbal communication (what I called involuntary expression in Chapter Three) believe that persons perceived as charismatic were simply more animated than other people (Friedman, Prince, Riggio, and DiMatteo, 1980). Therefore, a leader might simulate or create charisma by exaggerating head and body movements, touching others more, smiling more often, and talking faster and with greater clarity. Adolf Hitler diligently studied the work of the mass psychologists of his day and used some of their techniques to evoke the compliance of the masses. There is evidence that John Kennedy, after visiting with movie stars in his teens, intentionally set out to acquire charisma (Collier and Horowitz, 1984, p. 4).

Ronald E. Riggio (1987) has identified six dimensions of social skill associated with charisma: emotional expressivity, emotional sensitivity, emotional control, social expressivity, social sensitivity, and social control. He believes people can correct their deficiencies in these areas through exercise, as they would exercise their muscles.

Since the charisma some speakers have with large audiences can almost be equated with "presence" and spellbinding speaking ability, some believe that teaching effective public speaking techniques develops charisma. Dale Carnegie, in his day, and the organization that still bears his name have conducted a successful business on this foundation. However, this view brings us full circle—can one *make* a great speaker, or merely identify and evoke a great speaker's latent ability?

The series of psychological techniques identified by John Grinder and Richard Bandler and called neurolinguistic programming can apply to leadership. For example, *mirroring* can induce the same response as rapport. Mirroring builds rapport as one person matches his or her posture, movements, voice tone and tempo, and breathing with that of the individual with whom he is communicating. When two people find something in common, they develop rapport that breaks down barriers and facilitates cooperation. Applied with skill, mirroring builds instant rapport (Cohen, 1992, p.38–39). An organization can, of course, train people in such manipulative techniques.

The Points of Light Foundation found that high effectiveness in utilizing volunteers in community service organizations included combining inspiring leadership with effective management. As long as charismatics exercise their mysterious power, the organizations they lead need to understand how best to harness their potency. While charismatic figures lead and inspire, someone must be at hand to polish their armor, maintain their stock of silver bullets, feed, groom, and water their horses—and shovel the manure.

A Down Side

Charismatic leaders are not without their liabilities. They can so dominate an organization, as happened with the Branch Davidians, that the alternatives may appear limited to complete submission, elimination of the leader, or abandonment of the cause. We must also remember that a charismatic personality is not necessarily a good or admirable person. Adolf Hitler, Jim Jones, and David Koresh were charismatic leaders, yet they are not now admired by outsiders, and each brought his organization crashing down around him. However, in most cases, the entity benefits from charismatics, accepting their assets and adapting to their liabilities. Charisma does not correlate with righteousness. Because of their ability to communicate and mesmerize their audiences, charismatics have proven their ability to manipulate large numbers of followers to their detriment. Fortunately, most of the adverse aspects of charisma are not as dramatic as mass suicide.

Consider now some of these liabilities and some ways of harnessing these sometimes illogical leaders as they ride their spirited white horses. I do not undertake to identify all the liabilities of charismatic leaders, nor every effective adaptation of the organization to charismatic leadership, but I spotlight many important considerations.

Some horses are too wild to harness. They are either released into the wilderness or shot. Some charismatic human beings are also too wild to harness. Some types of charismatics in this category are incompetent, deranged, unethical, and untrustworthy; those who pursue lost causes; and those who abuse their power. Such individuals constitute a class without sufficient redeemable aspects to maintain the leader-follower relationship. If possible, appropriate action includes the discharge, commitment, or arrest of these leaders. (It is interesting that most targets of assassination are powerful charismatics.) If these alternatives are immoral or impossible, the ethical follower's only course is desertion or abandonment. The point here is that the presence of a powerful leader does not absolve the organization from its responsibility to develop checks and balances on the leader's power and blind spots.

There are other liabilities, however, that organizations can live with although they may require organizational adaptation for optimum results. I have placed them into two classifications. The first consists of weaknesses that require a complement. These weaknesses are typical of many charismatic personalities. The second group consists of corollary weaknesses, liabilities that are the other side of the coin of leader strengths.

Complementary Weaknesses

Ethical charismatic leaders may rapidly leapfrog to success, jumping over routine procedures and processes considered essential by more mundane managers. Charismatics, particularly in the short term, may lead organizations to great heights only to see their successes jeopardized by loose ends and blind spots. The charismatic crisis mode may suffice in the short term, yet the loose ends must be tied together eventually to prevent the fabric from unraveling in the long term. The loose ends and blind spots are rarely unethical or intentional but are sins of omission. The leader means no harm but has focused intently on the big picture, considering the "details" trivial.

Responses to my survey included the following remarks about certain charismatic leaders: "didn't build an organization," "weak on important administrative details," "neglected management skills," "did not follow through," "too loose and informal," and "didn't delegate." Such comments are symptomatic of complementary weaknesses. The following descriptions detail some complementary weaknesses that may be tolerable to a degree but that may also become intolerable.

Substitution of excitement for substance.   Leaders may spend much of their time inspiring those within the organization and advocating the cause to the public. Both activities may create a charismatic experience and excitement for followers. "The leader needs to project ideas into images that excite people, and only develop choices that give the projected images substance. Consequently, leaders create excitement in work" (Zaleznik, 1989, p. 129). Such an emphasis, while effective, may result in the kinds of neglect of task accomplishment complained about in my survey. However, as George Bernard Shaw observed, "Reasonable men adapt themselves to their environment; unreasonable men try to adapt their environment to themselves. Thus all progress is the result of the efforts of unreasonable men." And thus some "unreasonableness" in charismatic leaders of nonprofits, some task neglect, may be necessary to get progress.

However, organizations must be on the lookout for leaders who have become too unreasonable, too neglectful of tasks. In south Texas, we say, "All hat, no cattle." It refers to the drugstore cowboy, with the ten-gallon hat and cowboy boots and belt, who is all show and does not know a steer from a dogie. To coin a related term, there is a kind of charismatic cavalry that is "All bugle, no gun." An exclusive emphasis on generating excitement can wear thin. Expectations may be hard to back up.

Idealized visions that fly away from reality.   Idealistic charismatic leaders often have a heightened sense of destiny. However, this, too, can get out of hand. At times, the more idealistic they are, the more accolades they receive, and the more they drift away from reality and lose touch with the real world of what their followers are struggling to accomplish. They are emotionally disturbed by efforts to attract their attention to routine problems. Their idealistic view, the view from the clouds, is far more attractive than the grubby world below. The greater their commitment to their vision, the less willing they may be to see the viability of competing approaches. Charismatics are more likely to pursue failing goals than are other leaders (Conger, 1989, p.137).

Unawareness of fundamentals.   Charismatic leaders often wear intellectual blinders. They attain their objectives without learning the routine skills and disciplines required of their less gifted counterparts. They are like the beautiful girls and football heros who achieve popularity in high school without developing interpersonal skills that benefit them in adulthood. In the short term, charismatics may lead organizations to great heights, only to see their success jeopardized by their neglect of the orderly, professionally calculative approach to work that managerial leadership fosters (Berlew and LeClere, 1974).

Charismatic leaders tend to be unaware of and untutored in the fundamentals of administering an organization. This is particularly true in organizations that draw leaders from groups of persons whose educational background is in a specialized program discipline rather than general management. The mind-set of these leaders may blind them to standard ways of dealing with matters that they have successfully dealt with intuitively. They tend to delegate responsibility without relinquishing authority (Greenberg and Greenberg, 1990, p. 142). They are excited by ideas but, at times, may be poor implementers (Conger, 1989, p.157).

Neglect of real-world needs of followers.   The world of charismatic leaders is often one of the ecstasy of ideas, anticipation of fulfilled hope, and the adulation of disciples. They single mindedly pursue their dreams, often living ascetic lifestyles. They can easily forget that their followers may not have reached their level of dedication. Followers may live in a world of relationships with spouses and children; demands of mortgages, car payments, and unmown lawns; needs for days off and vacations. Neglect of real-world everyday needs of followers may lead to followers' short-term frustration and long-term disillusionment because of the commitment required of them and the personal risks involved.

Erratic, impetuous, and overstimulated behavior.   Many charismatics live in a field of dreams. Their minds are challenged and bombarded with mental and emotional stimuli of creative change, ideas, opportunities, and hopes. Their realm of innovation, persuasion, and initiation moves faster than their subordinates' realm of engineering the dreams of leadership to fit daily reality, the realm of nuts and bolts, problem solving, limited resources, and the nitty and gritty. Charismatics can stir up more to do in a week than can be done in a year, and next week, they may bring in another load. It is often the subordinates' job to sort through this wealth of opportunity, and prioritize, selecting what is possible for optimum implementation.

Ignoring of supporting systems and structure.   Some charismatic leaders take their organizations' systems and structures for granted. They act impulsively. Their personnel choices are based on the personal impressions rather than on the managerial competence of candidates. There is no systematic development of subordinates. Input from the managerial tier is neither sought nor heeded. The house is built on sand. As Zaleznik put it, "the presence of great leaders may undermine the development of managers who become very anxious in the relative disorder that leaders seem to generate" (1989, p. 125). Conger also notes the tendency to fail to consider contrary opinions or facts. He advises leaders, "You must learn to rein your enthusiasm in for a moment and coldly consider information that might challenge your mission. Finally, you have a great power in your hands—the dependence and commitment of your subordinates" (1989, p. 175). Indeed, subordinates are reluctant to disagree with one whose approval or disapproval is so vital, and in this way, potentially valuable ideas and information are stifled.

Warren Bennis relates a story about Nikita Khrushchev's appearance at the Washington Press Club that tells us much about the behavior of members of the inner circle of powerful personalities. The first written question for Khrushchev was: "Today you talked about the hideous rule of your predecessor, Stalin. You were one of his closest aides and colleagues during those years. What were you doing all that time?"

As he heard the question, Khrushchev's face grew red. "Who asked that?" he roared. No one answered.

"Who asked that?" he insisted. Again, silence.

"That is what I was doing," Khrushchev said (1991, p. 7).

Being close to a powerful charismatic leader is heavy wine. Proximity brings many benefits and much vulnerability. Confidants of impetuous personalities often have the opportunity to nudge them in one direction or the other. Such opportunities carry much responsibility for the ethical subordinate. Let me plead for balance. While a loose cannon may need to be secured, do not throw it overboard.

A present trend toward recreating voluntary and nonprofit organizations in the image of businesses incorrectly suggests that impersonal bureaucracy is superior to leadership (Derakhshan and Fatehi, 1985). Conger writes, "While famous for its creativity and

vision in the entrepreneurial sector, our business culture is woe-
fully unsupportive of these qualities in large corporations" (1989,
p. 162). A desire for more order and predictability also points in
the direction of the impersonal bureaucracy. Business almost
squeezed out the entrepreneurial spirit for this reason, and they
are now resurrecting it. I could name several major nonprofits that
intentionally and systematically restricted innovation and individual decision making to move to a riskless group-think posture. Year
after year, their membership numbers decline dramatically—but
predictably!

Denial of personal limitations.   Human beings developed organizations because groups can accomplish some things better than
individuals working alone. Charismatic leaders tend to forget this
fact. They have the same hours in each day as their colleagues.
They can lift a finite number of pounds, talk to a finite number of
people, occupy just one space at a time, keep up their interest only
so long, remember just so many facts, and go without food for a
finite number of hours. They are subject to fatigue and burnout.
If the charismatic is the only hub of the wheel, his or her limitations constrain an organization's capacity to function beyond those
limits (Nadler and Tushman, 1990).

Arrogance.   There are reasons why charismatic leaders become
arrogant. There is much glamour associated with charisma, but
arrogance is still dysfunctional. It is usually in the organization's
interests and in the interests of top aides to build the leader's image,
and feed his or her ego. The problem comes when the leader
begins to believe the press releases. "When cults develop around
leaders, they begin to believe in their own infallibility, and anyone
who believes that he or she can do no wrong is a menace to him- or
herself as well as to the rest of us. [Moreover] they behave like mini-
emperors, getting rid of dissenters or those who might have better
ideas, . . . building their individual power bases at the expense of
the greater community" (Bennis, 1989b, pp. 72–73).

Arrogance is counterproductive because it is distasteful to
those subjected to it and because it blinds the arrogant one. Arrogant people are so convinced they are right, they do not see the
reality of valuable alternatives or accept realistic limitations. They
begin to believe in their own infallibility. Charisma, with its sense
of preeminence, authority, and power, creates arrogance and a

great need for visibility. The most charismatic and probably ablest American military leader in memory was Douglas MacArthur. Yet in the end, his charisma made him so arrogant that he brushed aside orders from President Truman, his commander-in-chief, disregarded all the warnings of a Chinese counterattack in Korea, and blundered into disastrous—and totally unnecessary—defeat.

Alienation of valuable participants.   Charismatics' magnetic personalities attract people. Their strong personalities are hard to ignore. However, the qualities that attract some may repel others. Often those who are turned off as a group are more nearly the leaders' peers than the rank and file, are those who would have been good for the cause or organization. Charismatics also may repulse individual followers, peers, and superiors. "As unconventional advocates of radical reform, they may alienate whole segments of their organization" (Conger, 1989, p. 154). Many prominent Iranians welcomed and adored the Ayatollah Khomeini. At the same time, Iran experienced a brain drain with the mass exodus of hundreds of thousands of well-educated members of the new Iranian middle class.

Clay feet.   Charismatic leaders enjoy high visibility as representative symbols of their cause and organization. Trusting, adoring followers who perceive them as virtually infallible surround them. If they lapse or are perceived to be tainted through sexual, financial, or other failures, all hell breaks loose, and an organizational crisis ensues.

Corollary Weaknesses

By corollaries, I mean conditions or traits that are inversely related to other traits or conditions. The corollary liabilities described here are the consequences of charisma, the other side of the coin. They would not exist if the charisma did not exist. However, eliminating them absolutely might require abandoning positive charismatic benefits.

One who has the positive assets of a charismatic leader often has certain negative aspects as well. Members may elect to follow the charismatic in spite of the negatives and then must live with the bad as a correlate of the good that (in a voluntary organization) they have freely chosen.

Such responses to my nonprofit organization survey as, "He has a one-track mind," "Subordinates can't keep up," "She's always on stage," and, "We became too dependent," suggest the presence of negative corollaries to good traits. Among the negative corollaries to charismatic assets are the leader's subjective emotional appeal, the tendency to favor direct personal power over structure, limitations on success and growth, organizational overdependence on the leader, a successor vacuum, and a primary focus on change.

Subjective emotional appeal. Charismatic leadership involves an affective, illogical, subjective, emotional relationship between a leader and those who attribute charisma to that leader. Therefore all aspects of the organization must put up with this emotionally based relationship. One does not throw out the baby with the bath water. Organizations are well advised to compensate a right-brain approach with a left-brain supplement. Both heart and head are essential, especially if the organization seeks to recruit and retain a strong tier of capable elites. Organizations might follow Weber's counsel (1946) and begin a long-term process of routinization of charisma to dissipate power throughout organizational processes, making power impersonal rather than personal.

Direct personal power over adherents. Not only is charismatics' appeal emotional, but it is also communicated directly to the constituency. Charismatics express a dyadic love relationship in their communication with the rank and file (Lindholm, 1990). "They . . . transform the needs, values, preferences, and aspirations of followers," write House, Spangler, and Woycke. "These leaders motivate followers to make significant personal sacrifices in the interest of some mission and to perform above and beyond the call of duty. Followers become less motivated by self-interest and more motivated to serve the interests of the larger collective" (1991, p. 368).

In the same vein, Conger writes, "Through an appeal to higher-order need, perceptions of extraordinary ability, expressions of approval, high expectations, empowerment, and a sense of urgency, the charismatic leader is able to forge a bond with followers that can result in commitment and performance quite beyond the ordinary" (1989 p. 136).

We can visualize the tremendous power inherent in such a direct relationship. It depends on intervening systems only to the degree that the conduits between the leader and the masses control vital media and mailing lists. This is a threat to all who would maintain structural order. Without formal constraints or potent norms to the contrary, direct communication can be initiated with impunity, posing an awesome and intimidating problem. Charismatics regularly function outside formal structures and systems, ignoring channels of command and undermining and devastating the authority of intervening subordinates (Conger, 1989, p. 156).

In government and the independent sector, a Chairman Mao can always appeal to the base of the pyramid and begin a Great Leap Forward. Politically, followers perceive the charismatic leader representing the rank and file in the midst of bureaucracy. This perception is the major basis of the leader's power. (Another point to remember is that the threat of a direct appeal may be more potent than its actual exercise.)

Success and growth limitations. Weber (1946) noted that leadership can remain charismatic only as long as the followers are few. Johnson (1992), addressing the subject of leaders of new religious movements, also observed that as an organization grows in numbers, access to the charismatic leader diminishes in frequency and intimacy. To grow beyond the size at which everyone has intimate contact with the leader, an organization must develop substitutes for this face-to-face relationship. Often, these substitutes are symbolic. Two worlds develop, the world of the leader and his or her inner circle and the world of the followers. Another step is the differentiation of the world of the leader and the world of those who keep the organization operating (Johnson, 1992). For the good of the organization, the evolution of this process accompanying growth must move smoothly and harmoniously.

Overdependence. Charismatic leaders are potent. They get things done. They generally get them done quicker, better, and in a greater magnitude than would be possible with more pedestrian means. Therefore, others in the organization can become addicted to their leader's empowerment (Conger, 1989, p. 157). Subordinates come to depend on leaders both in times of difficulty and in the good periods, and the organization will fail to develop alternative means of fulfilling such tasks as recruiting, raising funds, innovating, and building morale. When the leader is the only initiator of action, the rest of the organization may become passive or reactive (Nadler and Tushman, 1990).

Successor vacuum.   Closely related to the overdependence just described is the most traumatic event in the life of many organizations—the loss of the charismatic leader with no successor of equal ability at hand. An unanticipated vacancy can devastate an organization that relied too much on the ability of one individual. Charismatic leaders are rarely followed with successors of equal personal magnetism. Yet organizations must face the fact that charismatic leaders never last forever. They get sick, lose their charisma, grow old, go elsewhere, or are usurped. A leader-dependent organization without an adequate successor may not survive the loss. Nonprofit organizations often fail to ask the right questions early enough: What kind of leader will we need? Where will he or she come from? Will the followers follow? When should the successor be named? How will we make the transition?

There is no such thing as a one-person organization. As described earlier, the presence of a powerful leader does not absolve the balance of the organization from its responsibility to develop checks and balances on the leader's power and blind spots.

Failure to lead in the absence of a crisis.   Weber and others have written that crises are necessary for charismatic leaders to emerge (Weber, 1946; Bass, 1985; Bradley, 1987, Conger, Kanungo, and Associates, 1988). Weber saw these leaders as change agents for radical innovation and as inherently unstable, creating new value systems that collide with existing structures. What if there is no crisis? Might a leader precipitate periodic crises as opportunities for him or her to renew his or her claim to savior status? H. L. Mencken said, "The whole aim of practical politics is to keep the populace alarmed (and hence clamorous to be led to safety) by menacing it with an endless series of hobgoblins, all of them imaginary" (*Correct Quotes*, 1991). At least one leader has confided to me that his fundraising strategy consisted of precipitating two financial emergencies a year!

Crises are an excellent environment for those who love excitement, adventure, enemies to conquer, and flowing adrenaline. They are also great for unilateral action, because rules and bureaucratic constraints are typically relaxed in a crisis, and power is transferred from formal structures and systems to the charismatic leader (Conger, 1989, p. 174). But is a series of disrupting crises always healthy for an organization? I cannot definitively answer the question: How does the crisis environment affect organizational health? For several years, I worked in such a milieu (not of my own making) and saw two organizations learn to swim rather than sink. Both survived by becoming leaner and more effective. I suspect the liabilities and benefits of multiple crisis depend on the organizations, their leaders, their causes, and the specific situations they have gotten themselves into.

An Organizational Agenda

The organizations I surveyed used six basic means to deal with all the corollary and complementary liabilities they experienced: independent boards, management teams, informal counselors, normative controls, dual leadership, and formal policies.

Independent Board

Boards of trustees and directors probably originated as checks and balances for strong leaders. An organization led by a charismatic should have a strong board, executive committee, or other body as a check and balance against the excesses and vacuums often associated with charismatics. These governing boards must not be dependent on the organizational leader. Compared to the organization leader, board members should ideally be of equal or higher status, with appropriate experience, clout, and initiative to anticipate and supplement the leader's shortcomings.

The nature of charismatic leaders militates against the establishment of strong governing bodies. Care must be taken that the group is neither designed nor perceived as a coup in progress or as an advocate for bureaucracy. Lack of patience or wisdom by such a body can kill the charismatic goose that lays the golden eggs. Ideally, the group should represent the best the organization can muster, willing to move with glacial profundity in becoming a true partner with the leader, and able to grasp the organizational reins tightly yet allow the leader maximum slack.

Management Team with Authority

Many leaders bless the establishment of a senior team of managers to handle day-to-day operations and are willing to work in tandem with the team. The charismatic handles the expressive leadership and the team the instrumental. At other times, the team works with the board as a counterbalance to the charismatic. A strong professional support team needs to be developed to accomplish the following tasks:

- Utilize talent. Some effective and potentially effective leaders may be turned off by the domination of the charismatic. The organization may need to be able to accommodate to this leadership drain to some degree, as long as the charismatic is essential to its success. But it is pawning its future if it does not attract and hold new talent. A strong, meaningful team tier is one means of utilizing and retaining such persons. "Encourage the charismatic to surround himself with subordinates who are especially skilled at operational details and have strong connections to other areas of the company" (Conger, 1989, p. 172).
- Manage the organization if the leader lacks management skills, building the structure required to fulfill the organizational purpose while also capitalizing on the charismatic's skills while he or she is available, though not becoming completely dependent on those skills.
- Provide training, testing, and incentives for potential successors. The eventual successor may or may not exercise a charismatic style. Neither "assistant" charismatics in the present leader's clique nor faithful detail-conscious bureaucrats may be optimum successors. "Most leadership skills are either too complex to train or else too poorly understood to be trainable" (Conger, 1992a, p. 49).
- Provide counsel to the charismatic leader to gently steer him or her away from disastrous courses or persistent attempts to ride "dead horses" (failed objectives or methodologies). Team members should coordinate the leader's agenda with program priorities, and otherwise provide an objective point of view, acting as trusted friends who are willing to advise the emperor of his lack of attire.
- Provide data and counsel to the board or other appropriate body concerning potential negative trends as manifested by the charismatic. Be available and capable of shouting, "Don't drink the Kool-Aid!"

Informal Counselors

Another method of guiding a charismatic leader is to form, off the organization chart, an inner circle of respected "senior statesmen" with whom the leader can communicate, bouncing ideas off these informal counselors while they, in turn, help keep his or her feet on the ground. Supplicants and lobbyists go through individuals in this group for help in influencing the leader.

Normative Controls

Leaders, especially founders, play a major role in establishing and maintaining organizational culture and norms. Once established, normative controls are of greatest value in harnessing a leader who tends to move out of the accepted path and go off on a tangent.

Dual Leadership

An inside-outside leadership dyad is typical of many organizations. The charismatic leader represents the organization to the public and a more routinized manager keeps the machinery running. In some cases, the charismatic may be the true subordinate, looking to the manager for direction. The hospice movement in Great Britain, for example, founded by Cicely Saunders, adapted to changing circumstances and the need for followers and stability by becoming increasingly routinized, with division of authority, hierarchy of offices, training, separation of official activities from private ones, and procedural rules (James and Field, 1992).

Formal Policies

Many charismatic leaders try to be laws unto themselves. Codes of ethics, mission statements, formal strategies, and policy manuals by themselves cannot deter these leaders. However, these formal policies are excellent tools for guiding charismatics when skillfully exercised by boards, managers, and advisers.

Critics and Organized Opposition

In addition to these six means of handling the weaknesses of charismatic leaders, I should mention that everyone has critics.

Largely outside the control of the leader, managers, or other elites, they exert a degree of control over the behavior of any leader. However, their influence may be neither constructive nor in the best interests of the organization.

Conclusion

"Who was that masked man?" asked the beneficiaries of the Lone Ranger's brief charismatic sojourns. We should know more of the answer to our own versions of that question and more about how to deal with the next leader who appears astride a white horse. Leadership probably plays a more crucial role in nonprofits with an expressive dimension than in other organizations. There are different styles of effective leadership, but the charismatic style, if properly harnessed, may evoke the most dramatic progress. And proven methods are available to snatch a difficult charismatic relationship from the jaws of disaster. Also, a nonprofit organization might benefit by heeding what we now know of the dual nature of leadership. At various places in the organization—perhaps even at the top—nonprofits might well consider employing a leader-manager expressive-instrumental team.

Needs for Further Research

Scholars might identify nonfinancial managers who have successfully led organizations in both the voluntary and business sectors and find out what their experience has taught them about normative leadership in each sector. Researchers might also explore the scars that destructive charismatics often leave. Many organizations have gone through a difficult management transition at the loss of a charismatic leader. A comparative study of successful and unsuccessful transitions should be productive and useful.

Do scholars have a bias against charismatics, as I suggest? Scholars should focus on the relationship of charismatics and their organizations if they are better to understand leadership in the sector and have a profound positive impact on our organizations. Can it be demonstrated that charismatic leaders are worth the problems they may cause? Research into the ways and means of creating visions, enunciating them, and symbolizing them in an environment of trust; and ways of dealing with the leaders who threaten to turn sour could be applied with great effectiveness.

Scholars who are concentrating on a single organization or field might research the degree to which organizations are using the various means of harnessing leaders that I have suggested. Managers who work with charismatics should do the same.

Actions for Practitioners

Managers might classify the degree to which leaders at several levels of their organizations use personal magnetism. They might ask which are the most appropriate positions for charismatics in their organizations. If I were to recommend that an organization take one action at this point, I would suggest that if it does not utilize charismatic leaders, it do so; if it already does so, it should make certain that constraints are in place.

Managers might think of themselves as talent scouts whose ultimate success depends on their ability to identify persons with charismatic leadership potential. Paid and unpaid staff need not fear the potent personal leaders they encounter once their organizations take steps to harness these leaders. The next time their organizations scan the environment for a titular head of a fundraising effort, managers might take a chance with a charismatic personality rather than a traditional subdued city father or social matriarch. Fundraisers might identify an appropriate self-contained project to test the charismatic leader. Certainly, those responsible for providing an organization's instrumental outputs can identify an appropriate self-contained project to test a leader with charisma.

Charismatics tend to act fast and to precipitate change. Utilizing leaders of this type does not take years of development, and organizations should be prepared for this speed and not be caught off guard with many members left standing in a cloud of dust when the charismatic leader mounts a white horse and takes off. That is what charismatics are supposed to do.

This chapter discussed leaders, the catalysts who will make things happen. It noted differences between managers and leaders, described different types of leaders, suggested the charismatic leadership style as optimum for instrumental-expressive organizations, and prescribed the cultivation, selection, placement, and constraining of charismatic leaders. To this point, we have identified a long string of sequential management functions, a basket full of tools for dealing with concurrent needs, and a method for strengthening the substance and style of leadership. The next chapter describes how leaders can wield these tools to achieve abundant instrumental and expressive outputs.

Chapter Ten

Growing a Nonprofit Organization

I like to tell a story about three friends, an American, a German, and a Frenchman, graduating from Oxford at the top of the class of 1962. The gregarious American suggests they periodically update each other on their unfolding lives. The systematic German insists they meet every decade on their graduation anniversary. The romantic Frenchman hosts their first meeting in Paris, in 1972, to which they bring their wives to introduce them to their comrades. At their 1982 Frankfurt meeting, the German suggests that since all of them are earning reputations as distinguished scholars, their next meeting should include a presentation on a subject of common interest—the elephant.

At their 1992 meeting in Houston, the German ponderously drops on the table two thick leather-bound tomes titled *Eine Kurz Geschichte aus Elefanten* (A Short History of Elephants). The Frenchman presents the American and the German with elegant morocco-bound, silk-sewn, India-paper volumes embossed in gold leaf: *L'Amour des Eléphants*. Finally, the American passes a cardboard carton around the table, encouraging his friends to take several copies of his paperback: *How to Grow Bigger and Better Elephants*.

Americans do tend to equate bigger with better, except for the size of our files at the IRS and our waistlines. Conversations among nonprofit executives at annual conventions are full of "Growth Since I Came" stories. And why not? Growth is usually as good an indication of general organizational health, vitality, and accomplishment as any other measure. *It is certainly a measure of an organization's attraction for people seeking opportunities for collective expressive activity.*

Besides increasing organizations' size, the growth process improves organizational life in many ways. There may be negative effects too, but the positive benefits usually predominate. This chapter uncovers reasons why expansion is important in nonprofit organizations seeking optimum expressive outputs, describes a proven means of growth through expressive groups that is rarely discussed outside of ecclesiastical circles, and illustrates how to apply that method through a program for building the conditions for natural growth into an organization's systems. The process I will describe also serves as an example of the power of intrinsic expressive motivation to transform organizations in ways other than enlarging their size.

Many voluntary enterprises have as little understanding of their growth process as Topsy in *Uncle Tom's Cabin*, who observed, "I 'spect I jest grow'd. Don't think nobody ever made me." Their growth is often a by-product of external factors, such as the availability of markets, an expanding population or economy, a need to respond to legislative decisions, a swing of public opinion, or a publicity windfall. All such stimuli are accidental from the point of view of organizational processes. Leaders cannot make them happen; they can only exploit the opportunity after it occurs.

Growth may also be a serendipitous result of intentional activities, such as improvement in services, increased funding, or the emergence of a new charismatic leader. Again, this growth is more a by-product than the direct result of an intentional effort. An intentional burst of activity in a membership drive, a volunteer recruitment effort, or a fundraising campaign may move an organization forward for the duration of the effort. Yet without propitious conditions, an organization can no more produce consistent growth than dogs can routinely walk on their hind legs or swimmers can make steady headway against a current. In each case, any progress is hard, uncertain, and short-lived. Dogs walk best on all fours, and swimmers swim best with no current. However, organizations can design natural expressive growth environments and stimulate growth as an integral part of its systems, just as growth occurs in a chicken because the design for growth is in its egg.

Before I discuss growth in more detail, lest the reader think that I mean bigger is better in every situation, I will say some good things about smallness. My earlier attention to the importance of small subgroups within organizations should provide some reassurance that I am not going to suggest abandoning the benefits of the bond between a group of friends united in a quest for a common goal, in shared values, and in appreciation of each other for what each person is, warts and all. Camaraderie, the sense of security, the learning from shared experiences, and the mutual support of a group of friends are qualities cherished and retained in the process we will explore. Furthermore, such expressive benefits of group participation are the key elements of the plan that follows.

Chester Barnard, the successful telephone company executive who wrote the insightful management classic *The Functions of the Executive*, observed that organizational growth comes only from the creation of new organizational units or the grouping of two or more existing units (1938, p. 110). When we start viewing a voluntary enterprise as a living system—an organism rather than a machine—we find it can reproduce itself. It is an open system, importing energy from its environment as it produces new units, like an organism producing living cells. Barnard wrote that many organizations can trace the roots of their structure to the early Christian church, the empire of Charlemagne, and the government of William the Conqueror. He saw that two of the ways new organizations begin are as "infant bodies set off by an existing parent organization" and as "the result of segmentation of existing organizations caused by schism, rebellion, or the interposition of an external force" (1938, pp. 101–102).

Organizations can enjoy the power, visibility, economies of scale, and other benefits of size and simultaneously enjoy the benefits of smaller groups by co-opting the advantages of smaller units under the umbrella of the larger whole. The beautiful aspect of this approach is that it enables and can facilitate the enlargement of the whole.

Organizations grow by drawing in from outside themselves more units than they lose. These units may be in the form of new members, of resources such as dollars and volunteer time, or of service units. An organization does its work by eliciting some form of outside energy, storing it, and then releasing it in accomplishing organizational tasks. This process builds growth into the nature of the organization itself.

Advantages of Growth

There are many desirable benefits of the growth process. Growth and life are virtually synonymous. Lack of growth in an organism is a symptom of impending death. Larger enterprises enjoy larger capacity and have more instrumental outputs to offer. People on the outside come inside. Assuming the organization is a good one, the society, the entity, members or clients, and new participants all benefit from a larger organization. Voluntary organizations frequently grow by encountering new needs and opportunities during their routine operations and seeing them as potential purposes. They tend to modify their existing purposes to incorporate some of these potential purposes. This is especially true when existing facilities and personnel can handle the new needs. Demand usually increases immediately after new services begin. For example, workers in a center established to feed poor senior citizens realize that the men and women who come to the center to eat are lonely and bored. With the same building and staff, they can provide an informal recreation program for the same clients. The center now has a broader purpose than feeding. Attendance grows. More food is needed. The seniors want more variety in recreation (Mason, 1988).

Larger size is an index of desirable incentives (Barnard, 1938, p. 159). New blood flows into the membership as new participants find the group's purposes as vital and as important as the old hands see them.

Growth counteracts entropy—the tendency for all organizations to move toward disintegration. All complex physical systems, including organizations, move toward random redistribution of their elements. Growth mechanisms counter this movement. Each year, a certain percentage of the contributors and workers in an organization will die. Others will move, retire, or divert their interest to another cause. If growth does not compensate for the forces of death, attrition, decay, and entropy, it is only a matter of time before the whole organism is dead. It is natural for organisms to run down and stop. Growth replaces their lost energy.

Larger organizations are usually more influential and powerful than small ones, and studies show that organizational leaders and other members benefit from growth (see Stolzenberg, 1978, for a review of the literature linking size to increased worker earnings, profitability, and decreased economic competition; see also McPherson, 1983, p. 520). Greater power can produce greater output. Bigger elephants are better elephants.

Larger size brings economies of scale. Larger organizations have specialized functions unavailable to smaller ones. Larger entities can usually buy goods at smaller unit costs. In a mechanical system, scaling up results in greater performance.

Growth enhances prestige. A stagnant organization is not just holding still but losing ground in an environment of economic inflation and rapid increases in the size of both public and private enterprises. It may be falling behind in relation to its competitors and in its ability to achieve its objectives even though management thinks that it is holding its own.

Growth enables an organization to accomplish its mission. An entity needs to reach a critical mass before it has enough resources to address its purpose seriously and effectively. Until it reaches that mass, it consumes much of its energy in the throes of surviving. Many contributors, volunteers, community leaders, and potential clients expect growth from organizations. When they see growth, they may well contribute more, work harder, and fuel still more progress. When organizations begin to decline, these same individuals wonder what bad thing or incompetent person has failed. People may desert the organization like the legendary rats leaving the sinking ship, withdrawing their support when the organization's needs are greatest. Growth provides an infusion of hope and expectancy. Participation accelerates because people do not want to miss any of the action. Participants' spirits improve as they perceive that the present will be better than the past and the future will be even better.

A continually expanding structure opens both paid and voluntary positions. These positions provide involvement for more people and a larger track for advancement as individuals move into the vacancies and grow in their capacity for greater responsibility. Advancement is a major opportunity for individuals to maximize expressive outputs. Apparently, self-actualization gets boring if an individual stays in the same job too long. Katz explored the relation of satisfaction and the time on a job. He found that in the early months, the significance of the task and the performance feedback produced ample satisfaction. As time passed, however, autonomy, the variety in the skills required, and the challenge of having a proper task with a beginning and an end became just as important as significance and feedback. Then, after five years on the job, none of these factors seemed to make much difference in satisfaction. Instead, contractual factors like pay, benefits, co-workers, and compatibility with the supervisor were more important (1977, p. 31). Though Katz studied paid employees, his findings should apply to people doing any work, pointing to the value of exposing people to the challenges of new jobs. New positions are continually opening in an expanding enterprise. Expressive outputs thrive as the most industrious and motivated participants prove themselves and move into more responsible and often more interesting and fulfilling positions with new challenges.

A growing organization tends to hold its better leaders and attract effective new leaders, both paid and unpaid. Leaders are usually ambitious. Organizations regularly try to entice the better ones to leave their current positions and come and work for them. When an organization is coasting and losing momentum, top employees may want to find greener pastures. But when leaders' responsibilities are growing with their present organization, these leaders will tend to stay and grow with the group they know best. When the organization looks beyond its boundaries for new talent, it will find that a growing organization with a reputation for vitality attracts the more intrinsically motivated people. When it looks internally, the larger its pool of personnel, the more people it has from which to choose new leaders at all levels.

Growth can lubricate the joints of arthritic entities rigidified by goal displacement. These organizations and their ruling coalitions have confused their means with their ends and elevated their outdated or inappropriate ways of doing things to the status of hallowed traditions. If some unintentional change somehow makes such an entity grow, it may begin to adapt and to restore its viability. Growth can prevent or forestall such arthritic conditions because growth instills fluidity, dethroning vested rights and diverting unhealthy preoccupations with internal politics. Organizations have little to fear from internal coalitions while they are growing fast. New groups form, old coalitions change, and there is as much for members to gain from an increase in the whole as from self-interest (Handy, 1988, p. 149).

Growth improves the psychological climate that directly and indirectly fuels the organization with energy. As I have already suggested, there is much to the adage that nothing succeeds like success. Some of the psychological attitudes engendered by a growing concern are the following:

Optimism.   Growth affects morale. Our society applauds growth and looks on an organization that is declining in size as failing (Mason, 1988). If an organization's contributors, a major energy source, see signs of growth, they may give more. Conversely, organizational decay demoralizes active participants. An expanding organization is vibrant and healthy. Many problems fade with the feelings of optimism, success, progress, and goodwill and a buoyant psychological tone.

Pride of membership.   Organizations want their participants to feel good about belonging, and individuals often enhance their self-image by appropriate affiliations. People feel better about themselves when their organization is vigorously attracting other people. Membership becomes more valuable, and the organization attracts a new wave of members.

Enthusiasm and excitement.   Growth precipitates changes. Every week one finds new people, new groups, new activities, and larger attendance at traditional events. Positive change and the anticipation of better things to come generates an increasing interest, excitement, and enthusiasm, regenerating activity among some long-standing participants.

Confidence.   A person will procrastinate or balk when faced with the prospect of failure in an assignment. But when good things are happening, when the prospect of success pervades the atmosphere, confidence tends to grow among all participants, and many will venture beyond their previous self-constraints.

Disadvantages of Growth

Napoleon and Hitler both failed on the road to Moscow because their troops outpaced their supply lines. There can be hazards and disadvantages in the growing process, especially if leaders do not intelligently plan expansion and execute their plans with excellence. In this area, forewarned is forearmed, because each disadvantage is manageable if anticipated. However, rapid growth does require unique management skills. Like blacksmiths who can shoe running horses, the best managers at managing growth are few and far between.

Proponents of the status quo act as if quality is always a trade-off with quantity. This is not necessarily so, for General Electric probably produces a better product than your local appliance repair shop and the Red Cross can marshal better resources to respond to disasters than most smaller relief agencies. However, change can unglue cohesion, separate colleagues who worked well together, and bring seemingly incompatible newcomers into once-effective teams. Growth can generate much activity without net gain if there is no program for integration. Enlargement can reduce efficiency as larger organizations become more centralized and waste the intelligence and initiative of their participants. The organization may not be able to keep up with some of the demands made on it. A significant number of members may become disgruntled or be left by the wayside. The more the organization does, the more expectations accelerate. Older participants understand the reasons behind old constraints, but newcomers become impatient with limitations that are slow in disappearing. Growth may mean more and/or harder work for a staff already working near capacity.

However, one organization's trash may be another's treasure. Enlargement may be bad for one entity in its particular situation but ideal for another in a different situation. In biological systems, size follows function. Drucker wrote, "It would surely be counterproductive for the cockroach to be big, and equally counterproductive for the elephant to be small. As biologists are fond of saying, 'The rat knows everything it needs to be successful as a rat.' Rats are way ahead of any other animal in what it takes to be successful as a rat" (1989a, p. 259).

Underlying Principles

James C. Coleman says, "Groups strive to maintain themselves and resist disintegration and to grow and develop their potentials. Like individuals, too, they may solve their problems in either task-oriented or defense-oriented ways, and if their problems are beyond their resources—or believed to be, they may show evidence of strain, decomposition and pathology" (1969, p. 298).

An organization is a group of groups; it is made up of groups of people who enjoy working together on a variety of tasks. Another way to view this group of groups is as an organism made of cells. It grows by adding workgroups (cells) that can attract and hold people and accomplish tasks with them. Leaders make growth an integral part of an organization by planting many small expressive groups, each of which can then grow to full size. If it is too small to do its job, a well-led group will attract enough workers. Once it has enough members to accomplish its tasks, and there are more individuals than can satisfactorily communicate and interact with each other, it will stop growing. So, for maximum growth, leaders should plan groups that are initially large enough to survive long enough to grow but are also too small for their tasks. When each group reaches full strength, leaders should start a new group around a nucleus taken from the old. This is the way that organizations grow. It can happen naturally in response to a need or it can happen accidentally. It can also happen as part of an intelligent, well thought out plan for building growth into the very nature of a voluntary enterprise.

An example of such a plan appears in the history of the Southern Baptist Convention. In 1919, Arthur Flake, an executive with the Sunday School Board of the Southern Baptist Convention, wrote *Building a Standard Sunday School*, the first of a series of manuals for the volunteer leaders of the convention's 25,303 churches with 2,961,348 members. He enunciated the principle that churches grew by creating new units. He also noted that new (expressive) groups tended to stop growing after about eighteen months. By that point, group members had bonded, and (unconsciously) they tended to stop recruiting and/or to exclude newcomers. Flake stressed the need for a system of continually starting new groups.

The Sunday School Board instituted a policy of grading Sunday school classes of all ages by sex and age. To perpetuate the system, the eldest group in each class moved up to the next older unit each fall. Many congregations also took advantage of promotion day reshuffling to subdivide their largest classes into smaller units to further stimulate the growth process. A controversy raged in local congregations for decades as members objected to the breakup of their comfortable primary social groups. Nevertheless, Flake's principle was gradually accepted and implemented. By 1959, this policy made the Southern Baptists the largest Protestant denomination in the United States, with 31,906 churches and 9,485,276 members, according to the Archives Department of the Sunday School Board of the Southern Baptist Convention (response to inquiry, October 1994). For a generation, it was the fastest growing denomination in the world.

Three basic natural tendencies underlie the growth process. First, individuals spontaneously join small affinity and task groups to satisfy some expressive need (I call these juvenile groups). Second, the groups grow to the limits of face-to-face interaction and optimum expressive gratification (becoming mature groups). Each group maintains the mature level for a time, and then, third, it fails to produce sufficient instrumental or expressive output and begins to lose more members than it gains (becoming an atrophied group) or it becomes too large to accommodate the face-to-face interaction that initially attracted the participants (becoming an old-age group) or it precipitates new juvenile units out of its membership, restoring face-to-face communication and opening new expressive opportunities (becoming a rejuvenating group). (This life-cycle is described in more detail below.)

Donald Anderson McGavran developed his own ideas of organizational growth independently, as a missionary in India. He enlarged and refined them through observations and research on six continents from 1936 through 1955. McGavran found that people joined churches by a homogeneous unit process. He saw that the fewer boundaries people had to cross, the more likely they were to join a group. Inevitably, he developed a strategy similar to that of the Southern Baptists. McGavran shared his ideas in many speeches, articles, and books (see especially McGavran, 1955, 1970). His concepts and terminology became a part of church-growth vocabulary, especially in the rapidly growing evangelical wing of U.S. Christianity.

This organic method of growth is consistent with the growth

of churches from the beginnings of Christianity. The earliest small Christian communities met in members' homes, then grew by attracting new members from preexisting friendship networks. These expressive friendship networks were a convenient means of communication within "affective bonds" that often carried over to a new church group.

Similarly, small expressive groups usually account for growth in nonprofit organizations. These groups usually contain fewer than ten people. They think of themselves as a unit, enjoy being with each other, and work together to accomplish some specific job for the larger organization. If readers picture the history and experience of their own organizations, how people came to join, how they function in the various activities, and how they do their work, more often than not they will see that their own organizations are made up of, and grow through, individuals working as participants in many small groups, some formally constituted, but many quite informal, just gatherings of members who like to work with each other.

There are important points to understand about each stage in the growth of groups.

Juvenile Stage

Juvenile groups form because individuals spontaneously join together. Some juvenile groups are informal and purely expressive, say, a group of men who breakfast together every morning at the T&C Café. Some are formal, like the Overeaters Anonymous chapter, an instrumental-expressive organization, that might meet on Fridays at the same café. The group of five secretaries from a large insurance agency who gather for lunch at the T&C on workdays is an informal expressive group within a larger instrumental organization. All juvenile groups exist because of the basic human need to affiliate with others with whom we have an affinity.

Juvenile groups grow as members invite others to join. In 1938, Barnard observed that interpersonal ties at their best create what he called a "condition of communion." He saw this condition as the opportunity for commandership and mutual support, forming the "basis of informal organization that is essential to the operation of every formal organization" (p. 148). Barnard also noted the innate propensity of organizations to expand (pp. 158–159). The reader will remember that Elton Mayo's Hawthorne investigations also documented the role of social factors in functions of the small informal groups that formed within a large Western Electric plant.

Individuals tend to join newly formed groups. Once a group establishes itself and works out its pecking order, the members become comfortable with the arrangement. Newcomers then feel like outsiders. It takes time for them to find their place in the fully established network of relationships. Thus, people find it easier and faster to care and share with a comparatively new group in which a network of relationships is not yet fully in place (Callahan, 1983, pp. 36–37). Tuckman (1965), summarizing fifty studies of small-group research, suggested a four-step group developmental sequence. He called the first stage "forming"; it corresponds to this juvenile phase in which participants have time to get to know each other and to make their mark. Eventually, everyone will participate. Until a person speaks or does something, he or she will not feel part of the group.

Lyle E. Schaller, who has explored thoroughly the part played in growth and decline by small church groups, found that while members joined for a variety of reasons, their friends or relatives brought in from 60 to 90 percent of new members. Most subsequent surveys consistently show a 70 percent figure (McGavran, 1970, p. 165). This phenomenon illustrates the way organizations with growing groups actively bring in new members.

Mature Stage

Individuals may continue to join a group as long as it provides expressive relationships or until it is large enough to perform its instrumental task while providing satisfaction in working with others striving toward the same goal. At this point, it is a mature group providing expressive experiences.

As described earlier, individuals continue to join an expressive affinity group until it reaches a limit for intimate face-to-face communication, and we can see the persistence of groups of this size throughout history: think of primitive hunting groups; Jesus and his disciples; cricket, football, and baseball teams; the Communist cell; army squads; and management theory regarding span of control.

The point when members freely communicate with each other on a face-to-face basis is the stage that Tuckman called "storming." Once groups have finished their forming stage, the storming stage fulfills affiliation. People drop their polite facades and frankly speak their minds. Sometimes, the storm is within the group itself. Sometimes the whole group storms against the wider organization. Either way, storming is a sign that the group is coming to terms with itself and its task. In the next phase identified by Tuckman, "norming," the mature group will start to decide how it is going to work, when to meet, who does what, and who can tell whom what to do. In the final and "performing" phase, the mature group gets down to producing significant outputs (Kormanski, 1985, p. 217). *Given sufficient expressive incentives or a sufficiently motivating task, groups will grow up to the limit of face-to-face communication* (Mason, 1988).

Old-Age Stage

To this point, all is well. The group is fulfilling its expressive purpose (and in the case of a task group, its instrumental purpose as well). Then, as the mature group slowly grows beyond the limit of intimate interaction, it faces a crisis. It loses the appeal that first attracted the members. To be sure, the leader and his or her inner circle are still in the center of activity, relating to the largest number; but members on the fringe participate less and less. This crisis occurs when a group gets beyond eight to ten individuals. Some believe that the critical point occurs when group size grows beyond seven. In any case, the crisis in communication causes the group to flow down one of several branches. It may atrophy, subdivide, or rejuvenate.

Atrophy. Since there is a limited size for an optimum group, its growth rate slows as it approaches that carrying capacity. When it reaches the carrying capacity, the growth rate may be zero and the system in equilibrium (McPherson, 1983, p. 522). In some cases, the group will continue to grow in apparent size (membership), but its real size (the number of individuals participating) remains constant. Inevitably, atrophy sets in. Members die, move, shift to other groups, or become inactive. At this point, the group may once again become small enough to facilitate interaction for all; it may take on new vitality and enjoy a spurt of growth until the cycle repeats itself. It is more likely, however, that the remaining members will continue to interact and enjoy each other but that the group will no longer appeal to potential newcomers. It will dwindle away, as members reminisce and mourn.

Subdivision.   As a vital growing workgroup exceeds the limits of intimate interaction for all, subgroups often form. The group still appears to be one, but it is really an organization of two or more groups, each providing expressive satisfactions. If each subgroup accepts the group leader, if various cohesive factors are functioning, and there are compelling tasks, this small organization may continue to grow with a life of its own and without any calculated growth strategy. Such subdivision may be desirable, but it may eventually stifle growth, lead to a competing organization within the overall organization, or inhibit the establishment of new freestanding groups.

Members tend to "free ride" more in large groups than in small ones, so larger units are the more inefficient of the two. In larger units, it is harder to tie efforts to rewards. Shirking is easier. Group members do not notice another member's participation or absence as easily as they would in a small group. "Members of a large group will not contribute to activities on behalf of the collectivity unless . . . some separate incentive, distinct from the achievement of the common or group interest, is offered to the members of the group individually" (Olson, 1965, p. 2).

Tuckman's forming, storming, norming, and performing model was a starting point for further investigation. Almost every subsequent model added a fifth stage concerning the termination of the group (Lacoursiere, 1980). In 1977, Tuckman and Jensen examined twenty-two of the subsequent studies and updated the original model to include an "adjourning" stage (Kormanski, 1985, p. 217).

However, rather than adjourning, groups that exceed the communication limit may rejuvenate by subdividing or by the calculated intentional process described in the following section.

Rejuvenation Stage

The underlying principles described in this chapter, appropriately adapted, permit the nonprofit manager to build within the distinctiveness of his or her own enterprise. When leaders understand the principles of building growth, they find that most nonprofit organizations can adapt them.

Voluntary enterprises do not have to depend on the stimulus-response relationship of a business to its customers. A business expends a given amount of money with the expectation that, spent effectively, it will produce more income than the cost, that is, a profit. Each time the business attempts to grow, there is a relatively low exchange ratio of stimulus to response—for instance, 1:1.5, meaning that for each dollar spent there is a dollar and a half return. Even in cases when the profit is considerable, there must still be an expenditure of organizational capital as a stimulus.

A voluntary enterprise has a constituency on which it can draw for resources, and it uses volunteers to accomplish its tasks. It has a relatively unlimited access to resources, and it is not necessarily constrained to the business degree of stimulus and response expenditure. For nonprofits, a ratio of 1:10 is routine, that is, one dollar spent in fundraising produces ten dollars in contributions. Dramatic ratios can occur, featuring virtually no direct cost, when an endorsement, an idea, or an effective appeal by an unpaid volunteer results in income.

An organization enlarges by adding more units than it loses. These units may be in the form of dollar income, the input of time, the growth of its constituency, an increase in the number of clients served, or other forms. How then do we stimulate this importation of units? Is it only a matter of will and work?

A commonly held belief is that organizations grow simply by trying harder. Without any thought for modification of the structure of the organization, its purposes, or its methodology, someone suggests: "If everyone would just . . ." Over and over, I have witnessed the same scenario in different organizations. The discussion is somber. Most of the comments reveal frustration at trying to come forth with a way to reach some worthy goal. A relative newcomer, figuring rapidly on a yellow legal pad, brightens as though his or her switch was just turned on. The newcomer then proposes the solution: "If each one of us will just get two a week, and if each one of them will get two more, why, in just a month, we will have . . ." Usually, such efforts are futile. The arithmetic is there; the motivation is not. But growth can occur in an organization that has a commitment, is willing to learn how growth takes place, and then implements a program for growth.

As we have seen, informal groups will develop within a larger organization automatically and informally. In other cases, the organization deliberately and formally subdivides into work-groups. Whether the forming into groups is informal and spontaneous or formal and calculated, the resulting groups represent the cells of the encompassing organism. Since the organization is built of such groups, it will grow as the groups grow or die as the groups die. If an organization wishes to build expressive growth into its systems, it will create a climate for rejuvenating itself, for continually forming groups in which expressive outputs flourish.

Eleven Steps Toward Organic Growth

I learned the principle of growth by means of multiplying small expressive cells by reading and participating in seminars and workshops from 1954 through 1962. In 1964, I began to elaborate on the concept and refined its application by using an eleven-step approach in a variety of organizational settings, with marked success. The most dramatic was perhaps the expansion of tutor training at the Laubach Literary organization, of which I was the CEO. We increased the number of tutors we trained annually from five thousand in 1965 to twenty-five thousand in 1967.

Commit to Growth by Official Action

The organization must make a top-level commitment to enlargement. Appropriate official action should formally sanction the new program. In some organizations, this will be routine, while in others, it may be the most difficult step of all because it has to do with the *why* of growth. Nevertheless, until official action initiates a growth program, enlargement is nothing but a dream in someone's mind.

In some organizations, the formal commitment is a legal

requirement. Even if it is not, official action can serve several valuable purposes.

- It has informational value. In preparing for the vote, people will have healthy discussion that will familiarize them with the growth process proposed.
- It will sanction the project, paving the way for the leaders to begin to implement the program.
- It will provide strong moral support to those responsible for forming the new groups. This support is key to enlargement.

The best way for a leader in an organization to initiate the formal action is to bring his or her own group of co-workers, friends, and confidants together to discuss the entire growth plan. This inner circle can provide support and reactions and help the leader resolve problems before formally presenting the plan for adoption.

The ensuing official commitment to growth signals to the rank and file that the bandwagon is ready to roll and it is time for everyone to climb on board. Prestige-suggestion studies show that people will believe or do what prestigious sources suggest, as in the "Hello, Good-bye" effect in psychotherapy, in which patients who merely have contact with a prestigious medical authority improve significantly and almost as much as those who get prolonged therapy (Frank, 1961). "A potential activist," says Chong, "will assess the prospects of collective action and decide to join only when he feels that 'enough others' have already joined to make it viable . . . What is needed under the circumstances are some highly dedicated, morally-committed activists who will contribute to collective action when few others are willing to do so. They provide the leadership in the movement and they constitute its critical mass. However, such self-starters who are willing to support collective action in its earliest, least promising stages, are relatively rare" (1987, p. 361).

Define Objectives

Leaders define, in writing, their most important organizational objectives at this point in the organization's development. They may have prepared these organizational objectives earlier, but in any case, they will not want to start a vigorous growth program without being sure where they want to go, what the institution is all about, and what it wants to accomplish. As an institution expands and enlarges, leaders must align its new structure with its overall objectives and purposes. The new units should contribute toward the reaching of those objectives, and if the objectives are not clearly defined and understood, there will be much confusion. The organization will be like the ship that was making good time but had lost its direction.

Plan Precipitant Activity

Leaders should develop a program around an activity that is highly likely to succeed. This activity will precipitate the interest and energy that is already in the organization and give everyone a clear target. It is a lot easier to go forward and make progress when the enterprise has something very clear and near to aim for. The long-range purpose may be to expand and to grow a bigger and better organization with optimum expressive outputs, but an excellent means of reaching the long-term goal is to have shorter-term events that command the attention and release the energy of the membership. The event could be a new building, a major public event, or any difficult challenge that will require a coordinated, whole-hearted effort of the entire organization. It has to be big enough and difficult enough to get everyone's attention!

Identify Existing Groups

The total organization is really a group of expressive groups, whether the formal organization chart shows them or not. Leaders may not have trouble at all identifying the groups or units that are already operating. First, they should review the organization chart. It should be easy to list the official groups, such as the executive committee, special task forces, boards, other committees, and other formal groups. Beyond that, informal groups that are not on the chart may come to mind as leaders study the charts and think of key individuals within the organization. Leaders can think of recent meetings, social occasions, or projects and try to remember the informal groupings of people who like to associate and work together. They can think of certain physical locations to see whether they bring to mind any informal groups associated with those sites. They can review certain sports and special interests and discover whether there are people who form groups because of these common interests. They can scan the current list of projects, activities, and purposes, seeking existing groups interested in these specific items. In short, leaders should use any type of memory-jogger they can to help identify existing formal and informal groups.

Choose Group Format

Next, leaders should decide what kind of groups to form to be the basis for establishing new groups. They should answer such questions as, What kinds of tasks are we going to give to these new groups that will make up the enlarged organization? and, What kind of expressive bond is going to hold the members of each group together as a cohesive whole? They should decide the classification basis for the new groups. For example, let us say that the purpose of the organization is to teach people how to swim, and leaders want to greatly increase the number of people who participate for this purpose. The leaders should decide at this point whether they are going to form groups of people according to people's ability to swim (beginner, intermediate, advanced) or according to age (five-year-olds, ten-year-olds, twenty-year-olds) or according to the schools they go to, the churches they belong to, or the parts of town in which they live. For some, this step will be easy and obvious while others will need to put in a great deal of time and thought to choose a basis for forming the new groups. But it is at this point in the enlargement program that leaders must decide what types of groups the organization is going to start.

Expand Capacity

Leaders should enlarge the organization structure to accommodate the first stage of anticipated growth. It is disastrous to stimulate growth at the group level and not have a structure sufficient to handle the increase. A failure at this point may result in splintering the organization. People may join but find insufficient structure to hold them together. (This will not only be bad in itself; it will also tend to discourage future attempts at enlargement and progress.) Leaders must look at their goals for growth and design a structure sufficient for the anticipated growth. They must change the structure of the organization itself, the organization chart, to what it will need to be when the organization reaches the size the leaders hope it will be at the end of its first stage of growth. Changing the structure now means that there will be a ready structural receptacle for the new groups.

Staff Groups

The next step is to form a nucleus with motivated individuals committed to the enlargement program and the purpose and objectives of the organization. (These individuals will not be much help if they commit to the purposes of the organization but not to its growth. Conversely, if participants commit to growth but not to the organization, leaders may find they have labored only to have someone else walk off with some of their new members.) Good judgment is crucial in this step, since leaders will be drawing the people who will form the nucleus of new groups from existing parts of the organization. Leaders have to plan for the future of the groups and tasks that these individuals may be leaving behind. They must also consider whether the persons they are going to put together as the nucleus of a new group will get along well with each other and whether they will be capable of attracting new members. The leadership selected will largely determine the number of successful new groups. Therefore, leaders should staff the new groups with motivated people who commit to both the larger organization and to the enlargement program and who consider what effect people's new roles will have on your total system. Every group should have one member primarily concerned with the task and someone else primarily responsible for the process (Handy, 1988, p. 55). For example, when small fundraising teams are being built for a campaign, businesses may loan executives with a lot of energy and community clout but with little knowledge of the organization. Leaders often officially assign such persons to key positions, but unofficially ask a loyal organization veteran to work within the team to harmonize the group's effort with the encompassing organizational culture.

Target Prospect Sources

Leaders should identify sources of new member prospects outside of the organization. Leaders will have already decided the basis on which to build the new groups and the types of groups targeted. Now, they match the blank group spaces with prospects on the outside who can be motivated to fill those spaces. But before picking individuals, they should first identify types and classifications of likely people. To follow up on the earlier example of the swimming classes, if groups are to be formed according to where the learners go to school, then schools will be the prospect source. But if classes are going to form by neighborhoods, the organization should identify neighborhoods of people who are likely to want to learn how to swim and who have access to the organization's pool.

Prospect lists develop faster and more thoroughly if done systematically. Leaders can prepare them on a wholesale basis by thinking first of categories of people rather than trying to list the names of individuals.

Prepare Leaders

The next step is to orient and train the group leaders. Obviously, those who have the responsibility for building the new groups need to learn specific skills. The program must assure the group leaders of the backing and support of the leadership and membership, and the leadership must communicate the overall purpose of the enlargement program to the group leaders in depth. Each person will need training in the skills required to recruit new members, to integrate those new members, and to begin work toward his or her specific job assignment. Training not only teaches specific information, it helps people work out problems before they occur, and it builds everyone's enthusiasm, confidence, and anticipation. The program will want not only to supply initial training or orientation but also to give psychological and spiritual support to the group leaders on whom the organization leaders are so dependent. The organization is investing in the success of the program; training and support protects that investment and will ensure that it pays good dividends.

Initiate Personal Contacts

Next comes the initiation of a program for personally contacting prospects. If organizational leaders have done everything else— defined their objectives, enlarged the organization structure, selected and trained group leaders, and defined where to look for prospects, then they must initiate a program of personally contacting the prospects. If they do not, they are like a farmer who plows his fields and sows his seed but does not reap the harvest. The process of enlargement will idle in neutral until its gears are engaged by personal contacts. If the step of personal contact fails, the new groups will not be able to develop into full strength and accomplish their objectives.

In my own experience, I have found that making the personal contacts is often the weakest link in the chain of events. To not spur forward vigorously at this point is to forfeit all that has gone before. There is a tremendous temptation to substitute almost anything for personal contact because people do not like the possibility of being rejected, but this must be done. Without it, the bridge is nine-tenths of the way across the river, and the car is ready, but it will never cross the river. Groups must invite prospects to come and join in accomplishing tasks. Moreover, as Rothschild-Whitt has observed, "Where personal and moral appeals are the chief means of social control, it is important, perhaps necessary, that the group select members who share their basic values and world view" (1979, p. 513).

Develop and Upgrade Competency

Leaders must develop the competency of the new expressive groups and upgrade the skills of the membership, for these new groups are now a capital asset that the leaders have spent much time, money, and energy in establishing and operating. This investment is worthwhile because the more a participant becomes emotionally involved, especially at the level of beliefs, the harder it will be to change him or her later (Berelson and Steiner, 1964, p. 575). The leaders must protect this capital so it will increase rather than diminish in value. They accomplish this task by establishing a formal training ground for group leaders to study group processes and by constantly raising the level of group tasks. Leaders will also want to give attention to the factors that contribute to cohesion within the groups. By upgrading the capability and quality of these new groups, leaders will ensure that the groups will mature and become capable of sponsoring or providing leadership for another generation of new groups.

Three Nonprofit Tools for Growth

Just as other sectors have unique tools for making their organizations more effective, so expressive organizations have unique tools for managing expressive behavior. For example, consider the following tools, which are not as appropriate for managing business employees' instrumental behavior: the multiplication of subordinates, empire building, and per-project participation.

Multiplication of subordinates occurs when individuals who feel overwhelmed by their work seek help by adding subordinates. Recruiting subordinates, usually two, increases the superior's value as the only person who comprehends both subordinate functions. This phenomenon is expressed in Parkinson's law of "multiplication of subordinates" and is expanded in his law of "multiplication of work" (1957, pp. 2–4). The latter is based on the premise that the more workers, the more internal work they make for each other. Additional workers cost money for organizations that do not use volunteers, so higher management tries to minimize the practice. In nonprofits, however, adding subordinates can be beneficial when they are recruited from outside the organization because that action enlarges the organization, involves more people in the work, and produces more expressive satisfaction.

Empire building happens because the larger and more important an organization or one of its components, the more powerful and prestigious that entity's leader. Leaders, it follows, tend to enlarge and enhance the importance of their units. They build empires. In a business, a larger unit may produce less profit than a leaner one, and the empire-building process itself can generate wasteful practices (Hicks and Gullett, 1972, p. 424). Nonprofits, however, can harness the expressive empire-building tendency and use it to generate contributions, recruit additional participants, and provide additional services or the same services in new ways.

Per-project participation can also benefit a voluntary nonprofit enterprise. Businesses find few compensating benefits to offset the waste often encountered when they experience an uneven demand for their services. When they must adjust their capacity for current demand, they may end up having too many or too few resources to meet later demand. However, sudden overdemand presents many nonprofits with several benefits. Intrinsically motivated participants respond positively to a short-term challenge, and their productivity increases. Short-term volunteers are more easily recruited under such pressure, and they provide the organization with an enlarged pool of resources that may be subsequently used for longer-term efforts. Overwhelming demand presents an advantageous fundraising opportunity—again establishing a larger resource pool that may be tapped later.

Conclusion

An organization is a group of workgroups of people who enjoy being together. Though these individual workgroups themselves grow by attracting individuals, the larger organization grows not by adding individuals but by adding groups that attract and retain people as they interact and accomplish tasks. Growth evolves as an integral part of an organization when leaders plant small groups, each of which can then grow to full size, following a process such as the eleven-step plan described here. Growth by a process resembling cell division in an organism can be built into an organization's system. Several Protestant denominations and individual congregations have successfully employed this methodology.

Growth has been a traditional means of evaluating an organization because it not only meters progress but also enhances capacity for both expressive and instrumental outputs. As leaders go through the steps involved in an organization's growth and development and commit to growth by taking official action, defining objectives, planning precipitant activity, identifying existing groups, choosing group format, expanding capacity, staffing groups, targeting prospect sources, preparing leaders, initiating personal contacts, and developing and upgrading competency, they will care for and nurture their new groups and develop mature members capable of subsequently separating from their established groups to form the nuclei for new groups. Like the cells of any organism, the groups can divide and start the entire growth process again.

Overall, perhaps *involvement* is the most important factor in nurturing groups and keeping them healthy—involvement of the group itself in the mainstream of the life of the larger organization and the involvement of every member of the group in the group's life. Groups are perfectly capable of protecting themselves from overwork; therefore, leaders should worry about not involving groups enough rather than too much. Groups stand to lose more members to "rustout" from insufficient involvement than they ever will lose to burnout from too much involvement. Leaders must continue the process to get ready for another cycle and a new generation of new groups in an ever-growing and improving organization.

Needs for Further Research

Scholars need to integrate what religious organizations have learned about expressive growth principles into the balance of nonprofit organizations. An analysis of dramatic growth in other types of organizations might also be conducted on the basis of the principles outlined here. The homogeneous group concept should be studied to see if an otherwise heterogeneous group might behave homogeneously when compelled by an overarching common goal. Researchers who confine their work to a single organization or field might examine their subject to see the degree to which it is a group of groups.

Actions for Practitioners

Leaders and managers can identify their constituent groups. They might structure their organization to include expressive groups. They might test the process with a time-limited project. If organizational leaders and managers were to implement only one thing at this point, I suggest they implement a pilot project in one organizational unit—a chapter, program, or project. For example, I have observed dozens of youth groups grow dramatically when multiple-age units are first subdivided into smaller groups by grade level. Leaders should remember this point in particular from this chapter about growing a workgroup: if at the beginning it is too small to do its job, a well-led group will attract enough workers. Once it has enough and there are more than can satisfactorily communicate and interact on a face-to-face basis with all the other group members, its growth will stop. So for greatest growth, leaders should plan groups that are large enough to survive long enough to grow, but that need more members in order to complete their tasks.

Conclusion
For the Joy of the Work

Forty-three years ago, I began a career managing local, regional, and international organizations—all of which sought instrumental goals. Twenty-seven years ago, I began systematically studying nonprofit management. I might have done better had the study preceded rather than overlapped the practice. However, when I started, where was the body of nonprofit theory? Where were the courses? Where were the journals and books? I learned by discovering what worked—and did not work. I learned what I could adapt from business management principles. I reflected on what was happening in my own organizations, in the boards on which I served, in the organizations of my collaborators and competitors, and in the good and bad cases I heard about on grapevines. I reflected on the results, then adapted my leadership according to what I observed. It has been a creative and stimulating experience, rooted in reality.

A Different Paradigm

What was the hardest lesson to learn? What took longest to bore into my deeper consciousness? Up until my last employment, organizations prospered *in spite of* my struggle to squeeze the expressive behavior of others out of the way of my instrumental objectives. I felt diverted from serious instrumental goals by what then appeared to be time-consuming expressive demands of members.

   I have always been profoundly influenced by Christian

teachings, the Judeo-Christian values of stewardship, accomplishment, self-discipline, delayed gratification, and particularly, the Protestant work ethic. I saw my culture as favoring instrumentality and relegating expression to a tiny recreational role. I perceived humankind's rational productive forces struggling against its natural expressive desires.

In retrospect, I now recognize that all the while, I was immensely exulting in the processes of my work. I awoke every morning eager to grasp opportunities, wrestle with problems, create new solutions, and mobilize people. I was intrinsically motivated by expressive activity toward instrumental ends! It was not until the last twelve years of my management career that I realized that opportunities for expressive behavior were a valuable organizational output. What the organization provided workers was one of the most important things it was producing. Enlightenment converted me and showed me the benefits of this expressive behavior. I discovered the transforming power of understanding that expressive behavior is an output that feeds back to an organization—enriching it and thrusting it forward. Since I could not quench the fires of expressive forces, I eagerly joined those forces to spread the blaze.

Expressive-Assisted Instrumentality

I learned that expressive outputs vitalize the organizations that produce them. When an organization provides a vehicle for expressive behavior, it envelops more and more participants into its body, and their activity enriches the enveloping organization and propels it toward even its instrumental goals. In these concluding pages, I reemphasize that direct gratification of needs for expressive action can also be instrumental for other ends. *The opportunity for expressive activity attracts and motivates participants to work enthusiastically and industriously for instrumental purposes.*

Among voluntary and nonprofit organizations are some that exist specifically for facilitating expressive behavior. Others traditionally use the intrinsic motivation of direct expressive satisfaction to achieve indirect instrumental goals. All leaders, especially those with significant commitments to measurable instrumental outputs, should appreciate expressive outputs as a major source of energy.

Without their expressive outputs, many organizations would be impoverished, and whole fields of endeavor would be severely inhibited. For example, what would Scouting organizations be without the volunteer den mothers and scoutmasters for whom they provide expressive opportunities? Would there be churches on every other corner if all choirs consisted of paid performers and every class were taught by professional teachers? Would Rotary International have more than one million members in 27,173 clubs in over 150 nations if it denied members the opportunity to fill offices and serve on committees? How much money would be raised if fund drives were left to paid solicitors with mere rational appeals?

A Valid Output

Expression is the process of directly manifesting, or pressing out, what people feel because they *want to do* something for themselves, for other individuals, or for the society as much as because they *want something done.* This concept of expression is much broader than a facial contortion or a manual gesture, much more than letting out emotions by painting a picture or singing in the shower. Expression is all those activities that are *ends in themselves;* it is doing something for the direct gratification of doing.

From the baby's birth cry to the octogenarian's death moan, individuals express themselves involuntarily. We obviously require expression psychologically and find it immensely satisfying. As we move from childhood to old age, we also move beyond simple individual involuntary expression and voluntarily choose organizations for group-facilitated expressive behavior. We choose the company of others because it is in our nature as human beings to do so. Early on, humans joined other humans for the instrumental purposes of personal safety, child care, and shared labor in hunting and gathering. But they also joined groups for the expressive purposes of sharing feelings and finding meaning as well as for the instrumental purpose of accomplishing more and better work. Groups grow or join other groups to acquire added resources to survive competitive forces and to undertake larger, more complex cooperative undertakings that will endure beyond a human lifetime. Organizations are a wonderful means of enhancing our lives, extending our grasp, and making us more potent. These activities are natural, legitimate and ubiquitous, pervading all organizations to some degree. Voluntary nonprofit organizations are particularly appropriate stages for displaying such activity. When appropriately bridled and guided, expressive motivations drive organizations to prosper and dramatically increase their effectiveness. Expressive enterprises are not second-choice alternatives to other formats, they are the first-choice preference of their participants.

Even so, the value of expressive motivations is not acknowledged as much as it should be. Expressive motivations have been hidden from view. The participants themselves sometimes often deny their motivations. The difficulty of measuring the effects of expressive behavior encourages others to neglect it. The relative youth of voluntary sector inquiry has attracted scholars whose primary orientation is to cultures other than the nonprofit culture. And since congregations and other religious institutions dominate the sector, our Western "culture of disbelief" has hidden a mammoth arena of expressive activity from the general view of scholars and managers.

Different actors play different roles on organizational stages. Some roles are more instrumental, others more expressive, and one role may segue into the other from time to time, creating a kaleidoscopic mix of roles from one organizational level to another. All voluntary nonprofit organizations generate expressive outputs, but the magnitude of those expressive outputs varies with the organization. And the impact varies according to whether personnel are paid or volunteer and according to the functional class of each individual. Some mixes of behavior are more effective than others for particular purposes, so organizations, and their roles, range from the purely expressive to the purely instrumental. We can understand expressive outputs better by roughly categorizing organizations along a continuum from purely expressive through expressive-instrumental and instrumental-expressive to purely instrumental. Most of the many human needs that experts describe are expressive, especially the "higher" ones. Scholarly literature shows that expressive behavior is old and takes various forms, thus pointing to its underlying ubiquitous presence. Research substantiates the inherent naturalness of expressive behavior and underlines its legitimacy as a subject worthy of continued serious investigation.

Observers can come to better understand this intrinsic human motivation, and leaders can learn to harness its power in shaping organizations. Policies and practices based on a natural phenomenon that leaders thoroughly understand are more likely to develop effective processes than policies and practices that ignore human needs and desires.

The way leaders visualize organizations affects what the organizations become. The more potent the leader, the more influential the leader's guiding metaphors. Images conducive to expressive behavior are more likely to exploit people's natural expressive motivation. When a leader pictures the entity he or she leads as having "heart," the organization is more likely to develop heart. An intentional, calculated orientation around an expressive-friendly metaphor helps all participants visualize what they want their organization to become. Leaders can shift the habitual way they think about a organization and its management, learning to think of the organization as a transformational natural organism, a social system of many informal expressive groups of Theory Y, intrinsically motivated participants. Organizations that use norms to get people to act, as most nonprofits do, concentrate on developing an optimum culture. That culture, in turn, "manages" the participants to fulfill the organizational purposes. The broadly conceived cultural "box" with its constraining boundaries is the most profound influence on participants. It is best implemented by leaders when they utilize certain techniques with expressive groups. Leaders can steer groups of people in a desired direction when these leaders understand organizational culture, the power of values, normative compliance, and the magnetism of the small groups in which the culture resides.

Cohesiveness is a prerequisite for a solid sustained effort to facilitate expressive outputs. Leaders who understand the factors that build cohesion and the factors that contribute to disintegration have an advantage. They learn to diagnose an organizations' status and better predict its actions and its potential for attracting and recruiting participants. Cohesion is both an end and a means. It is an end because it enhances expressive outputs to constituencies and to the society. It is a means because it is essential to organizational achievement. Voluntary nonprofit organizations contribute to individuals' lives by providing a vehicle for expressive experience. Individuals will join and remain in those organizations and the organizations will remain viable when cohesive forces are stronger than disruptive forces. Human beings are naturally gregarious, so even a little forethought and encouragement by management can facilitate cohesion and expressive outputs.

At first glance (and, indeed, often after persistent study) managing expressive behavior may seem as helter-skelter as herding cats. And when leaders do not implement an intentional plan, the resulting unbridled expressive behavior is likely to produce anarchy. However, with expressive-friendly images and a target culture in mind, a sequential management process can modify an organization during the course of a management cycle. Herding cats in a desired direction requires such an instrumental process, even when the destination is a more innovative expressive environment. Besides the activities that are steps in a management sequence, all managers should also perform the concurrent functions that enhance both the expressive and instrumental aspects of organizations all day every day. Some of these concurrent functions are universal, but others are characteristic of the voluntary sector specifically. Some are especially important in managing volunteers.

The voluntary nonprofit sector is a special venue for leadership. Leaders are the essential catalysts for transforming organizations; theirs are the hands that guide organizations to a better future. Leaders can incorporate the reality of expressive goals and objectives into the structures and output evaluations of their management systems. They can take full advantage of expressive energy by means of implementing a normative cultural focus and utilizing more participative decision making. They can co-opt informal leaders and start affinity and task groups in a strategy for organizational growth. They can develop a more intentional socialization and cohesiveness development program. Leaders might also consider the potential for meeting the expressive needs of new categories of unpaid participants, perhaps a whole range of middle managers between the staff and direct service volunteers. The special leader that we call the charismatic personality best elicits expressive energy. Such leaders are the founders of most nonprofits and are responsible for most surges of dramatic growth in nonprofits. Organizations that have avoided charismatic leaders can learn more about the assets of charismatic personalities and learn how to harness charismatics' dynamic energy. They must be loosely harnessed, but harnessed nonetheless by means of an array of inducements and constraints.

There are many advantages to organizational growth, including the enrichment of expressive outputs. Organizations can take advantage of the characteristic of small expressive groups to add members up to the point of diminishing expressive outputs. This characteristic increases an entity's expressive dimension while at the same time building an organic process of enlargement into the organizational systems.

Educators and students preparing for leadership in voluntary sector organizations can explore expressive needs and activity, intrinsic motivation, normative culture and compliance, socialization and institutionalization processes, system design, cohesion development, and small voluntary task groups. The tendency to gravitate to the currently more measurable and readily accessed data, which largely concern other topics, skews formal theory and research in the sector. Scholars who factor expressive aspects into current theory will push forward the frontier.

Once we acknowledge that an expressive output is not only legitimate but also essential for the traditional strength of voluntary and nonprofit organizations, research opportunities will virtually double as some of our most insightful scholars apply their abilities to exploring what has previously been almost as unregarded as the dark side of the moon. Many questions require more inquiry. To what degree does the organizational clientele include persons with expressive needs? How does the research on intrinsic motivation apply to organizations as arenas for expressive activity? Why and to what degree are expressive goals unstated in instrumental-expressive organizations that have stated instrumental goals? Why and to what degree do avowed expressive organizations eventually undertake some instrumental goals? What has drawn scholars to study the nonprofit and voluntary sector? Why do such a disproportionate number of voluntary sector scholars and other commentators on the sector come from outside rather than inside established nonprofit fields? How do individuals embedded in the real nonprofit and voluntary world evaluate current scholarship concerning their sector? How does the intermittent work of unpaid participants mesh with the more sequential work of paid personnel, and what are the span-of-control and other management implications of intermittent workers? What are appropriate criteria for filling organizational positions with unpaid versus paid personnel? How can an organization measure expressive outputs? Are expressive outputs simply parallel to instrumental outputs, or do good expressive outputs actually improve the instrumental ones? How can one demonstrate that charismatic leaders are worth the problems they may precipitate?

We begin, nourish, work for, and support many organizations because we want to do something as much as because we want something done. Voluntary nonprofit organizations are a positive, chosen expressive arena, not a last resort. Instead of tolerating activity for the sake of the activity as an incidental phenomenon or covering it from view, organizations can put it on today's agenda and uncover its potency as a positive attribute worthy of enhancement and exploitation.

The Oregon Trail

Recognizing the transforming power of paradigms and images, I want to leave you with two more. Consider the settling of the American West from the perspective of the European Americans of that time, and particularly recall the two contrasting images of the Oregon Trail and the railroad.

The Oregon Trail was an instrumental system along which pioneers moved to the Northwest. The system consisted of trails, wagon trains, frontier forts, army units, and primitive communications. If we believe our folklore, colorful trappers and adventurers blazed the trails. Professional wagon masters led the wagon trains, moving the pioneers along an optimum route. Herdsmen, wranglers, and still more adventurers assisted the wagon masters. They sought to protect the wagons from the Native Americans across whose hunting grounds they trekked and to woo the widows, schoolmarms, and farmers' daughters. Gallant army officers and their troops protected the wagon trains and stragglers and staffed the garrisons at the forts. Express riders carried mail from fort to fort, from station to station. The system protected the settlers from a hostile environment, facilitated their getting from where they were to where they wanted to be, and ultimately moved a vast number of people to the Northwest. Management concerned itself with the essential perimeters but did not address what took place inside each wagon or fort.

In addition, however, the settlers had their own diverse reasons for utilizing the system. Some wanted to set up farms or ranches. Bankers wanted to bank, merchants wanted to sell, blacksmiths wanted to shoe horses, saddlers wanted to make saddles, and schoolmarms wanted to teach school. Missionaries wanted to evangelize and minister, gamblers wanted to gamble, entrepreneurs wanted to get rich, and families wanted to experience a grand enterprise together. Some were drawn by the hope of a new land, and some were driven by a sheriff back East. Along the trail, mothers and fathers raised families and planned their futures; youths learned, flirted, and made love; and adventurers adventured. Both instrumental and expressive behaviors abounded. In the forts, bartenders tended bar, bankers banked, preachers preached, doctors doctored, bakers baked, and haberdashers haberdashed. Each individual was responsible for his or her own livelihood, recreation, food, clothing, and daily activity. The Oregon Trail, then, was a loose confederation of shared power and responsibility; no one entity controlled the others. Each component was an arena for people to interact, perform, or struggle. The wagon masters and fort authorities managed the conditions under which activities took place, but not the outcomes of the interactions. It worked.

Once the West was sufficiently populated, the government and private enterprise found it feasible to shuttle trains west and east. The railroad, too, was a successful instrumental enterprise, carrying mail, goods, and passengers rapidly from one end of the country to the other. Trains were run by professional railroad men, and passengers were the cargo. Trains ran on schedule along rigid tracks from one established station to the next. Someone back East determined their schedule and destination. There was time for passengers to play a few card games, shoot a few bison in the fields, and surrender a few brooches or gold watches to train robbers.

I suggest that leaders visualize the Oregon Trail as opposed to the railroad as a pattern for a varied mix of expressive and instrumental outputs.

Remember, people create organizations for people. Yet as all sorts of organizations gather steam and move forward with increasing momentum, some people begin to think that somehow people were created for operating the organizations. People create some entities to get something done for society, some for direct gratification through affiliating with others, and still other organizations do things for society by employing the motive power of direct expressive gratification. Let us all maximize the usefulness of our organizations to people. Let us give to our work the significance that Kipling envisioned as paradise when he wrote (1892):

> And no one shall work for money, and no one shall work for fame,
> But each for the joy of the working, and each, in his separate star,
> Shall draw the Thing as he sees It for the God of Things as They are!

The joy of working is what the expressive dimension of work is all about.

References

Aberback, J. D. "Alienation and Political Behavior." *American Political Science Review,* Mar. 1969, *63,* 86–100.

Ackroyd, S., Hughes, J. A., and Soothill, K. "Public Sector Services and Their Management." *Journal of Management Studies,* 1989, *26*(6), 603–619.

Adams, D. S. "Voluntary Action: Speculations on the Thing Itself." *Volunteer Administration,* 1976, *9,* 8–12.

Adams, D. S. "Why Is Volunteering Fun? Some Notes on Play, Work, and Voluntary Action." Paper presented at the meetings of the North Central Sociological Association, Ohio State University, Cleveland, 1981.

Adams, D. S. "Toward a Model of Voluntary Action as Ritual Action." Paper prepared for the meetings of the Midwest Sociological Society, Chicago, 1984a.

Adams, D. S. "Voluntarism and Civil Religion: Doing Good as Ritual Action." Paper presented at the meetings of the Midwest Sociological Association, Chicago, 1984b.

Adams, D. S. "The Imperative to Volunteer: A Theme in American Civil Religion." Paper presented at the meetings of the Association for the Sociology of Religion, 1986.

Adams, D. S. "Issues and Ideas in the Culture of American Voluntarism." Paper prepared for the meetings of the American Sociological Association, Washington, D.C., Aug. 1990.

Ader, R. "The Effects of Early Experience on Subsequent Emotionality and Resistance to Stress." *Psychological Monographs,* winter 1959, pp. 2–32.

Adler, A. *The Practice and Theory of Individual Psychology.* London: Kegan Paul, 1925.

Allport, F. H. *Theories of Personality and the Concept of Structure.* New York: Wiley, 1955.

Ardrey, R. *The Territorial Imperative.* New York: Atheneum, 1966.

Argyris, C. "The Individual and the Organization." *Administrative Science Quarterly,* June 1957, pp. 1–24.

Ashbrook, J. B. "The Relationship of Church Members to Church Organization." *Journal for the Scientific Study of Religion,* 1966, *5,* 397–419.

Athos, A. G., and Coffey, R. E. *Behavior in Organizations.* Englewood Cliffs, N.J.: Prentice-Hall, 1968.

Avolio, B., and Bass, B. M. "Charisma and Beyond: Research Findings on Transformational and Transactional Leadership." In J. L. Hunt and others, *Emerging Leadership Vistas.* Lexington, Mass.: D. C. Heath, 1987.

Babchuk, N., and Booth, A. "Voluntary Association Membership: A Longitudinal Analysis." *American Sociological Review,* Feb. 1969, *34,* 31–45.

Bales, R. F. *Interaction Process Analysis: A Method for the Study of Small Groups.* Chicago: University of Chicago Press, 1950.

Bales, R. F. "The Equilibrium Problem in Small Groups." In T. Parsons, R. F. Bales, and E. A. Shils, *Working Papers in the Theory of Action.* New York: Free Press, 1953.

Bales, R. F. "Adaptive and Integrative Changes as Sources of Strain in Social Systems." In A. P. Hare, E. F. Borgatta, and R. F. Bales (eds.), *Small Groups, Studies in Social Interaction.* New York: Knopf, 1955.

Barnard, C. I. *The Functions of the Executive.* Cambridge, Mass.: Harvard University Press, 1938.

Barry, V. *Moral Issues in Business.* Belmont, Calif.: Wadsworth, 1979.

Bass, B. M. *Leadership and Performance Beyond Expectations.* New York: Free Press, 1985.

Beauchamp, T. L., and Bowie, N. E. (eds.). *Ethical Theory and Business.* Englewood Cliffs, N.J.: Prentice-Hall, 1979.

Becker, H. "Notes on the Concept of Commitment." *American Journal of Sociology,* 1960, *66,* 32–40.

Beer, M., and others. *Human Resource Management: A General Manager's Perspective.* New York: Free Press, 1985.

Bell, J. *The Anatomy and Philosophy of Expression.* In T. Parsons, E. Shils, K. Naegele, and I. R. Pitts (eds.), *Theories of Society.* New York: Free Press, 1961.

Bennis, W. G. "The Four Competencies of Leadership: Using Research to Improve Practice." *Training and Development Journal,* 1984, *38*(8), 14–19.

Bennis, W. G. "Leading Through Inspiration." *Executive Excellence,* 1989a, *6*(3), 13–14.

Bennis, W. G. *Why Leaders Can't Lead: The Unconscious Conspiracy Continues.* San Francisco: Jossey-Bass, 1989b.

Bennis, W. G. "Leading Followers, Following Leaders." *Executive Excellence,* 1991, *8*(6), 5–7.

Bennis, W. G., and Nanus, B. *Leaders: The Strategies for Taking Charge.* New York: HarperCollins, 1985.

Berelson, B., and Steiner, G. A. *Human Behavior: An Inventory of Scientific Findings.* Orlando, Fla.: Harcourt Brace Jovanovich, 1964.

Berlew, D. E., and LeClere, W. E. "Social Intervention in Curaçao: A Case Study." *Journal of Applied Behavioral Science,* 1974, *10*(1), 29–52.

Billis, D. "What Can Nonprofits and Businesses Learn from Each Other?" In D. C. Hammack and D. R. Young, *Nonprofit Organizations in a Market Economy: Understanding New Roles, Issues, and Trends.* San Francisco: Jossey-Bass, 1993.

Blake, R. R., and Mouton, J. S. *The Managerial Grid.* Houston, Tex.: Gulf, 1964.

Blau, P. M. *The Dynamics of Bureaucracy.* Chicago: University of Chicago Press, 1955.

Blau, P. M. *Exchange and Power in Social Life.* New York: Wiley, 1964.

Blau, P. M., and Meyer, M. W. *Bureaucracy in Modern Society.* New York: Random House, 1987.

Blau, P. M. and Scott, W. R. *Formal Organizations: A Comparative Approach.* San Francisco: Chandler, 1962.

Boal, K. B., and Bryson, J. M. "Charismatic Leadership: A Phenomenological and Structural Approach." In J. G. Hunt, B. R. Baliga, H. P. Dachler, and C. A. Schriesheim, *Emerging Leadership Vistas,* 1988.

Bradley, R. T. *Charisma and Social Structure: A Study of Love and Power, Wholeness and Transformation.* New York: Paragon, 1987.

Burns, J. M. *Leadership.* New York: HarperCollins, 1978.

Callahan, K. L. *Twelve Keys to an Effective Church: Strategic Planning for Mission.* New York: HarperCollins, 1983.

Cattell, R. B. *The Description and Measurement of Personality.* New York: World Book, 1946.

Cattell, R. B., Saunders, D. R., and Stice, G. F. "The Dimensions of Syntality in Small Groups." *Human Relations,* 1953, *6*, 331–336.

Channing, W. E. *Lectures on the Elevation of the Labouring Portion of the Community.* Boston: W. D. Ticknor, 1840.

Chong, D. *Collective Action and the Civil Rights Movement.* Chicago: University of Chicago Press, 1987.

Clary, E. G., Snyder, M., and Ridge, R. "Volunteers' Motivations: A Functional Strategy for the Recruitment, Placement, and Retention of Volunteers." *Nonprofit Management and Leadership,* 1992, *2*(4), 333–349.

Coch, L., and French, F.R.P., Jr. "Overcoming Resistance to Change." In Society for the Psychological Study of Social Issues, *Readings in Social Psychology.* (Rev. ed.) Troy, Mo.: Holt, Rinehart & Winston, 1952.

Cohen, W. A. "The Potential Revolution in Leadership." *Business Forum,* winter 1992, pp. 37–39.

Coleman, J. C. *Psychology and Effective Behavior.* Glenview, Ill.: Scott, Foresman, 1969.

Collier, P., and Horowitz, D. *The Kennedys: An American Drama.* New York: Summit Books, 1984.

Conger, J. A. *The Charismatic Leader: Behind the Mystique of Exceptional Leadership.* San Francisco: Jossey-Bass, 1989.

Conger, J. A. "The Dark Side of Leadership." *Organizational Dynamics,* autumn 1990, *19,* pp. 44–55.

Conger, J. A. *Learning to Lead: The Art of Transforming Managers into Leaders.* San Francisco: Jossey-Bass, 1992a.

Conger, J. A., Kanungo, R. N., and Associates. *Charismatic Leadership: The Elusive Factor in Organizational Effectiveness.* San Francisco: Jossey-Bass, 1988.

Cooley, C. *Social Organizations.* New York: Charles Scribner's Sons, 1906.

Cornuelle, R., and Finch, R. *The New Conservative Liberal Manifesto.* San Diego, Calif.: Viewpoint Books, 1968.

"Correct Quotes." San Rafael, CA: Wordstar, 1991.

Coser, L. *The Functions of Group Conflict.* New York: Free Press. 1956.

Covey, S. R. *Principle-Centered Leadership.* New York: Summit Books, 1991.

Darwin, C. *The Expression of the Emotions in Man and Animals.* London: John Murray, 1872.

Davis, K. "Management Communication and the Grapevine." In *People: Managing Your Most Important Asset.* Boston: Harvard Business Review, 1987.

Davis, S. M. *Managing Corporate Culture.* Cambridge, Mass.: Ballinger, 1984.

Deal, T. E., and Kennedy, A. A. *Corporate Cultures: The Rites and Rituals of Corporate Life.* Reading, Mass.: Addison-Wesley, 1982.

Deci, E. L. *Intrinsic Motivation.* New York: Plenum, 1975.

Derakhshan, F., and Fatehi, K. "Bureaucracy as a Leadership Substitute: A Review of History." *Leadership and Organization Development Journal* (UK), 1985, *6*(4), 13–16.

Deutsch, M. "The Effects of Cooperation and Competition upon Group Process." In D. Cartwright and A. Zander (eds.), *Group Dynamics: Research and Theory.* New York: HarperCollins, 1968.

Drucker, P. F. *Management! Tasks, Responsibilities, Practices.* New York: HarperCollins, 1974.

Drucker, P. F. *The New Realities.* New York: HarperCollins, 1989a.

Drucker, P. F. "What Business Can Learn from Nonprofits." *Harvard Business Review,* 1989b, *67*(4), 88–93.

Drucker, P. F. *Managing the Non-Profit Organization.* New York: HarperCollins, 1990.

Durkheim, E. *The Division of Labour in Society.* (W. D. Hall, trans.) New York: Free Press, 1938. (Originally published 1893.)

Durkheim, E. *Suicide: A Study in Sociology* (J. A. Spaulding, trans., G. Simpson, ed.). New York: Free Press, 1951. (Originally published 1897.)

Ellis, S. J. *From the Top Down: The Executive Role in Volunteer Program Success.* Philadelphia: Energize Associates, 1986.

Erbe, W. "Social Involvement and Political Activity: A Replication and Elaboration." *American Sociological Review,* Apr. 1964, *29,* 198–215.

Ethics Commission of the Independent Sector. *Obedience to the Unenforceable: Ethics and the Nation's Voluntary and Philanthropic Community.* Washington, D.C.: Independent Sector, 1990.

Etzioni, A. *A Comparative Analysis of Complex Organizations.* (Rev. ed.) New York: Free Press, 1975.

Etzioni, A. *The Moral Dimension: Toward a New Economics.* New York: Free Press, 1988.

Falbe, C. M., and Yukl, G. "Consequences for Managers of Using Single Influence Tactics and Combination of Tactics." *Academy of Management Journal,* 1992, *35*(3), 638–652.

Fayol, H. *General and Industrial Management.* London: Pitman, 1949.

Festinger L. *A Theory of Cognitive Dissonance.* Stanford, Calif: Stanford University Press, 1957.

Fiennes, R. *To the Ends of the Earth.* New York: Arbor House, 1983.

Fischer, P. H. "An Analysis of the Primary Group." *Sociometry,* 1952, *16,* 272–276.

Fisher, J. C., and Cole, K. M. *Leadership and Management of Volunteer Programs: A Guide for Volunteer Administrators.* San Francisco: Jossey-Bass, 1993.

"The Forbes Nonprofit 500: Businessmen with Halos," *Forbes,* Nov. 26, 1990, pp. 100–114.

Frank, J. *Persuasion and Healing.* Baltimore, Md.: Johns Hopkins University Press, 1961.

Freud, S. *Psychopathology of Everyday Life.* New York: Macmillan, 1914.

Friedman, H. S., Prince, L. M., Riggio, R. E., and DiMatteo, M. R. "Understanding and Assessing Nonverbal Expressiveness: The Affective Communication Test." *Journal of Personality and Social Psychology,* 1980, 39(2), 333–351.

Fromm, E. *Escape from Freedom.* Troy, Mo.: Holt, Rinehart & Winston, 1968.

Gager, J. G. *Kingdom and Community: The Social World of Early Christianity.* Englewood Cliffs, N.J.: Prentice-Hall, 1975.

Gamson, W. A. *Simulated Society.* New York: Free Press, 1967.

Georgopoulos, B. S., and Tannenbaum, A. S. "A Study of Organizational Effectiveness." *American Sociological Review,* 1957, *22,* 535–540.

Golembiewski, R. T. "Excerpts from 'Organization as a Moral Problem.'" *Public Administration Review,* Mar.-Apr. 1992, *52*(2), 95–103.

Gordon, C. W., and Babchuk, N. "A Typology of Voluntary Associations." *American Sociological Review,* Feb. 1959, *24,* 22–29.

Gouldner, A. W. "Organizational Analysis." In R. K. Menton, L. Brown, and L. S. Cottrell, Jr. (eds.), *Sociology Today.* New York: HarperCollins, 1959.

Greenberg, J., and Greenberg, H. "Charisma Isn't Always Enough." *Sales and Marketing Management,* Oct. 1990, *12,* 142.

Grodzins, M. *The American System: A New View of Government in the United States.* Skokie, Ill.: Rand McNally, 1966.

Gudykunst, W. B. *Bridging Differences: Effective Intergroup Communication.* Newbury Park, Calif.: Sage, 1991.

Gulick, L., and Urwick, L. *Papers on the Science of Administration.* New York: Institute of Public Administration, Columbia University, 1937.

Guy, M. E. *Ethical Decision Making in Everyday Work Situations.* New York: Quorum Books, 1990.

Handy, C. *Understanding Organizations.* New York: Facts on File, 1985.

Handy, C. *Understanding Voluntary Organizations.* New York: Viking Penguin, 1988.

Hansmann, H. "Economic Theories of Nonprofit Organizations." In W. W. Powell (ed.), *The Nonprofit Sector: A Research Handbook.* New Haven, Conn.: Yale University Press, 1980.

Harris, M. L. *Cultural Materialism.* New York: Random House, 1979.

Hershberg, T. "Universities Must Devote More Time and Money to Policy Research at the State and Local Levels." *Chronicle of Higher Education,* Nov. 8, 1989, pp. 74–75.

Herzberg, F. *Work and the Nature of Man.* Cleveland, Ohio: World Publishing, 1966.

Hicks, H. G., and Gullett, C. R. *The Management of Organizations: A Systems and Human Resources Approach.* New York: McGraw-Hill, 1972.

Hodgkinson, V. A., and Weitzman, M. S. *The Charitable Behavior of Americans.* Washington, D.C.: Independent Sector, 1992.

Homans, G. C. *The Nature of Social Science.* Orlando, Fla.: Harcourt Brace Jovanovich, 1951.

Horney, K. *Neurosis and Human Growth.* New York: Norton, 1950.

House, R. J. "All Things in Moderation." *Academy of Management Review,* 1987, *12,* 164–169.

House, R. J., Spangler, W. D., and Woycke, J. "Personality and Charisma in the U.S. Presidency: A Psychological Theory of Leader Effectiveness." *Administrative Science Quarterly,* Sep. 1991, pp. 364–396.

Inkson, K., and Moss, A. T. "Transformational Leadership—Is It Universally Applicable?" *Organization Development Journal,* 1993, *14*(4), i–ii.

Jacoby, A. P., and Babchuk, N. "Instrumental and Expressive Voluntary Associations." *Sociology and Social Research,* 1957, *47,* 461–471.

James, J. "Clique Organization in a Small Industrial Plant." *Research Studies, State College, Washington,* 1951, *19,* 125–130.

James, N., and Field, D. "The Routinization of Hospice: Charisma and Bureaucratization." *Social Science and Medicine,* June 1992, *34,* 1363–1375.

Jeavons, T. H. "When Management Is the Message: Relating Values to Management Practice in Nonprofit Organizations." *Nonprofit Management and Leadership,* 1992, *2*(4), 403–417.

Jeavons, T. H. "Ethics in Nonprofit Management: Creating a Culture of Integrity." In R. D. Herman and Associates, *The Jossey-Bass Handbook of Nonprofit Leadership and Management.* San Francisco: Jossey-Bass, 1994.

Johnson, B. "On Founders and Followers: Some Factors in the Development of New Religious Movements." *Sociological Analysis,* 1992, *53,* No. S Supplement, pp. S1–S13.

Josephson, M. *Ethical Obligations and Opportunities in Philanthropy, Grantmaking and Fund Raising.* Marina Del Rey, Calif.: Joseph and Edna Josephson Institute for the Advancement of Ethics, 1986.

Katz, D. "Social Disaffection Among Deprived Groups." *International Journal of Intercultural Relations,* 1977, *1*(1), 12–39.

Katz, D., and Kahn, R. L. *The Social Psychology of Organizations.* New York: Wiley, 1966.

Kets de Vries, M.F.K. "Origins of Charisma: Ties that Bind the Leader and the Led." In J. A. Conger and R. N. Kanungo (eds.), *Charismatic Leadership: The Elusive Factor in Organizational Effectiveness.* San Francisco: Jossey-Bass, 1988.

Kipling, R. "L'Envoi." In *The Seven Seas,* 1892.

Klein, J. *The Study of Groups.* London: Routledge & Kegan Paul, 1956.

Knowles, H. P., and Saxberg, B. O. *Personality and Leadership Behavior.* Reading, Mass.: Addison-Wesley, 1971.

Knowles, M. *The Adult Learner: A Neglected Species.* Houston, Tex.: Gulf, 1973.

Koontz, H., and O'Donnell, C. *Principles of Management.* New York: McGraw-Hill, 1961.

Kormanski, C. "A Situational Leadership Approach to Groups Using the Tuckman Model of Group Development." *Developing Human Resources,* 1985, pp. 217–225.

Kotter, J. P. *A Force for Change: How Leadership Differs from Management.* New York: Free Press, 1990.

Kouzes, J. M., and Mico, P. M. "Domain Theory: An Introduction to Organizational Behavior in Human Service Organizations." *Journal of Applied Behavioral Science,* 1979, *15*(4), 449–469.

Kouzes, J. M., and Posner, B. Z. *The Leadership Challenge: How to Get Extraordinary Things Done in Organizations.* San Francisco: Jossey-Bass, 1987.

Kramer, R. M., and Specht, H. *Readings in Community Organization Practice.* (2nd ed.) Englewood Cliffs, N.J.: Prentice-Hall, 1975.

Kroeber, A. L., and Kluckhohn, C. *Culture: A Critical Review of Concepts and Definitions.* New York: Vintage, 1952.

Kuhnert, K. W., and Lewis, P. "Transactional and Transformational Leadership: A Constructive/Developmental Analysis." *Academy of Management Review,* 1987, *12,* 648–657.

Lacoursiere, R. *The Life Cycle of Groups: Group Developmental Stage Theory.* Springfield, Ill.: Human Sciences Press, 1980.

Langer, E. J., Blank, A., and Chanowitz, B. "The Mindfulness of Ostensibly Thoughtful Action: The Role of 'Placobic' Information in Interpersonal Interaction." *Journal of Personality and Social Psychology,* June 1978, *36*(6), 635–642.

Lawler, E. E. III. *The Ultimate Advantage: Creating the High-Involvement Organization.* San Francisco: Jossey-Bass, 1992.

Lewin, K. *Resolving Social Conflicts.* New York: HarperCollins, 1948.

Lewin, K., Lippitt, R., and White, R. K. "Patterns of Aggressive Behavior in Experimentally Created 'Social Climates.'" *Journal of Social Psychology,* 1939, *10,* 271–299.

Likert, R. *New Patterns of Management.* New York: McGraw-Hill, 1961.

Lindeman, E. C. *The Community.* New York: Association Press, 1921.

Lindholm, C. *Charisma.* Cambridge, England: Basil Blackwell, 1990.

Lohmann, R. A. *The Commons: New Perspectives on Nonprofit Organizations and Voluntary Action.* San Francisco: Jossey-Bass, 1992.

Lorenz, K. *On Aggression* (M. K. Wilson, trans.). San Diego, Calif.: Harcourt Brace Jovanovich, 1966.

Loveman, A. *The Saturday Review of Literature,* Nov. 3, 1951, p. 17.

Lundberg, G. A. *Foundations of Sociology.* Westport, Conn.: Greenwood, 1934.

McClelland, D. C. *The Achieving Society.* New York: Van Nostrand Reinhold, 1961.

McClelland, D. C., Constantian, C. A., Regalado, D., and Stone, C. "Making It to Maturity." *Psychology Today,* 1978, *12,* 42–43.

Maccoby, M. *The Gamesman: The New Corporate Leaders.* New York: Simon & Schuster, 1976.

Maccoby, M. *Why Work?* New York: Simon and Schuster, 1988.

MacDuff, N. "Principles of Training for Volunteers and Employees." In R. D. Herman and Associates, *The Jossey-Bass Handbook of Nonprofit Leadership and Management.* San Francisco: Jossey-Bass, 1994.

McGavran, D. A. *The Bridges of God: A Study in the Strategy of Missions.* London: World Dominion Press, 1955.

McGavran, D. A. *How Churches Grow: The New Frontiers of Mission.* New York: Friendship Press, 1970.

McGregor, D. *The Human Side of Enterprise.* New York: McGraw-Hill, 1960.

Machiavelli, N. *The Prince.* London: Dent, 1958. (Originally published 1513.)

McKinney, J. C. "The Application of Gemeinschaft and Gesellschaft as Related to Other Typologies." In F. Tönnies, *Community and Society.* East Lansing, Mich.: Michigan State University Press, 1957.

McPherson, M. "An Ecology of Affiliation." *American Sociological Review,* 1983, *48,* 519–532.

Madden, M. *Blessing: Giving the Gift of Power.* Nashville, Tenn.: Broadman Press, 1988.

Maslow, A. H. *Motivation and Personality.* New York: HarperCollins, 1965.

Marrow, A. J., Bowers, D. G., and Seashore, S. E. *Management by Participation: Creating a Climate for Personal and Organizational Development.* New York: HarperCollins, 1967.

Maslow, A. H. *Motivation and Personality.* New York: HarperCollins, 1965.

Mason, D. E. *The Compulsive Christian.* Grand Rapids, Mich.: Zondervan, 1969.

Mason, D. E. "Factors That Build Cohesion in a Nonprofit Organization." Paper presented at the conference of the Association for Voluntary Action Scholars, Virginia Polytechnic Institute and State University, 1984a.

Mason, D. E. *Voluntary Nonprofit Enterprise Management.* New York: Plenum, 1984b.

Mason, D. E. "Dealing with Anti-Management Bias in the Third Sector." In D. Hyman, R. Warren, and T. Borkmann, *Coproduction Prosuming and Appropriate Technology for the Nonprofit Sector,* Proceedings of the annual meeting of the Association of Voluntary Action Scholars, Oct. 6–9, 1985. New Orleans: Association of Voluntary Action Scholars, 1985a.

Mason, D. E. "A Square Peg in a Round Hole." Program in the *Forward Together* television series, broadcast on VUE-TV, New Orleans, Nov. 18, 1985b.

Mason, D. E., "Building Growth into the Systems of Voluntary Sector Organizations." Paper presented at the annual conference of the Association of Voluntary Action Scholars, Chevy Chase, Md., Oct. 1988.

Mason, D. E. "Ethical Issues in the Nonprofit Sector." In *Towards the 21st Century.* London: London School of Economics, 1990a.

Mason, D. E. "Nonprofits Well Managed!" In *Towards the 21st Century.* London: London School of Economics, 1990c.

Mason, D. E. "Water or Gasoline: Allocating Resources Between the Service-Providing and the Resource-Providing Systems." Paper presented at the annual conference of the Association of Voluntary Action Scholars, London, July 1990b.

Mason, D. E. "Charismatic Leadership: An Appropriate Style." Paper presented at the annual conference of the Association for Research on Nonprofit Organizations and Voluntary Action, Chicago, Oct. 1992.

Mason, D. E. "Harnessing the White Horse: Effective Organizational Adaptations to Charismatic Leadership." In V. Hodgkinson (ed.), *Transmitting the Tradition of a Caring Society to Future Generations.* Washington, D.C.: Independent Sector, 1993.

Mason, D. E. "Synagogue and Church as the Organizational Prototype of Contemporary Nonprofits." Paper presented at the annual conference of the Association for Research on Nonprofit Organizations and Voluntary Action, Cleveland, Ohio, Nov. 1995.

Mason, D. E., and Harris, M. "An Embarrassed Silence: Research on Religious Nonprofits." Paper presented at the annual conference of the Association for Research on Nonprofit Organizations and Voluntary Action, Berkeley, Calif., Oct. 1994.

Mink, O. G., Shultz, J. M., and Mink, B. P. *Developing and Managing Open Organizations.* Austin, Tex.: Catapult Press, 1979.

Mintzberg, H. "Planning on the Left Side and Managing on the Right." *Harvard Business Review,* 1976, *54,* 49–58.

Mintzberg, H. *The Rise and Fall of Strategic Planning.* New York: Free Press, 1994.

Mitchell, J. G. *Re-Visioning Educational Leadership.* New York: Garland, 1990.

Mooney, J. C., and Reiley, A. P. *Onward Industry.* New York: HarperCollins, 1931.

Moore, J. W. "Patterns of Women's Participation in Voluntary Associations." *American Sociology,* May 1961, *66,* 592–598.

Morgan, G. *Images of Organization.* Newbury Park, Calif.: Sage, 1986.

Morgan, G. *Imaginization: The Art of Creative Management.* Newbury Park, Calif.: Sage, 1993.

Morgan, G. "Human Resources Practices in Transforming Organizations." Address at Case Western Reserve University, Cleveland, Ohio, Nov. 1994.

Morris, D. *The Human Zoo.* New York: McGraw-Hill, 1969.

Murray, H. A. *Explorations in Personality.* New York: Oxford, 1938.

Murray, H. A., and Kluckhohn, C. (eds.). *Personality in Nature, Society, and Culture.* New York: Knopf, 1948.

Nadler, D. A., and Tushman, M. L. "Beyond the Charismatic Leader: Leadership and Organizational Change." *California Management Review,* winter 1990, *32*(2), 77–97.

Nelson, R. "Authority, Organization, and Societal Context in Multinational Churches." *Administrative Science Quarterly,* 1993, *38,* 653–682.

Ohmae, K. *The Mind of the Strategist: The Art of Japanese Business.* New York: McGraw Hill, 1982.

Olson, M. *The Logic of Collective Action.* Cambridge, Mass.: Harvard University Press, 1965.

Ouchi, W. G. *Theory Z: How American Business Can Meet the Japanese Challenge.* Reading, Mass.: Addison-Wesley, 1981.

Palisi, B. J., and Jacobson, P. E. "Dominant Statuses and Involvement in Types of Instrumental and Expressive Voluntary Associations." *Journal of Voluntary Action Research,* 1977, *6*(1–2), 80–88.

Parkinson, C. N. *Parkinson's Law: And Other Studies in Administration.* Boston: Houghton Mifflin, 1957.

Parsons, D. R. "Bi-Component Intra-Task Transfer in Motor Learning." Unpublished doctoral dissertation, University of California, Berkeley, 1968.

Parsons, T., *Structure and Process in Modern Societies.* New York: Free Press, 1960.

Parsons, T. "Culture and Social System Revisited." In L. Schneider and C. M. Bonjean (eds.), *The Idea of Culture in the Social Sciences.* Cambridge, England: Cambridge University Press, 1973.

Parsons, T., and Edward, A. S. *Toward A General Theory of Action.* Cambridge, Mass.: Harvard University Press, 1962.

Pascarella, P., and Frohman, M. A. *The Purpose-Driven Organization: Unleashing the Power of Direction and Commitment.* San Francisco: Jossey-Bass, 1989.

Payton, R. L. *Philanthropy.* New York: Macmillan, 1988.

Pereroy, E. "Expectational Composition and Development of Group Cohesiveness Across Time Periods." *Psychological Reports,* 1980, *47*(1), 243–249.

Peters, T. J. "Symbols, Patterns and Settings." *Organizational Dynamics,* 1978, *7,* 3–22.

Peters, T. J., and Waterman, R. H., Jr. *In Search of Excellence.* New York: HarperCollins, 1982.

Peterson, K. S. "Poll: 59 Percent Call Religion Important." *USA Today,* Apr. 11, 1994, p. 1.

Pfeffer, J. *Management as Symbolic Action: The Creation and Maintenance of Organizational Paradigms.* Greenwich, Conn.: Jai Press, 1981.

Pondy, L. R. *Leadership is a Language Game.* Durham, N.C.: Duke University Press, 1978.

Porter, L. W., and Lawler, E. E., III. *Managerial Attitudes and Performance.* Homewood, Ill.: Richard D. Irwin, 1968.

Porter, L. W., Steers, R. M., Mowday, R. T., and Boulian, P. V. "Organizational Commitment, Job Satisfaction, and Turnover Among Psychiatric Technicians." *Journal of Applied Psychology,* 1974, *59*(5), 603–609.

Powell, W. P. *The Nonprofit Sector: A Research Handbook.* New Haven, Conn.: Yale University Press, 1987.

Putnam, R. D., "Bowling Alone," *Journal of Democracy,* Jan. 1995, *6*(1), 32–38.

Radcliffe-Brown, A. R. "The Nature and Functions of Ceremonials." In *The Andaman Islanders.* New York: Free Press, 1948.

Radcliffe-Brown, A. R. *Structure and Function in Primitive Society.* New York: Free Press, 1952.

Rahim, M. A. "A Strategy for Managing Conflict in Complex Organizations." *Human Relations,* 1985, *38*(1), 81–89.

Rahim, M. A. *Managing Conflict in Organizations.* (2nd ed.) New York: Praeger, 1992.

Rawls, J. R., Ullrich, R. A., and Nelson, O. "A Comparison of Managers Entering and Reentering the Profit and Nonprofit Sectors." *Academy of Management Journal,* 1973, *18*(3), 616–623.

Riggio, R. E. *The Charisma Quotient.* New York: Dodd, Mead, 1987.

Roberts, N. C., and Bradley, R. T. "The Limits of Charisma." In J. A. Conger and R. N. Kanungo (eds.), *Charismatic Leadership: The Elusive Factor in Organizational Effectiveness.* San Francisco: Jossey-Bass, 1988.

Rogers, C. R. *On Becoming a Person.* Boston: Houghton Mifflin, 1961.

Rose, A. *Theory and Method in the Social Sciences.* Minneapolis: University of Minnesota Press, 1954.

Rose, A. *The Power Structure.* New York: Oxford University Press, 1967.

Rosenthal, P. *Words and Values.* Cambridge, England: Cambridge University Press, 1984.

Rothschild-Whitt, J. "The Collectivist Organization: An Alternative to Rational-Bureaucratic Models." *American Sociological Review,* Aug. 1979, *44,* 509–527.

Rubin, I. M., and Beckhard, R. "Factors Influencing the Effectiveness of Health Teams." *Milbank Memorial Fund Quarterly,* July 1972, pt. 1, 317–335.

Schein, E. H. *Organizational Culture and Leadership: A Dynamic View.* San Francisco: Jossey-Bass, 1985.

Schumpeter, J. A. "Robinson's Economics of Imperfect Competition." *Journal of Political Economy,* 1934, *42,* 249–257.

Scott, W. R. *Organizations: Rational, Natural, and Open Systems.* Englewood Cliffs, N.J.: Prentice-Hall, 1987.

Selznick, P. *Leadership in Administration.* New York: HarperCollins, 1957.

Sheler, J. L. "Spiritual America," *U.S. News & World Report.* Apr. 4, 1994, p. 50.

Sherif, M. "Superordinate Goals in the Reduction of Intergroup Conflict." *American Journal of Sociology,* 1958, *63*(4), 349–356.

Shils, E. A., and Janowitz, M. "Cohesion and Disintegration in the Wehrmacht in World War II." *Public Opinion Quarterly,* 1948, *12*(2), 280–315.

Simon, H. A. *Administrative Behavior.* (3rd ed.) New York: Free Press, 1976.

60 Minutes. CBS Television News, May 29, 1994.

Slater, P. E. "Role Differentiation in Small Groups." In A. P. Hare, E. F. Borgatta, and R. F. Bales (eds.), *Small Groups: Studies in Social Interaction.* New York: Knopf, 1955.

Smircich, L., and Morgan, G. "Leadership: The Management of Meaning." *Journal of Applied Behavioral Studies,* 1982, *18,* 257–273.

Smith, A. *The Theory of Moral Sentiments or, An Essay towards an analysis of the Principles by which men naturally judge concerning the conduct and character, first of their neighbors, and afterwords of themselves.* New Rochelle, N.Y.: Arlington House, 1981. (Originally published 1822.)

Smith, C., and Freedman, A. *Voluntary Associations: Perspectives on the Literature.* Cambridge, Mass.: Harvard University Press, 1972.

Smith, D. H. "Ritual in Voluntary Associations." *Journal of Voluntary Action Research,* 1972, *1*(4), 39–53.

Smith, D. H. "Dimensions and Categories of Voluntary Organizations/NGO's." *Journal of Voluntary Action Research,* 1973, *2*(2), 116–120.

Smith, D. H. "The Impact of the Non-Profit Voluntary Sector of Society." In T. D. Conners (ed.), *The Non-Profit Organization Handbook.* New York: McGraw-Hill, 1980.

Smith, D. H. "Four Sectors or Five? Retaining the Member Benefit Sector." *Nonprofit and Voluntary Sector Quarterly,* summer 1991, pp. 137–150.

Solomon, R. C., and Hanson, K. *It's Good Business.* New York: Athenaeum, 1985.

Sorokin, P. A. Foreword to F. Tönnies, *Community and Society.* East Lansing, Mich.: Michigan State University Press, 1957.

Spencer, H. *The Study of Sociology.* In *Works of Herbert Spencer.* Osnabrück, Germany: Adler's Foreign Books, 1966.

Stebbins, R. A. *Amateurs on the Margin Between Work and Leisure.* Newbury Park, Calif.: Sage, 1979.

Stolzenberg, R. M. "Bringing the Boss Back In: Employer Size, Employee Schooling, and Socioeconomic Achievement." *American Sociological Review,* Dec. 1978, *43,* 813–828.

Sullivan, H. S. "Conceptions of Modern Psychiatry." *Psychiatry,* 1940, *3,* 1–117.

Tannenbaum, R., and Schmidt, W. H. "How to Choose a Leadership Pattern." *Harvard Business Review,* May/June 1973, pp. 162–164.

Taylor, D. W., and Faust, W. L. "Twenty Questions: Efficiency in Problem Solving as a Function of Size of Group." *Journal of Experimental Psychology,* 1952, *44,* 360–368.

Taylor, F. W. *Principles of Scientific Management.* New York: HarperCollins, 1911.

Thomas, E. J. "Role Conceptions and Organizational Size." *American Sociological Review,* 1959, *24,* 30–37.

Thompson, V.A. *Modern Organizations.* New York: Knopf, 1961.

Tichy, N. M. *Managing Strategic Change.* New York: Wiley, 1983.

Tiger, L. *Men in Groups: A Controversial Look at All-Male Societies.* New York: Marion Boyars, 1989.

Tinbergen, N. "Derived Activities: Their Causation, Biological Significance, Origin and Emancipation during Evolution." *Quarterly Review of Biology,* 1952, *27*(1), 1–26.

Tönnies, F. *Community and Society* (C. P. Loomis, trans.). East Lansing: Michigan State University Press, 1957. (Originally published as *Gemeinschaft und Gesellschaft,* 1887.)

Tuckman, B. W. "Developmental Sequence in Small Groups." *Psychological Bulletin,* 1965, *63*(6), 386–399.

Tunstall, W. B. "Cultural Transition at AT&T." *Sloan Management Review,* 1983, *25*(1), 15–26.

Turner, F. J. *The Frontier in American History.* Troy, Mo.: Holt, Rinehart & Winston, 1937.

Van Gigch, J. P. *Applied General Systems Theory.* New York: HarperCollins, 1974.

Van-Hoof, J.A.R.M. "Facial Expression in Higher Primates." *Symposia of the Zoological Society of London,* 1963, *10,* 103–104.

Van Til, J., and Associates. *Critical Issues in American Philanthropy: Strengthening Theory and Practice.* San Francisco: Jossey-Bass, 1990.

Vineyard, S., and Lynch, R. *Secrets of Leadership.* Downers Grove, Ill.: Heritage Arts, 1991.

Waerness, K. "The Rationality of Caring." In *Economic and Industrial Democracy,* Vol. 5. Newbury Park, Calif.: Sage, 1984.

Walker, M. "Limits of Strategic Management in Voluntary Organizations." *Journal of Voluntary Action Research,* 1983, *12*(3), 39–56.

Walton, R. E., and Lawrence, P. R. (eds.). *Human Resource Management Trends and Challenges.* Boston: Harvard University Press, 1985.

Warner, W. L., and Associates. *Democracy in Jonesville.* New York: HarperCollins, 1949.

Warriner, C. K., and Prather, J. E. "Four Types of Voluntary Associations." *Sociological Inquiry,* spring 1965, *35,* 138–148.

Weber, M. *Essays in Sociology.* New York: Oxford University Press, 1946.

Weber, M. *The Theory of Social and Economic Organization.* New York: Oxford University Press, 1947.

Weber, M. *The City.* New York: Free Press, 1966.

Weisbrod, B. A. *The Nonprofit Economy.* Cambridge, Mass.: Harvard University Press, 1988.

White, R. K., and Lippitt, R. *Autocracy and Democracy.* New York: HarperCollins, 1960.

Whyte, W. H., Jr. *The Organization Man.* New York: Doubleday, Anchor Books, 1956.

Wirth, L. "Urbanism as a Way of Life." *American Journal of Sociology,* 1938, *44*(1), 1–24.

Wolin, S. S. *Politics and Vision: Continuity and Innovation in Western Political Thought.* Boston: Little, Brown, 1960.

Wolpert, J. "Fragmentation in America's Nonprofit Sector." Paper presented at the 1993 Spring Research Forum of the Independent Sector, San Antonio, Tex., Mar. 18, 1993.

Wortman, M. S. "A Radical Shift from Bureaucracy to Strategic Management in Voluntary Organizations." *Journal of Voluntary Action Research,* Jan.-Mar. 1980, *10,* 62–81.

Wuthnow, R. *Acts of Compassion: Caring for Others and Helping Ourselves.* Princeton, N.J.: Princeton University Press, 1991.

Yalom, I. D. *The Theory and Practice of Group Psychotherapy.* (2nd ed.) New York: Basic Books, 1975.

Yankelovich, D. *New Rules: Searching for Self-Fulfillment in a World Turned Upside Down.* New York: Random House, 1981.

Yoon, B. S. "Effects of Feedback on Intrinsic Motivation: The Role of Communication Style, Feedback Message, and Individual Differences." Unpublished doctoral dissertation, Georgia Institute of Technology, 1991.

Yoon, J. "Interpersonal Attachment and Organizational Commitment." *Human Relations,* Mar. 1994, 329–351.

Young, D. R. "What Business Can Learn From Nonprofits." In D. Hyman and K. Parkum (eds.), *Models of Health and Human Services in the Nonprofit Sector.* University Park: Pennsylvania State University, 1986.

Yukl, G. A. *Leadership in Organizations.* Englewood Cliffs, N.J.: Prentice-Hall, 1989.

Zald, M., and McCarthy, J. "Religious Groups as Crucibles of Social Movements." In M. Zald and J. McCarthy (eds.), *Social Movements in an Organizational Society.* New Brunswick, N.J.: Transaction, 1987.

Zaleznik, A. *The Managerial Mystique: Restoring Leadership in Business.* New York: HarperCollins, 1989.

Name Index

Hillary, E., 54
Hitler, A., 121, 242, 243, 265
Hobbes, T., 84
Hochschild, A. R., 54–55
Hodgkinson, V. A., 14
Holmes, O. W., 53
Homans, G. C., 139, 140
Horney, K., 50
Horowitz, D., 242
House, R. J., 236, 250
Hughes, J. A., 40

I

Ibn Khaldun, 55
Iglesias, J., 54
Inkson, K., 96

J

Jackson, M., 235
Jacobson, P. E., 69, 74
Jacoby, A. P., 31, 64–65
James, J., 145
James, N., 255
Janowitz, M., 143
Jeavons, T. H., 11, 52, 109
Jensen, 272
Jesus, 84, 86, 121, 270
Johnson, B., 251
Johnson, L. B., 23
Jones, J., 98, 121, 235, 243
Josephson, M., 108
Jung, C. G., 49

K

Kahn, R. L., 121
Kanungo, R. N., 236, 237, 252
Katz, D., 121, 263–264
Kennedy, A. A., 103, 105, 119
Kennedy, J. F., 235, 242
Kets de Vries, M.F.K., 236
Khomeini, R., 121, 249
Khrushchev, N., 247
King, M.L., Jr., 121, 145–146, 235
Kipling, R., 294
Klein, J., 71
Kluckhohn, C., 103, 119

Knowles, H. P., 84, 85, 87
Knowles, M., 113
Koontz, H., 190
Koresh, D., 98, 138, 235, 243
Kormanski, C., 271, 272
Kornhauser, W., 63
Kotter, J. P., 158, 230
Kouzes, J. M., 108, 110
Kramer, R. M., 87
Kroeber, A. L., 103
Kuhnert, K. W., 236

L

Lacoursiere, R., 272
Langer, E. J., 242
Lawler, E. E., III, 85, 100, 145, 193, 214
Lawrence, P. R., 106
Lawrence of Arabia, 21–22
LeClere, W. E., 246
Lenin, V. I., 84, 121, 238
Lewin, K., 50, 144, 233
Lewis, P., 236
Likert, R., 91, 92, 234
Lindeman, E. C., 61–62
Lindholm, C., 250
Lippitt, R., 144, 186, 233
Lohmann, R. A., 4–5, 8, 106, 108–109, 135
Lorenz, K., 48
Loveman, A., 113
Lundberg, G. A., 61, 62
Lynch, R., 220–221

M

MacArthur, D., 121, 249
McCarthy, J., 94
McClelland, D. C., 35, 53
Maccoby, M., 51, 95–96, 105
MacDuff, N., 185
McGavran, D. A., 140, 268, 270
McGovern, G., 204
McGregor, D., 22, 90–91, 92, 99, 239
Machiavelli, N., 83–84, 98
McKinney, J. C., 57, 58
McPherson, M., 263, 271

Subject Index

A

Accountability, emphasis on, 23–24

Achievement, need for, 53

Activity, need for, 53, 71

Affiliation: and cohesion, 128; and groups, 116; leaders' need for, 225; need for, 70

Alamo, as symbol, 133

Alienation, by charismatic leaders, 249

Amateurism, in expressive organizations, 70

American Automobile Association, as instrumental organization, 32, 74

American Cancer Society, and culture, 102–103

Arrogance, of charismatic leaders, 248–249

Assessing, management step of, 160–162

Association for Research on Nonprofit Organizations and Voluntary Action (ARNOVA), 43, 77

Atrophy, in groups, 271–272

B

Beatles, 121

Behavior: of charismatic leaders, 246; expressive, 46, 61–69; involuntary and voluntary, 46–49

Blinders, of charismatic leaders, 245–246

Boards: and charismatic leaders, 253; concept of, 37–38; planning retreat for, 164

Boy Scouts, resources of, 203

Brain hemispheres: and leadership, 230, 250; and management metaphors, 82

Budgeting, in planning, 171–173

Bureau of Alcohol, Tobacco and Firearms, 138

Bureaucracy, as formal organization, 88

C

Caring, need for, 54–55

Cats, metaphor of herding, 40–41

Ceremonies: for cohesion, 132–133; for recruiting key personnel, 182

Challenge, need for, 53–54

Change: and growth, 265; leadership for, 231–232

Charismatic experiences, need for, 54

Charismatic leadership: aspects of, 235–258; characteristics of, 235–243; and cohesion, 143; complementary weaknesses of, 244–249; corollary weaknesses of, 249–253; and democracy, 98; development of, 241–243; liabilities of, 243–253; organizational agenda for, 253–256; and personal limitations, 248; and vision, 237–239, 245

Chlorophytum comosum metaphor, 177–178

Clients, concept of, 39–40

Cognitive dissonance, and expressive-instrumental organizations, 72

Cohesion: aspects of building, 128–156; background on, 128–132; benefits of, 129–131; conclusion on, 154–156; as end and means,